Hitchcock as Philosopher

Hitchcock as Philosopher

ROBERT J. YANAL

McFarland & Company, Inc., Publishers
Jefferson, North Carolina, and London

All photographs provided by Photofest.

LIBRARY OF CONGRESS CATALOGUING-IN-PUBLICATION DATA

Yanal, Robert J.
   Hitchcock as philosopher / Robert J. Yanal.
      p.   cm.
   Includes bibliographical references and index.

   ISBN 0-7864-2281-5 (softcover : 50# alkaline paper)

   1. Hitchcock, Alfred, 1899–[1980]— Criticism and
interpretation.   2. Philosophy in motion pictures.   I. Title.
PN1998.3.H58Y36   2005
791.4302'33'092 — dc22   2005014055

British Library cataloguing data are available

Cover illustration by Mark Durr

Manufactured in the United States of America

McFarland & Company, Inc., Publishers
   Box 611, Jefferson, North Carolina 28640
   www.mcfarlandpub.com

For my mother, Elizabeth,
who first introduced me to Hitchcock,
and
Herb Granger, whose insights into these films
enriched this book

Acknowledgments

I would like to thank the people who read (or heard) various parts of the manuscript and who had helpful and encouraging comments, in particular Anthony Ambrogio, Lesley Brill, Noël Carroll, Ken Dewey, Alessandro Giovannelli, Gina Granger, Mark Huston, and Deborah Knight. The philosophy and film faculties of Wayne State University and the faculty of the philosophy department of the University of Windsor responded enthusiastically to a reading of the chapter on *Suspicion*. I want also to thank Larry Spencer not only for his comments but also for his support and encouragement at home. Herb Granger's insights into these films constantly enriched my own, and I owe him great thanks. Work on *Rebecca* and *Suspicion* was supported by a Wayne State Liberal Arts Research Fellowship. *Shadow of a Doubt*, *Strangers on a Train*, and *Marnie* were completed during a sabbatical leave. I am most grateful to my university for this support.

Thanks, too, to Photofest in New York City for help in acquiring the photos included in this book; and to the Humanities Center and Philosophy Department of Wayne State University for reimbursement of photo fees.

The third chapter, "*Rebecca*'s Deceivers," appeared in substantially the same form (and under the same title) in *Philosophy and Literature* 34 (2000): 67–82. The fourth chapter on *Suspicion* appeared, again in substantially the same form, as "The End of *Suspicion*: Hitchcock, Descrates, and Joan Fontaine," in *Film and Knowledge: Essays on the Integration of Images and Ideas*, ed. Kevin Stoehr (Jefferson, N.C.: McFarland, 2000).

Contents

Acknowledgments vii
Preface 1

1. Hitchcock as Philosopher 3

I. DECEPTION

2. The Problem of Deception 13
3. *Rebecca*'s Deceivers 16
4. The End of *Suspicion* 31
5. *Vertigo* 47
6. *North by Northwest* 67

II. MIND

7. On Knowing a Mind 81
8. *Shadow of a Doubt* 84
9. *Strangers on a Train* 100
10. *Psycho* 115
11. *Marnie, Spellbound* 126

III. KNOWLEDGE

12. Problematic Knowledge 145
13. *Rear Window* 148
14. *The Man Who Know Too Much* 163
15. *The Birds* 175

Chapter Notes 191
Bibliography 199
Index 203

Preface

The ideas for *Hitchcock as Philosopher* came indirectly. While writing a book on emotion and fiction,[1] I happened to choose some examples from Hitchcock films. The examples could have come from nearly any fiction, but Hitchcock came readily to mind. Besides, I could reasonably expect my readers to know at least some of the more popular Hitchcock movies, such as *Psycho* (1960) or *North by Northwest* (1959). The resulting book, *Paradoxes of Emotion and Fiction*, in fact begins with a description of the crop duster scene in *North by Northwest*, and introduces the paradox by asking how it is that viewers could feel anxiety for the plight of Roger Thornhill (Cary Grant) and feel relief that he survives the attack — all the while knowing that there is no Roger Thornhill, and therefore knowing that no one is really in danger.

But other examples from Hitchcock came up. I was struck by something I had not noticed in *Psycho*: the similarities between Marion Crane (Janet Leigh) and Norman Bates (Anthony Perkins), and how both have in a sense lost themselves. This led to reflections on *Strangers on a Train* (1951): how similar Bruno Anthony (Robert Walker) and Guy Haines (Farley Granger) are, and how well Bruno seems to know what Guy wants — perhaps better than Guy himself. Eventually I began to see that Hitchcock was illustrating a kind of solution to the philosophical problem of knowing a mind, one's own or another's.

Another philosophical avenue opened when I happened to catch Hitchcock's first American film, *Rebecca* (1940), on television, and by now was in a frame of mind conducive to seeing philosophical issues in Hitchcock's work. The deceptions worked on the heroine of the film reminded me of the famous "evil deceiver" hypothesized by René Descartes. The second Mrs. de Winter (Joan Fontaine) is brought to believe that her husband is still in love with his deceased first wife — in somewhat the same way that Descartes' evil genius might bring the illusion of sitting in front

1

of a fire when there is in reality no fire. What Hitchcock brings to the problem of deception is an investigation of the psychology of the deceived. The second Mrs. de Winter lacks self-esteem, which makes her a perfect target of deception. And then I reflected on the next Hitchcock film that starred Joan Fontaine, *Suspicion* (1941), in which she again plays a woman of low self-esteem who cannot let go of a husband who may have tried to murder her.

So the project of writing on Hitchcock as philosopher began. Besides *Psycho* and *Strangers on a Train*, *Shadow of a Doubt* (1943), *Marnie* (1964), and *Spellbound* (1945) fell into place as further investigations of the problematic of knowing a mind. Hitchcock's greatest work, *Vertigo* (1958), and his most popular, *North by Northwest*, joined *Rebecca* and *Suspicion* as illustrating various aspects of deception (with *Vertigo* adding the problematic of *self*-deception). Eventually, two films about the ethics of knowing — *Rear Window* (1954) and *The Man Who Knew Too Much* (1934, 1956) — and a film about unknowability, *The Birds* (1963), finished out the project.

Some of Hitchcock's better films did not make it into this book: most notably *Notorious* (1946), but also *Rope* (1948), *Dial M for Murder* (1954), and *To Catch a Thief* (1955). (*The Thirty-Nine Steps* [1935] is in effect covered as it has been in a sense re-made as *North by Northwest*.) *Notorious*, *Rope*, and the others did not strike me as having philosophical implications, and it may well be that this accounts for their lightness relative to some of the philosophical films I discuss. I hasten to add that having philosophical implications does not always lift a film higher. *Notorious* is superior to *Spellbound*, despite the fact that the latter has some ramifications for the problem of knowing a mind. Nonetheless, who would deny that the philosophical implications of the dozen or so Hitchcock films discussed here are an added value — that they give these films greater depth?

I should like to comment on several aspects of the book. The first chapter argues that Hitchcock really *is* a kind of philosopher. Subsequently, each part — Deception, Mind, and Problematic Knowledge — begins with a brief account of the philosophical problematic in which I fit the films that follow. Finally, the chapters on individual films begin with a summary of the film.

1

Hitchcock as Philosopher

The title *Hitchcock as Philosopher* drops the master of suspense into a philosophical context dominated by, among others, Descartes, Hume, Kant, and Wittgenstein. How can the *auteur* of films about dangerous spies, psychotic killers, *femmes fatales*, compulsive thieves, amoral liars, haunted aristocrats, and murderous sea gulls possibly belong there? Even granting Hitchcock's greatness as a film director — even granting that he is one of the greatest of twentieth-century artists in any medium — we may still reasonably ask, How is Hitchcock a philosopher?

Aristotle wrote that "poetry is more akin to philosophy and is a better thing than history; poetry deals with general truths, history with specific events. The latter are, for example, what Alcibiades did or suffered, while general truths are the kind of thing which a certain type of person would probably or inevitably do or say."[1] The poet, in other words, shows us how a person of thus-and-such a temperament and character, when placed in these-or-those circumstances, would act. If the character is realistic or plausible, then we will come to see that he or she exemplifies general truths about human nature. And it is this exemplification of general truths that led Aristotle to call poetry "akin to philosophy" (though today we might prefer to call it "akin to psychology").

One doesn't usually think of a Hitchcock film as being a character study. And yet there are many memorable and deeply-drawn characters: the heroine of *Rebecca* and her husband; the Aysgarths and Beaky Thwaite of *Suspicion*; the two Charlies of *Shadow of a Doubt*; Guy and Bruno (especially Bruno) of *Strangers on a Train*; Jeff, Lisa, and Stella of *Rear Window*; Scottie Ferguson of *Vertigo* (perhaps Hitchcock's deepest character study); Lydia Brenner of *The Birds*; and of course Marnie. If these films illustrate "general truths" about how a type of person acts— and I think they do— then they are films "akin to philosophy" in Aristotle's sense. However, in Aristotle's sense there are many "poets" who are philosophical: Sophocles,

Dickens, Jean Renoir, Tennessee Williams, and others. Hitchcock, I want to say, is philosophical in a further sense.

Can a film be philosophical beyond presenting characters that illustrate general truths about human behavior? A film can, of course, show a philosophy lecture. For example, Richard Linklater's animated *Waking Life* (2001) has a scene in which the philosopher Robert Solomon explains the importance of existentialism. Hitchcock's characters, too, occasionally articulate some philosophy — Uncle Charlie of *Shadow of a Doubt* expresses a philosophy of "useless women" and Lisa Fremont in *Rear Window* voices qualms about the moral propriety of "peeping" into other people's windows. But, philosophical speeches aside, is it possible that philosophy be done by means of a narrative fictional movie of the sort Hitchcock made?

Metaphilosophy is the philosophy of philosophy. According to the customary metaphilosophy (CMP), the proper subjects of philosophy are matters of morals or metaphysics. On CMP, something is philosophy only if it does at least some of the following: (1) it raises a problem of morals or metaphysics; (2) it solves such a problem; (3) it defends its solution; or (4) it refutes other solutions. One might also think of (1) through (4) as marking points on a continuum, from (1) minimal philosophy through (4) maximal philosophy.

Consider (1), raising a problem of morals or metaphysics. It is uncontroversial to hold that a film can raise such problems. For example, Kurosawa's *Rashômon* (1951) raises the issue of the reliability of memory and the difficulty of overcoming subjectivity, as four different and conflicting accounts are given of a violent crime. Francis Ford Coppola's *The Godfather* (1972) raises the problem of an individual's primary loyalties: should they be to one's clan or to one's wife? The Wachowskis' *The Matrix* (1999) raises the skeptical possibility that we are being fed our "reality" by computers. A film raises a problem of morals or metaphysics when this problem is an answer to the question, What is this film about?, an answer justified by appeal to salient elements of the film. So some films are minimally philosophical.

Raising a problem of morals or metaphysics is one thing; solving it and justifying the solution another. Can a film solve a problem and justify its solution? In his *Rhetoric*, Aristotle held that the two common modes of persuasion are the enthymeme (a syllogism with missing parts) and the "paradigm" or "example."[2] (The enthymeme is a deductive argument and the paradigm turns out to be an induction; hence the two common modes of persuasion are, in effect, deduction and induction.) Good speakers use enthymemes rather than complete syllogisms because, Aristotle tells us, not everything needs to be stated; else the speaker would become "tiresome."[3]

However films are not enthymemes (though they may occasionally incorporate one into a script); they are better seen as, in Aristotle's sense, examples.

There are two kinds of examples, Aristotle tells us, one drawn from history, the other made-up: what Aristotle calls a "fable." "Fables are suitable in deliberative oratory and have this advantage, that while it is difficult to find similar historical incidents that have actually happened it is rather easy with fables. They should be made in the same way as comparisons, provided one can see the likenesses, which is rather easy from philosophical studies."[4] Here is one of Aristotle's examples:

> Aesop, when speaking on behalf of a demagogue who was on trial for his life in Samos, told how a fox, while crossing a river, was carried into a hole in the bank. Not being able to get out, she was in misery for some time and many dog-ticks attacked her. A hedge-hog came wandering along and, when he saw her, took pity and asked if he could remove the ticks. She would not let him and, when asked why, [said], "These are already full of me and draw little blood, but if you remove these, other hungry ones will come and drink what blood I have left." "In your case too, O Samians," said [Aesop], "this man will no longer harm you; for he is rich. But if you kill him, other poor ones will come who will steal and spend your public funds."[5]

"If one does not have a supply of enthymemes," Aristotle advises, though he did not tell us whether Aesop had any in defense of his unsavory client, "one should use paradigms as demonstration; for persuasion [then] depends on them."[6]

How does the example — especially the fable — work in persuasion? Again, we'll repair to Aristotle, who tells us that examples are "similar to an induction."[7] As Aristotle defines it, "Induction is a passage from individuals to universals."[8] The example he gives is, "The skilled pilot is the most effective, and likewise the skilled charioteer, then in general the skilled man is the best at his particular task." The example, in other words, can serve as a beginning of an induction to a general truth. The use of examples, Aristotle thought, is "more convincing and clear" and clear than deductive reasoning, and this because the example "is more readily learnt by the use of the senses, and is applicable generally to the mass of men, though reasoning is more forcible and effective against contradictious [*sic*] people."

Why are examples more effective in general than arguments? Aristotle's explanation — that examples are "more readily learnt by the use of the senses" — is at best incomplete. It's true that an example is a particular case, hence one can imagine or picture it, which is probably what is meant by "the use of the senses." But why is this more convincing than reasoning? Why is it convincing at all? Here's the beginning of an answer. To grasp something as an *example*— rather than just a story or isolated fact — one must grasp what it is an example *of*. And an example (*qua* example) is an illustration — an instantiation — of some general truth. Hence to grasp what something is an example of one must understand what general truth it illustrates. If the audience thinks the example is believable — plausible — then the audience will also think the general truth is believable.

It is not only ancient rhetoricians like Aesop who make use of examples. Contemporary philosophers with some frequency make use of them. Indeed, sometimes what is most memorable about certain books or essays is their engaging examples.

- Sartre's examples of bad faith (the woman who simultaneously knows and denies that her male companion has a sexual interest in her, the homosexual who has sex with men but who treats his case as "different," etc.) which show that bad faith is possible, though its necessary condition, namely that a person "know the truth very exactly *in order* to conceal it more carefully," would appear impossible to satisfy, and hence without Sartre's examples we might not agree that there could be such a thing as bad faith.[9]
- Judith Jarvis Thompson's pro-abortion example in which a person wakes up one morning, her kidneys plugged into the kidneys of a famous violinist. She's been kidnapped by a society of music lovers, and her kidneys are being used to extract poisons from the blood stream of the violinist. She's told it will only be for nine months. But it's obvious that she don't *have* to stay even though the violinist will die. Being pregnant is like being hooked up to the violinist. And if she doesn't have to donate a portion of her life to the violinist, she doesn't have to donate a portion of her life to her fetus.[10]
- Hilary Putnam's example of "twin earth" which has a substance that appears identical to water (wet, colorless, odorless) though is chemically different from earth's water — the liquid on twin earth is of chemical makeup xyz, the liquid on earth is H_2O. Both earthlings and twin earthlings use "water" to refer to this liquid. When an earthling thinks about water he thinks about what in fact is H_2O (though he is unaware of its chemical structure); when a twin earthling thinks about water he thinks about what in fact is xyz (though he too is unaware of its chemical structure). The only way to determine the contents of their thoughts is, therefore, by reference to their environment, i.e. meaning is external to thought.[11]

- Robert Nozick's "Wilt Chamberlin example," which begins with a society that has had an enforced equal distribution of wealth. Then 100,000 basketball fans from that society freely pay Wilt Chamberlin 25¢ each to watch him play, leaving Chamberlin with $25,000 more than other members. This is supposed to show that freedom "upsets" and hence is incompatible with equality.[12]

It is in this context important to point out that the fictional aspect of these examples is irrelevant to their persuasive force. It entirely misses the point to say that no one was really hooked up to a famous violinist, or that there is no such place as twin earth. If we understand the twin earth example, then we may well be persuaded that meaning is external to thought regardless of the fictitiousness of twin earth and its water-like xyz. And if we are not, ultimately, persuaded by a particular example, it does not reflect badly on the use of examples in general.

I think Hitchcock's films are fables in Aristotle's sense. They are examples that serve as the beginning of an inductive argument to a general truth. Thus Hitchcock gets at least to philosophical level (3). At least, I hope that subsequent chapters will show this. It is interesting that the philosopher with whom Hitchcock has most affinity is Wittgenstein, whose mode of doing philosophy conspicuously involves the use of fables—the builder who calls out "block" and "slab" to his assistant; the person who keeps a diary about a certain sensation he cannot define; the picture of the boiling pot emitting steam; etc.[13] Of course, Sartre, Thompson, Putnam, and Nozick do not simply offer their fables; they couch their examples in a theory which among other things does the inductive generalization for their audience, much as Aesop did for his: "In your case too, O Samians…" (Wittgenstein is less inclined to explicitly draw out the lesson of his parables, sometimes leaving that as an exercise for the reader.) In other words, when a philosopher uses an example as a means of persuasion he typically tells us what it means. Hitchcock of course does not draw out the lessons of his films explicity (in the films, anyway). But Aristotle thought telling us what the examples mean is not necessary "provided one can see the likenesses, which is rather easy from philosophical studies." Consider the chapters to follow, the philosophical studies that enable the reader to see the meaning of the example.

* * *

Did Hitchcock intend for the dozen or so films discussed here to be read philosophically? The question is ambiguous. If it means, Did Hitchcock intend to allude to Descartes, Wittgenstein, and other philosophers?, the answer is, Probably not. On the other hand, if it means, Was Hitchcock aware enough of the human condition that he could point up the issues that other canonical philosophers have wrestled with even if Hitchcock either did not read or did not intend to allude to those philosophers?, then the answer is, Certainly so. Descartes did not invent his deceiver out of whole philosophical cloth, but begins his *Meditations* with a kind of auto-biography of past deceptions: "the multitude of errors that I had accepted as true in my earliest years... Now I have sometimes caught the senses deceiving me.... How often, in the still of the night, I have the familiar conviction that I am here, wearing a cloak, sitting by the fire — when really I am undressed and lying in bed?" And then the awful thought, "How do I know [God] has not brought it about that, while in fact there is no earth, no sky, no extended objects, no shape, no size, no place, yet all these things should appear to exist as they do now?"[14] Could not Hitchcock have also thought about deception without explicit reliance on Descartes? Indeed, that *Rebecca* is a film about deception and its heroine's way out of decep-tion seems incontrovertible. Reading this film with or through Descartes and Wittgenstein is not a diversion from the narrative; it is a way *into* the story. In this way I hope to be consonant with Hitchcock's intentions.

Hitchcock's superior intelligence and erudition are evident in his films. Consider what I take to be his allusions to Hesiod (*Strangers on a Train*) and to the Tristan legend (*Vertigo*). Consider, too, the artistic heights to which he raised a louche French thriller in creating *Vertigo*. His intelligence surfaces but does not dazzle in his published writings and interviews. Sidney Gottlieb has put together a collection of Hitchcock's essays, *Hitchcock on Hitchcock*, and of course there are Truffaut's and Bogdanovich's wonderful interviews.[15] Dan Auiler has recently published a fascinating set of documents he calls *Hitchcock's Notebooks*, which contains story boards, versions of scripts for some of the films, memos to and from Hitchcock, and so on. Hitchcock's keen dramatic sense is shown here, for example in his letter to Evan Hunter on the script for *The Birds*, and his breath-taking technical savvy in his notes on the sound for the 1955 remake of *The Man Who Knew Too Much*.[16]

In the Gottlieb collection Hitchcock is unfailingly charming and witty but rarely philosophical. One exception is his essay "The Enjoyment of Fear," initially published in 1949 in *Good Housekeeping*, of all places. There Hitchcock explores what is today called "the paradox of horror." Hitch-cock begins with the observation that "millions of people every day pay huge sums of money and go to great hardship merely to *enjoy* fear seems paradoxical."[17] His solution runs as follows:

> The pleasant fear sensation experienced by a roller-coaster rider as the car approached a sharp curve would cease to exist if he seriously thought for

one moment that the car might really fail to negotiate the curve. The audience at a motion picture is, of course, entirely safe from that point of view. Though knives and guns may be used on the screen, the audience is aware that no one out front is going to be shot or stabbed. But the audience must also be aware that the characters in the picture, with whom they strongly identify themselves, are not to pay the price of fear. This awareness must be entirely subconscious; the spectator must *know* that the spy ring will never succeed in pitching Madeleine Carroll off London Bridge, and the spectator must be induced to *forget* what he knows. If he didn't *know*, he would be genuinely worried; if he didn't *forget*, he would be bored.[18]

This is a solution which in the recent literature on the topic would be called a "control theory,"[19] and while a control theory may not be ultimately the correct solution to the paradox of fear, it shows that Hitchcock can do philosophy if he chooses.

The Truffaut and Bogdanovich interviews are important and interesting for any number of reasons, though they only rarely lead Hitchcock to wax philosophical. Truffaut is interested in the history of the films—for example, "Did you select Thorton Wilder [to write *Shadow of a Doubt*] or did someone suggest him to you?"[20] Sometimes he will suggest an interpretation with which Hitchcock generally agrees, though in the following exchange Hitchcock shows he had something close to a philosophical view in mind.

> TRUFFAUT: At one time I was under the impression that *Lifeboat* intended to show that everyone is guilty, that each of us has something to be ashamed of, and that your conclusion meant that no one man is qualified to pass judgment on others. But now I believe that I was mistaken in that interpretation.
>
> HITCHCOCK: You were indeed; the concept of the film is quite different. We wanted to show that at that moment there were two world forces confronting each other, the democracies and the Nazis, and while the democracies were completely disorganized, all of the Germans were clearly headed in the same direction. So here was a statement telling the democracies to put their differences aside temporarily and to gather their forces to concentrate on the common enemy...[21]

Peter Bogdanovich more explicitly engages with philosophy when he puts this statement to Hitchcock: "*Vertigo* really is about the conflict between illusion and reality." "Oh, yes," Hitchcock responds, and proceeds to describe how and why he bathed Kim Novak in a green light. "She had come back from the dead, and he felt it, and knew it, and probably was even bewildered — until he saw the locket — and then he knew he had been tricked."[22]

I do not mean to pounce on these fragments with glad cries to show that Hitchcock is a philosopher after all. Hitchcock may not have engaged much in explicit philosophizing. But it should not be forgotten that Hitchcock always aspired to be, and generally was, a *commercially successful* filmmaker. His most important films were made in Hollywood, whose anti-intellectualism in Hitchcock's American years was summed up by Samuel Goldwyn, "Pictures are for entertainment, messages should be delivered by Western Union." In his public persona Hitchcock was intellectually light (as the pieces in Gottlieb's volume show). And he was remarkably successful at marketing himself. Hitchcock's name as director, perhaps even more than his stars, brought audiences to his films. What was in it for him publicly to explicate the depths that he certainly knew ran through his films? Another Hollywood philosopher, Louis B. Mayer, said, "Be smart, but don't show it." Orson Welles learned what it cost to flash intelligence in Hollywood.

* * *

This book looks at twelve films which it portions among three philosophical topics: (I) Deception, (II) Mind, and (III) Knowledge. The introductory chapter to each section describes the philosophical issues that Hitchcock's films address. Subsequent chapters draw out the philosophical implications from the individual films in detail.

This is a book intended for fans of Hitchcock and fans of philosophy, and it is perhaps mainly for the latter that I introduce most films with a plot summary. Readers who know the films well are invited to skip these.

I

DECEPTION

2

The Problem of Deception

Modern philosophy begins with René Descartes (1596–1650) who wondered how we could have knowledge if we were sometimes deceived: by received "knowledge" that proved wrong, by our senses, by dreams, and especially if we were deceived by an "evil spirit," who is the most worrisome skeptical hypothesis Descartes raises in the first of his *Meditations*. While it might seem plainly certain and indubitable that he, Descartes, is "sitting by the fire, wearing a winter cloak, holding this paper" in his hands, and so on, it is possible that all these —fire, cloak, paper, even hands— are illusions. "I will suppose, then, not that there is a supremely good God, the source of truth; but that there is an evil spirit, who is supremely powerful and intelligent, and does his utmost to deceive me. I will suppose that sky, air, earth, colors, shapes, sounds and all external objects are mere delusive dreams, by means of which he lays snares for my credulity."[1]

I have called the evil deceiver a skeptical *hypothesis*, and for Descartes the deceiver is a mere possibility, raised so as to motivate the reconstitution of knowledge that follows. That there *might* be a powerful deceiver is itself a threat to knowledge for Descartes. Indeed even the possibility of an evil deceiver is so potent a threat that Descartes must do nothing less than prove God's existence to reestablish certainty. "But now I have discerned that God exists, and have understood at the same time that everything else depends on him, and that he is not deceitful; and from this I have gathered that whatever I clearly and distinctly perceive is necessarily true."[2] Descartes is relieved to find the certainty he sought. "So I ought not to be afraid any longer that all that the senses show me daily may be an illusion; the exaggerated doubts of the last few days are to be dismissed as ridiculous."[3]

Descartes's consistently and cosmically deceptive genius is inconsistent with God's existence. Yet deceivers who hide or manipulate the truth, now and again, on certain matters are a fact of life — as consistent with

God's existence as are dreams. This is not an "exaggerated" and "ridiculous" skeptical doubt, but a simple observation. Illusionists, con men, and seducers have deceived multitudes. One can even deceive oneself. While such real deceivers may not have the enormous power Descartes attributes to his "evil spirit" they can deceive us nonetheless.

Descartes's evil deceiver works in a fairly specific and powerful way. He offers false perceptions—hallucinations, really—that seem true, presumably because they are so detailed and consistently maintained. There are other deceptive possibilities. A deceiver can make what is true appear to be false. Or a deceiver can keep us from the truth, not by making what is true seem false or what is false seem true, but by disabling our faculty of judgment, rendering us so cognitively enfeebled that we cannot arrive at a judgment though we may be in possession of sufficient evidence. Or a deceiver can withhold information and thereby let us draw a conclusion that is not true, a conclusion we would not have drawn had we had fuller information. Or a deceiver can make us leap to conclusions, taking scant evidence and inflating it in our minds so that we think we know when we don't. Or a deceiver can lure us into ignoring evidence so that we think we don't know when we do. And here's another difference. Descartes's evil sprit is an invisible sniper who zaps his unsuspecting targets with false perceptions. We wouldn't have a chance against him were he actual. Human deceivers in the real world, on the other hand, must have some cooperation from their targets, for mere humans cannot exercise a Cartesian evil spirit's total control over their victims.

In the quartet of films that follow—*Rebecca*, *Suspicion*, *Vertigo*, and *North by Northwest*—there is a series of deceptions that are worked on the main character. Part of what these films demonstrate is the psychology of the deceived, that is, what character traits enable the deceptions to take hold. (*North by Northwest* is an exception: there is little there of the psychology of deception that is so apparent in the other three films.) Descartes in explaining error pointed towards a sort of rush to judgment: "my will extends more widely than my understanding ... not only to things that the understanding knows absolutely nothing about, but in general to everything that the understanding does not know clearly enough at the time when the will deliberates."[4]

In other words, we sometimes *want* to believe more than we're entitled by the evidence. The heroines of *Rebecca* and *Suspicion* are fed information that plays into their insecurities. They react in opposite ways. The Fontaine character of *Rebecca* is only too willing to believe anything that confirms her sense of inferiority, seizing on anything that aggrandizes her predecessor or humiliates her. She ultimately pulls herself out of her insecurity, in part because she is given information that contradicts much of what she had been led to believe, but also because she has found a new expression of her sense of inferiority: she will be the helpmate of her irascible and dependent aristocratic husband. *Suspicion*'s Lina Aysgarth is unwilling to believe anything that would confirm what she fears: namely that her handsome and charming husband does not love her, and may have tried to murder her. Her sense of inferiority leads her back gladly into whatever her marriage brings next, which may be nice or it may be nasty.

The hero of *Vertigo* is also deceived, though in his case the deception works on him not because he is possessed of low self-esteem but because of his romantic longing. He wants more than "beers with Midge." He is a bit like Don Quixote who thinks the world to mirror the chivalrous romances he's read (not that Scottie is presented as much of a reader). Scottie is even more like the Tristan of that most romantic of tales, falling in love with another man's wife and then later again with a simulacrum of that woman. The entrancing story of Madeleine Elster, possessed by the spirit of Carlotta Valdez, is just what his romantic longings need. And later these same romantic longings bring him to explicit and conscious self-deception by dressing (and bedding) Judy Barton as Madeleine Elster. Scottie is deceived because he needs to be.

North by Northwest, possibly Hitchcock's most beloved film, plays fast and furious with the idea of deception. Nearly every character either is pretending to be someone else or is taken to be other than who he is. *North by Northwest* is about the perils of deception to be sure, but also about deception's lighter side. Descartes thought deception could have no end except falsehood; his cosmic deceiver is an *evil* genius (*genium aliquem malignum*). The principal deceiver of *North by Northwest* is the Professor, who might be seen as a Cartesian evil genius: his deceptions land Roger Thornhill in grave danger and the Professor leaves him there for much of the film. And yet this isn't the whole story. The Professor is not exactly evil; he's a spy working on behalf of his country (and also a utilitarian: he intended to sacrifice Thornhill for the greater good). Eventually Thornhill endangers the Professor's spy operation, and this forces him to bring Thornhill and Eve Kendall together. Of course without the Professor's deceptions Thornhill would have been left on Madison Avenue phoning his mother and supporting several bartenders; and there would have been no fun for him or the audience.

3

Rebecca's Deceivers

"Some years ago now I observed the multitude of errors that I had accepted as true in my earliest years, and the dubiousness of the whole superstructure I had since then reared on them; and the consequent need of making a clean sweep for once in my life, and beginning again from the very foundations…"
— René Descartes, *Meditations on First Philosophy*[1]

"Knowledge is in the end based on acknowledgement."
— Ludwig Wittgenstein, *On Certainty*[2]

Alfred Hitchcock in his first American film, *Rebecca* (1940), closely based on the novel by Daphne du Maurier, explores the idea of deceit and of deceivers who inhibit knowledge, specifically the heroine's knowledge as to her role in her marriage to Maxim de Winter. While the heroine's deception is not on the global scale Descartes attributes to his hypothetical evil spirit, her deception is carried through in ways Descartes never explored.

Hitchcock described du Maurier's tale as "quite close to 'Cinderella,'"[3] and Jack Favell (George Sanders) even refers to the new Mrs. de Winter as "Cinderella." *Rebecca* does have some points in common with that tale: a young girl, cast adrift in life, of at best modest background and stuck in a demeaning job, meets and marries a rich Englishman, who is lord of a castle; there is a wicked stepmother (Mrs. Van Hopper) and a wicked stepsister (Mrs. Danvers); there is a costume ball with an unhappy denouement; there is even a sort of glass slipper, though it is a broken cupid and leads away from not towards marriage — but no pumpkin coach, no good fairy godmother; and *Rebecca* has ghostly and murderous elements that are not part of the Cinderella story. Cinderella had a simpler task: she must get to the ball, meet her prince, and afterwards wait for the prince to find her, for she knows that he loves her. The second Mrs. de Winter, not really trying for a prince, has nonetheless been found by one; hers becomes the harder task of coaxing love out of him. *Rebecca* is a Cinderella story after the prince has found Cinderella when it turns out he's still recovering from his first marriage. *Rebecca*'s plot, unlike the Cinderella story, is furthered by deception and deceivers. And the heroine of *Rebecca*, unlike Cinderella, wrests a kind of knowledge out of doubt.

If the story-line of *Rebecca* resembles a fairy tale, its narrative structure is operatic. There is a prologue (musical overture and recitative), followed by three acts. Each act contains a principal deceiver, and each deceiver is more powerful than the one before. Each act ends with an emotional bang: a marriage proposal, a shipwreck, a fire. There is a grand house, infidelity, family honor, a mad scene in the west wing, a storm, arias of jealousy and rage, a suicide, a trial, musical *leitmotifs* for Rebecca and Manderley, and a *Götterdämmerung*-like fiery climax complete with self-immolation (though David O. Selznick, *Rebecca*'s producer, hoped only that it would rival the prior year's burning of Atlanta in *Gone with the Wind*). *Rebecca* is operatic in length, too: at 130 minutes, it is outlasted in Hitchcock's *oeuvre* only by *North by Northwest*.

Prologue. The film opens with dreamy scenes of woods, clouded over here and there with mist, and accompanied by Franz Waxman's wonderful, moody score. We then hear a female voice who begins, "Last night I dreamt I went to Manderley again." Hitchcock's camera takes us through the dream. An iron gate bars her way, though through the "supernatural powers" of the dreamer she passes through. The driveway, now overgrown, twists and turns, "and finally there was Manderley." Yet even within her dream she is further deceived — an illusion within an illusion:

> Moonlight can play odd tricks upon the fancy and suddenly it seemed to me that light came from the windows and then a cloud came upon the moon and hovered an instant like a dark hand before a face. The illusion went with it. I looked upon a desolate shell with no whisper of the past about its staring walls. We can never go back to Manderley again, that much is certain. But sometimes, in my dreams, I do go back to those strange days of my life, which began for me in the south of France.

The voice is spoken in (from) the present, and the dream it describes was dreamt in the present (or recently), though the dream concerns the past. The dream concerns the events the film is about to relate; and it is tempting to take the deception implied by a dream and illusion as prefiguring the deceptions of the story that follows. While the prologue tells of being caught in the devices of deception — a dream, a trick of the moonlight — the dreamer who relates the dream is not then dreaming, is speaking of a dream of a time past, and is not in the present, some time after the events of the film, deceived. Or is she?

Act one: the south of France. The female voice belongs to Joan Fontaine, whose character famously has no name apart from "Mrs. Maxim de Winter," acquired only after she marries Maxim de Winter. Fontaine — I will use this way of reference — is a companion (Fontaine gives the term the fanciful etymology of "friend of the bosom") to Mrs. Van Hopper (Florence Bates), a wealthy woman vacationing on the Riviera. Fontaine is a shy, timorous young woman, somewhat "mousy" despite her physical attractiveness. In her position as servant-secretary-companion to the bossy Mrs. Van Hopper, Fontaine has little life of her own. This will soon change for the recently widowed Maxim de Winter (Laurence Olivier) happens to be staying at the same hotel. While Mrs. Van Hopper attempts to make social and possibly romantic connections with Maxim — we learn from Mrs. Van Hopper that Maxim's wife, the "beautiful Rebecca," has recently drowned — it is Fontaine who captures his attention. Maxim, obviously older than Fontaine, takes her for a drive; that night they go dancing; the next day another drive. But Fontaine is uncertain of Maxim's motives. "Why did you ask me, Mr. de Winter?" He grows angry. "I asked you to come out with me because I wanted the company. But if you think I asked you out of kindness or charity you can get out of the car and find your own way back."

Suddenly Mrs. Van Hopper receives word of her daughter's marriage and decides that she will leave immediately for New York. Fontaine rushes to Maxim's room to tell him that she must accompany her employer, whereupon Maxim asks her to marry him (out of her sight and ours, from his bedroom, where he has gone to dress):

> MAXIM: Which would you prefer, New York or Manderley?
>
> FONTAINE: Please don't joke about it. Mrs. Van Hopper's waiting and I'd better say goodbye now.
>
> MAXIM: I repeat what I said. Either you go to America with Mrs. Van Hopper or you come home to Manderley with me.
>
> FONTAINE: You mean you want a secretary or something?
>
> MAXIM: I'm asking you to marry me, you little fool.

The camera shows Fontaine, radiant, sinking into a chair. But almost immediately she questions her happiness.

> FONTAINE: I'm not the sort of person men marry...
>
> MAXIM: Of course if you don't love me...
>
> FONTAINE: I do love you. I love you most dreadfully...
>
> MAXIM: Bless you for that. I'll remind you of this one day. You won't believe me. It's a pity you have to grow up.

The proposal is brusque, but that may be excused since it is made to pre-empt Fontaine's imminent departure. Even under such hurried circumstances, however, the proposal is made indirectly ("New York or Manderley"), and notably does not include a declaration of love. Nor through Maxim's courting did he ever tell her he loved her. Fontaine is never sure just what's going on. Why is he taking her for drives? Is he asking her to Manderley because he needs a secretary or "something"?

Indeed, Fontaine's inquiries into Maxim's motives inspire some of the later plot. She later becomes fascinated with Rebecca and Rebecca's things, and her curiosity, while eventually taking on a life of its own, springs initially from a desire to know just what Maxim sees in her, Fontaine. It is as if Fontaine is a Cartesian who wants to know, with certainty, whether Maxim loves her (and isn't just being kind or paternal or something else). Now the evidence before Fontaine at the time of Maxim's proposal is not entirely conclusive. Maxim is often solicitous, sometimes tender; he seeks out her company day after day; he sends flowers; he at least tells her he is grateful that she loves him; he proposes marriage; certainly he has saved her from the awful Mrs. Van Hopper and is taking her to a grand house which she knows from picture postcards. But he never declares his love for her.

To heighten Fontaine's doubts, deceivers intervene. The first is Mrs. Van Hopper. When Maxim tells her about the marriage Mrs. Van Hopper professes herself delighted and wishes the couple her best. Privately, after Maxim leaves the room, Mrs. Van Hopper's voice drops to the lower register she uses for servants and nurses. "How'd you manage it?" she asks Fontaine.

> I always did say that Englishmen have strange tastes. But you certainly have your work cut out for you as mistress of Manderley. To be perfectly frank with you, my dear, I can't see you doing it. You haven't experience. You haven't the faintest idea of what it means to be a great lady. Of course you know why he's marrying you, don't you? You haven't flattered yourself that he's in love with you? The fact is that empty house got on his nerves to such an extent, he nearly went off his head. He just couldn't go on living alone.

This speech prefigures the grander, more wicked deceptions from Mrs. Danvers in the west wing of Manderley. Perhaps Mrs. Van Hopper speaks truly when she says that she can't see Fontaine as mistress of Manderley. What little we know about Fontaine's background suggests that it is modest, and Fontaine presents herself as shy and timorous. But we already know that Fontaine is uncertain whether Maxim loves her, and

"You haven't flattered yourself that he's in love with you?" Mrs. Van Hopper (Florence Bates) tells the future Mrs. de Winter (Joan Fontaine, right) in *Rebecca* (1940).

while Mrs. Van Hopper can't quite know *that*, she makes up a hypothesis nearly out of whole cloth about Maxim's motives. Simply put, Mrs. Van Hopper tells Fontaine that it can only be that Maxim has gone "off his head" and that's why he's marrying her. (Later, Fontaine herself will offer an equally baseless hypothesis for why Maxim married her — he wants someone dull, someone who won't inspire gossip.) Descartes's evil deceiver makes what's false appear true. Mrs. Van Hopper makes what she can't really know and probably doesn't really believe, seem true, and she knows that she is speaking to an impressionable young woman, a "child" as she sometimes calls her. She has defined herself in part as acting in loco parentis, and now seizes on her mother role to undermine what small confidence in Maxim's affections Fontaine has attained.

Act two: Manderley. After a quick wedding and a honeymoon (alluded to in some home movies), Maxim and the new Mrs. de Winter drive to Manderley while Fontaine grows more and more anxious— and wet, as it has started to rain. Hair dripping, Fontaine and Maxim enter the great hall where the whole staff has been assembled. Fontaine is introduced to Mrs.

Danvers (Judith Anderson), Manderley's stiff and formidable housekeeper. It is immediately clear that Danvers dislikes and intimidates Fontaine. The second act portrays the discomfort the new Mrs. de Winter feels at Manderley, the gradual breakdown of her relations with her husband, and most dramatically the abusive relationship she enters into with Mrs. Danvers.

The new Mrs. de Winter is plainly ill at ease at Manderley. She enters the library to read and is told that in the morning the fire is lit in the morning room, but then she can't find the morning room. She answers the phone, "Mrs. de Winter? Oh I'm afraid you've made a mistake. Mrs. de Winter's been dead for over a year." In her nervous movement she breaks a valuable china cupid and hides the pieces in the desk. She can't seem to find out what she should be doing. Rebecca spent her mornings writing letters and making telephone calls, Mrs. Danvers informs Fontaine, though it is clear that Fontaine has no letter or calls to make. "I feel so uncomfortable," Fontaine confesses to Maxim, "I try my best everyday…"

Her relations with Maxim deteriorate. A happy walk the couple take with their dog ends up near the sea with Maxim forbidding Fontaine to go to the beach cottage, but she runs there anyway to retrieve the dog who's wandered off. Maxim is visibly angry, and when Fontaine returns, having briefly entered the cottage and seen Rebecca's touches everywhere, she tries to defuse Maxim's anger by telling him that she loves him very much. "Do you? Do you?" Maxim retorts. A tranquil moment while the couple view home movies of their honeymoon (in which both are obviously very happy) is interrupted when the matter of the broken china cupid is brought up by the butler and Fontaine is forced to admit that it was she who broke it and told no one. Her childishness angers Maxim.

Fontaine then delivers her hypothesis about Maxim's motives for marrying her, a hypothesis as made up of whole cloth as Mrs. Van Hopper's: "I suppose that's why you married me, because you knew I was dull and gauche and inexperienced, and there'd never be any gossip about me." This angers Maxim. "Gossip? What do you mean?" "I don't know. I just said it for something to say." Then comes Fontaine's question, "We're happy, aren't we? Terribly happy?" "How can I answer you when I don't know the answer myself? Happiness is something I know nothing about. If you say we're happy let's leave it at that." Ever willing to believe she isn't loved, Fontaine takes Maxim to mean that he isn't happy with *her*, but all he says is that *he* isn't happy (for reasons he doesn't specify). The story at this point becomes less *Cinderella* and more an inversion of *King Lear* in which it is now Cordelia who is trying to get an admission of love out of her father.

But the principal dynamic of this act comes in Mrs. Danvers's humiliations of Maxim's new bride. Others happen inadvertently to heighten

Fontaine's lack of self-confidence. Maxim's sister, Beatrice (Gladys Cooper), gives the well-intentioned advice that Fontaine "do something" with her hair, but then dismisses her own suggestion. "I can see by the way you dress you don't care a hoot about how you look." Beatrice's husband (Nigel Bruce) is surprised that Fontaine doesn't ride, and makes a joke when he is told that she sketches. To Frank Crawley (Reginald Denny), who manages Manderley, Fontaine confides that she "knows" that everyone always compares her unfavorably with Rebecca.

> FONTAINE: Everyday I realize things that she had that I lack — beauty and wit and intelligence and all the things that are so important.
>
> FRANK: There are other qualities that are just as important, more important if I may say so. Kindliness, sincerity, and if you'll forgive me, modesty, mean more to a husband than all the wit and beauty in the world...
>
> FONTAINE: Tell me, what was Rebecca really like?
>
> FRANK (after a pause): I suppose — I suppose she was the most beautiful creature I ever saw.

It is as if (to mix fairy tales) Cinderella had asked the mirror who's the fairest of them all, and the mirror responded, "Well, Rebecca, but you have good qualities too."

Mrs. Danvers deliberately plays on Fontaine's lack of confidence, not only in her abilities to be the mistress of Manderley, but especially in her husband's love. Danvers exhibits some surprise on finding out that Fontaine has no personal maid. "It's usual for ladies in your position to have a personal maid." She comes to Fontaine with the lunch menu for Maxim's sister and husband with the request that Fontaine specify the sauce (since Rebecca was very particular about sauces), but it is clear that Fontaine hasn't any idea what to recommend. Fontaine's bedroom is quite nice but Mrs. Danvers tells her that Rebecca's bedroom is "the most beautiful room in the house" — and *it* has a view of the sea. And when Fontaine finally enters that room, Mrs. Danvers is there to show her Rebecca's beautiful things: her underwear, hairbrushes, furs. Danvers reveals her intimacy with Rebecca, who called her "Danny," how she waited up for Rebecca, brushed her hair, laid out her nearly transparent nightgown from a case she embroidered for her mistress. "Do you think the dead come back and watch the living?" Mrs. Danvers asks the second Mrs. de Winter, who seems on the verge of believing that they do.

For a costume ball, Mrs. Danvers slyly suggests that Fontaine masquerade as one of the women in the de Winter family portraits, but it is not the first time someone wore that costume. "Rebecca!" Beatrice gasps as Fontaine enters the ballroom. Fontaine flees Maxim's anger and the

Mrs. Danvers (Judith Anderson, right) fans the insecurity of the second Mrs. de Winter (Joan Fontaine) in *Rebecca* (1940). The shadows in the background suggest the presence of the dead Rebecca (*Rebecca*, 1940).

scene of her humiliation, and follows Mrs. Danvers into the west wing. "I watched you go down just as I'd watched her a year ago," Mrs. Danvers says. "Even in the same dress, you couldn't compare." As Danvers tells her of how Maxim wandered Manderley "suffering torture because he'd lost her," Fontaine is brought to the point of emotional collapse. "You're over-wrought, madam. I've opened a window for you. The air will do you good." Mrs. Danvers takes Fontaine to the window overlooking the sea far below and delivers her poisonous final aria:

> Why don't you go? Why don't you leave Manderley? He doesn't need you. He's got his memories. He doesn't love you. He wants to be alone again, with her. [Softly.] You've nothing to stay for. You've nothing to live for, really, have you? Look down there. It's easy, isn't it? Why don't you? Why don't you? [Crooning, as if to a child.] Go on. Go on. Don't be afraid.

Fontaine seems on the verge of succumbing when suddenly a flare in the sky and cries of "Shipwreck! Ship on the rocks!" break the spell. Fontaine runs down to the beach leaving Danvers looking defeated.

Why does Fontaine fear and believe Mrs. Danvers? Maxim, Beatrice, and Frank Crawley each tell Fontaine that she needn't fear Mrs. Danvers, who is after all a servant (though Beatrice recognizes a certain danger about the housekeeper and advises Fontaine not to deal with her more than she has to). But Fontaine clearly fears Danvers more and more as time passes. Hitchcock plays up the haunted qualities of this character, lighting Judith Anderson's face from below, and having her suddenly appear in rooms. But such touches can only spook the audience. Within the fictional world of the film Mrs. Danvers isn't "lit" nor does she literally appear in rooms without entering them. Mrs. Danvers holds some power in her knowledge of how great ladies should behave and how Manderley is run, but this is not all of her power.

Her principal power is the power of the deceiver. It derives from the illusion she spins that Maxim still loves Rebecca, an illusion that Fontaine finds both appalling and appealing. This brings Danvers close to Descartes's evil genius. The deceiver of the First Meditation must spin perceptions; hence his modern philosophical counterpart is the scientist delivering sensations to an unsuspecting brain in a vat.[4] A truly convincing deceiver must not only deliver false impressions; he must offer false but convincing substitutes for the truth: mental impressions of an external world where there is none, for example. So, in place of the absent first wife, Mrs. Danvers offers to the second a narrative in which Rebecca was beautiful, loved by all, and especially beloved by Maxim. The mere memory of Rebecca will sustain Maxim in life. The illusion she creates is that Fontaine is

unwanted and unnecessary. Still, a deceiver can't deceive without the cooperation of his target, and Fontaine is very cooperative. Though she knows
Mrs. Danvers dislikes her and resents her very presence Fontaine believes
Danvers more than anyone — more than Beatrice and her husband, who
obviously are happy that Maxim married her; more than Frank Crowley,
who tells her kind things; more than Maxim, who remains solicitous
despite his moments of annoyance with her. Fontaine believes Mrs. Danvers because she fundamentally believes herself unworthy of being loved,
and Danvers's narratives play to her insecurity.

Act three: the inquest. The costume ball has become a scene for a shipwreck and confusion. Fontaine discovers Maxim in the beach cottage,
Rebecca's private space for sexual intrigue. Maxim tells her it's too late.
"We've lost our little chance at happiness." This is the entr'acte to a sort
of marital therapy session. Fontaine thinks, as usual, that whatever happened is her fault. "How could I even ask you to love me when I knew you
loved Rebecca still?" "You thought I loved Rebecca? You thought that? I
hated her." Maxim explains that Rebecca was a cruel and unfaithful wife
from the start, someone "incapable of love or tenderness or decency."
Rebecca offered him a "bargain" in which she would be allowed her friends
and sexual escapades, and in return she would make Manderley "the most
famous show-place in all the country." He accepted to preserve his "family honor." Their outwardly brilliant marriage was anything but. And
Maxim now makes the declaration of love that finally Fontaine can believe:
"I've loved you, my darling. I shall always love you." It is from this moment
on that Fontaine begins to attain knowledge: of who she is and what her
marriage will be. She will become a "friend of the bosom" to her husband.

Maxim tells Fontaine that the boat that Rebecca was sailing in when
she drowned has been found on the sea floor while the shipwreck was being
recovered, along with a body below deck. And he knows it to be the body
of Rebecca because he himself put it there. A year ago he confronted
Rebecca in the beach cottage. The camera's movements enact Maxim's narration of Rebecca's demise (thanks to Hitchcock's good taste, we are spared
a literal flashback). She had told him that she was pregnant by another
man; she laughed at him because this child which is not his would inherit
Manderley; she told him that towards her child she will be "'as perfect a
mother as she was a wife.... Well, Max, what are you going to do about
it? Aren't you going to kill me?'"

> I suppose I went mad for a moment. I must have struck her. She stood
> staring at me. She looked — almost triumphant. Then she started toward
> me again, smiling. Suddenly she stumbled, like that. When I looked

down, ages after it seemed, she was lying on the floor. She'd struck her
head on a heavy piece of ship's tackle. I remember wondering why she
was still smiling — she was dead.

Maxim then says that he put the body in the boat, took it out to sea, drilled
holes in the planking from the inside, opened the seacocks, and escaped
in the dinghy.

Rebecca was for over a year assumed drowned at sea after her boat
capsized — a body had even already been wrongly identified as Rebecca's.
But with the boat recovered, there are holes in the planks drilled from the
inside and open seacocks to explain. During the coroner's inquest it seems
as if Maxim de Winter will be accused of the murder of Rebecca de Winter, but it is learned from her London doctor that Rebecca knew she was
dying of cancer and the conclusion of the inquest is that she deliberately
killed herself. Mrs. Danvers, holding a candle and lit like a de La Tour Mag-
dalene, sets fire to Manderley and is shown consumed in the flames in
Rebecca's bedroom. (As Maxim and Frank approach the house in their car,
they echo the deceptions of the dream that opens the film. Maxim wonders whether the glow in the sky could be dawn. No, it's too early. Frank
thinks it might be the northern lights. But, no, it isn't winter. It's Manderley!)

There is a conspiracy of deceivers in this third act. Maxim de Winter colluded with his first wife to present a false front of a happy marriage,
brilliant parties, and smart friends, a deception that worked on nearly
everyone, most strikingly on his second wife. He continued the deception
when he failed to inform his second wife right from the start about what
really happened in his first marriage. It is the deception of a loving and
happy marriage that Mrs. Danvers enhances in the west wing. Maxim de
Winter had already deceived the first coroner's inquest (falsely identifying a stranger's corpse as Rebecca's, and withholding his knowledge of the
circumstances of her death). Now he and the second Mrs. de Winter con-
spire to keep hidden Maxim's role in Rebecca's death. Both are now guilty
of conspiracy of justice, and she is also possibly an accessory after the fact.
Jack Crawley, who doesn't fully believe in the inquest's verdict of suicide,
hides what he suspects (Maxim even makes a half-confession to Crawley).

Paradoxically, two of the deceivers of the film are now the truth-
tellers: Jack Favell produces the note from Rebecca that makes suicide seem
highly unlikely, and Mrs. Danvers names Rebecca's London doctor. Favell
even guesses the truth — that Maxim killed Rebecca thinking she was pregnant with another man's child. Their truth-telling, however, is not quite
done for the sake of duty: Favell sought to blackmail Maxim with the note,

and would have withheld it for cash; and the name of Rebecca's doctor had to be pried out of Mrs. Danvers, who finally reveals it to convict Maxim de Winter. Paradoxically, too, Danvers and Favell are deceived in the end, for they accept the inquest's verdict of Rebecca's suicide as the truth.

The pivotal deceiver in this third act, though, is really Rebecca herself: Rebecca, who deceived Maxim into marrying her (she had no intentions of being faithful or even a good companion to him —"Love was a game to her," Mrs. Danvers says); Rebecca, who knew Maxim would stay with her out of "family honor"; Rebecca, who made possible Mrs. Van Hopper's and Mrs. Danvers's deceptions of Fontaine; and Rebecca, who at the end deceived Maxim about her "pregnancy" and goaded Maxim into killing her, a sort of suicide, but also an act designed to leave Maxim burdened by guilt. Rebecca even managed to deceive her special confidants, Jack Favell, one of her lovers, and Mrs. Danvers too, Rebecca's confidant and enabler. "Rebecca held out on both of us," Favell tells Mrs. Danvers on the telephone. "She had cancer. Yes, suicide. Now Max and that dear little bride of his will be able to stay on at Manderley and live happily ever after." Descartes thought deceivers "evil," and they may well be; still, apart from dying young, Rebecca seems to have had more fun than anyone else in this story.

The lesbian overtones of Mrs. Danvers's— Danny's—feelings towards Rebecca have been noted. [5] It is incontrovertible that Mrs. Danvers, in Beatrice's words, "adored Rebecca." Certainly the rapturous look on Danvers's face as the flaming ceiling crashes down on her in the final shots of the film suggests that she welcomes the opportunity to destroy Manderley and revenge her mistress even at the cost of her own life (though we are meant to regard Mrs. Danvers as having gone mad). While the film implies that Mrs. Danvers was attracted to Rebecca, it does not establish that Rebecca reciprocated in kind. Maxim tells Fontaine that his first wife did "things I'll never tell a living soul," which might (or might not) be 1940's code for homosexuality. Mrs. Danvers may, as have many gay and lesbian people, been relegated to a role of confidant, allowed to brush her beloved's hair, embroider a case for her nightgown, and so on, without being allowed sexual contact. In other words Rebecca may have used Mrs. Danvers's affections for her own purposes as she used Maxim's.

Here I should like to take issue with an influential feminist writer on Hitchcock, Tania Modleski, who claims that Rebecca's "great crime ... was her challenge to patriarchal laws of succession."[6] But Rebecca, I believe, does much more than this. It is one thing to assert a right to define oneself or to challenge patriarchy; it is another to lie and hurt people to do it. Rebecca entered into her marriage with Maxim under false pretenses. Just days after the wedding she informed Maxim that she intended to be unfaithful. And she was a user: of her husband, of Frank Crawley, and even of her allies, Mrs. Danvers and Jack Favell. Even her "challenge to patriarchal laws of succession" is a lie. She is not pregnant, she has cancer.

* * *

If the first two acts of *Rebecca* enact Descartes's First Meditation, the third begins to work itself out of deception. But not by a proof of God's existence, as Descartes thought he needed. In the Cartesian system, there is a God who guarantees the truth of clear and distinct perceptions. Trust only in clear and distinct ideas and you will remain undeceived. The problem faced by Fontaine is that clarity and distinctness are in short supply in her neck of the woods. Either she remains in a muddle or she must do something else to extricate herself. And the latter is what she does. She comes to a decision — what Wittgenstein would call an "acknowledgment" — about her role in her marriage. In her search to know what Rebecca meant to Maxim, Fontaine has come to acknowledge what *she* means to her husband, which is to be his helpmate as she was Mrs. Van Hopper's. "Can't we start all over again?" Fontaine asks Maxim. "I don't ask that you love me. I won't ask impossible things. I'll be your friend, your companion. I'll be happy with that." Thus Fontaine offers Maxim a bargain, as did Rebecca, only this time it is the husband who will have the upper hand. And Maxim accepts. "I've loved you, my darling. I shall always love you," he says to Fontaine for the first time — now that he knows what the terms of their relationship are to be and what his declaration of love would mean.

Fontaine has seen that her role in her marriage to Maxim is to be his helpmate through the crisis that is to come. In particular she must shield Maxim from his self-destructive impulses: his temper, his guilt, even his possibly suicidal tendencies (we first see Maxim standing on the edge of a high cliff). Fontaine tries to assuage Maxim's guilt over the death of Rebecca. "But you didn't kill her. It was an accident." She comes to share Maxim's secrets about his role in Rebecca's death, and thereby to know some of what lay behind his strange moods. "You can't understand what my feelings were. Can you?" "Of course I can, darling, of course I can." She comes to know his weaknesses: his temper of course — it was his temper, after all, that led him to strike Rebecca — but also his willingness to give up when Rebecca's boat and body are found. Fontaine wants to go to the inquest and resists Maxim's entreaties to stay away. She advises him, twice, not to lose his temper. At the inquest Fontaine — conveniently if not deliberately — faints as Maxim begins to grow angry when asked, twice, whether relations between him and the late Mrs. de Winter were "perfectly happy," a question her faint leaves unanswered.[7] Fontaine was a servile and reluctant companion to Mrs. Van Hopper; she will henceforth be an active and ardent wife to Maxim de Winter. Fontaine will perhaps continue in her role as companion, though at least Maxim treats her better than Mrs. Van Hopper did. Fontaine has come to know who she is, and this is perhaps why Maxim tells her that she's "grown so much older."

Her maturing and its consequences—and indeed the entire arc of their relationship—are, I think, misunderstood by Robin Wood, who thinks that "Maxim de Winter marries the (unnamed) heroine because he sees her as a helpless child ... whom he can mold and dominate; in the course of the film she grows up, and romance abruptly evaporates."[8] Maxim is, initially, paternalist to Fontaine, for example telling her at lunch to eat something and during a drive to stop biting her nails. And he is attracted by her innocence in contrast with the infidelities of his first wife (he tells Fontaine he loves her "funny, young lost look"). However I don't see that Maxim wants to "mold and dominate" Fontaine. He installs her as the mistress of his huge ancestral home—and leaves her to her own devices. It is perhaps correct to say that their relationship is more father-daughter at the beginning. But this certainly changes after Maxim's revelations in the beach cottage. Maxim and Fontaine become partners in perjury. It is she who nurses him through the inquest. Certainly by this point they each know what the other is about, and if their partnership is not quite a conventional romance (despite their Hollywood kiss before the great fireplace at Manderley), their relationship has become at least honest when Fontaine "grows up."

We may not know how the lives of Mr. and Mrs. de Winter turn out after the fire. The prologue, spoken (long?) after the fire, says that "we" can never go back to Manderley, which suggests that the de Winters are still together, their bargain perhaps still honored. But of course we know little more than this about their relationship. Yet, the prologue may tell us something more about its speaker.

Fontaine has told us that "sometimes in her dreams" she goes back to those "strange days of her life," which implies that "sometimes" she has the Manderley dream. The prologue is spoken as a piece of nostalgia, a longing for a past irretrievably gone. But if dreams reveal a wish, and the prologue is nostalgic, why is it Fontaine would wish to relive what was a virtual nightmare of humiliation, deceit, and despair, followed by an inquest into whether her husband murdered his first wife, an ugly business fraught with publicity and blackmail, during which she must watch her husband commit perjury and herself become his co-conspirator? Possibly this: Fontaine has, in the "present" of the prologue, grown comfortable in her role as Maxim de Winter's companion, and revisits Manderley in her dreams as the scene of a personal success. After the beach cottage she is no longer deceived but the opposite: she has achieved knowledge of her circumstances and her role as Maxim's companion. In the "present" of the prologue she has become who she is. Her dream ignores what happened before the scene in the beach cottage as if it happened to someone she used to be but is no longer. As Fontaine overcomes her self-doubt she can see how she succumbed in the past to deception. Her dream, then, is not the illusion it seemed for it embodies Fontaine's self-knowledge; the dream reveals her triumph over her former deceived state.

* * *

Postscript: Daphne du Maurier's novel. David Selznick insisted that Hitchcock follow Daphne du Maurier's story closely — it was, after all, a best-seller — and rejected in harsh terms Hitchcock's first treatment of it. (Would that we had that treatment! The only detail known about it is that Hitchcock wanted to open with Maxim de Winter sailing to the Riviera, smoking cigars and bringing his fellow passengers to seasickness.[9]) But one plot point had to be altered. Maxim de Winter in du Maurier's novel quite deliberately shoots Rebecca after being goaded by her claim to being pregnant with another's child, then puts the body in the boat. When the body is found, it is too decomposed to discover a bullet, which conveniently hit no bone. According to Donald Spoto, Selznick and Hitchcock were forced to change the way Rebecca dies to satisfy the Hays office, which objected to a murderer getting away with it.[10] So, instead of getting away with murder, the film's Maxim de Winter gets away merely with manslaughter and obstruction of justice. Du Maurier in her novel gives a slightly stronger suggestion than the film that Rebecca had lesbian affairs. "She was not even normal," Maxim tells his second wife, which does seem like 1930's code for homosexuality. Also, du Maurier suggests that the de Winters after Manderley remain together, but live in a succession of sterile hotels. Maxim seems to have become a sort of emotional invalid.

4

The End of *Suspicion*

"'But if you are *certain*, isn't it that you are shutting your eyes in the face of doubt?'— They are shut."
— Ludwig Wittgenstein, *Philosophical Investigations*[1]

"For mightn't I be crazy and not doubting what I absolutely ought to doubt?"
— Ludwig Wittgenstein, *On Certainty*[2]

Whereas Hitchcock was initially reluctant to cast Joan Fontaine in *Rebecca*, he apparently saw the self-doubt she was able to project as the second Mrs. de Winter and wanted to reuse this persona to portray Lina McLaidlaw in *Suspicion* (1941), Hitchcock's fourth film made in America, though still set in England. Each of Fontaine's characters marries a man who, as Lina's husband might put it, is not up her alley. *Rebecca*'s Fontaine marries an older man of far higher social class; *Suspicion*'s Lina marries a man worldlier and more sexually experienced than she. In both stories, these women marry men whose affections for them are not clearly and distinctly evident. Indeed in Lina's case, she married a reckless playboy, Johnnie Aysgarth (Cary Grant), who gives signs of murderous intent directed at her (Maxim de Winter was murderous too, but only towards his first wife). Each Fontaine character is confused as to whether she is loved by her husband, though this is in some large part due to her respective husband's confusing behavior. While the doubts of the second Mrs. de Winter are fanned by deceivers and prove false, the first Mrs. Aysgarth's doubts are produced by a combination of her husband's lies and the accretion of certain facts— and may well be correct. The anxieties these doubts generate make each marriage all the worse, though Mrs. de Winter was at worst headed for divorce court, while Mrs. Aysgarth might have wound up in the morgue. *Suspicion* thus ups the ante of deception. If *Rebecca* presents a mystery over who Rebecca was and what she still means to Maxim, *Suspicion* is a suspense story whose principal question is whether Johnnie

Aysgarth will murder his wife. The suspense in *Rebecca* largely concerns whether a dead woman will break up a marriage. The suspense in *Suspicion* is whether Lina will survive her marriage alive.

*

Suspicion is narrated in two parts of unequal length. The first, and shorter, describes the courtship between Lina McLaidlaw (Joan Fontaine) and Johnnie Aysgarth (Cary Grant). The second, and longer part, tells the story of their marriage. The courtship has a generally upward trajectory as Lina finds herself the center of Johnnie's attentions. Their marriage has a generally downward trajectory as Lina's suspicions mount: first the suspicion that Johnnie continues to gamble, next that he is in deep financial trouble, then the suspicion that Johnnie has murdered his friend Beaky, and finally the suspicion that he is going to murder Lina herself. Whether her suspicion is justified or fantastical is the main issue raised by this film, and the answer turns on the evidence available to Lina (and to the audience). To exhibit this evidence requires a summary of this film's rather convoluted plot.

The courtship. Johnnie Aysgarth enters Lina's life asking for money (he's barged into her first class train compartment with a third class ticket and lacks funds to make up the difference). She's reading *Child Psychology* (and will later tell Johnnie that he's a "baby" for being so cavalier about money). Something about Lina has piqued Johnnie's interest, for in the next scene Johnnie sees her at a hunt and asks to be introduced. "She's not up your alley," a female friend tells him.

But Johnnie drops in on Lina at her parent's home. "I'm told the sight of a really eligible male is a rare treat in this part of the country." He takes Lina for a walk. The next scene abruptly gives us a long shot of what appears to be a struggle between Lina and Johnnie on a windy hilltop, though what exactly went on is unclear. He says, "What did you think I was trying to do? Kill you?" Lina says that she thought he wanted to kiss her. He says he only wanted to fix her hair.

On Lina's return home she and Johnnie overhear her parents agree that Lina is "rather spinsterish." Impulsively Lina kisses Johnnie. During lunch her father tells her that John Aysgarth is "wild," though he can't quite remember if he cheated at cards or if he were a correspondent in a divorce action. Johnnie calls and cancels their afternoon date to Lina's visible disappointment. He is nowhere to be found for a week, but he surfaces at the Hunt Club ball. Lina invites him home for a drink. At Lina's home before a huge portrait of her father in military uniform Johnnie proposes by "asking" the portrait for his daughter's hand in marriage. Each seems aware that the General will disapprove. "It doesn't matter," Lina

"I'm told the sight of a really eligible male is a rare treat in this part of the country."
Johnnie Aysgarth (Cary Grant) and three unidentified bit players invite Lina McLaidlaw (Joan Fontaine, far left) to go to church, in *Suspicion* (1941).

says. "Poor Monkey-face," Johnnie answers. Lina's and Johnnie's courtship
is about as swift as Maxim's and Fontaine's in *Rebecca*, and the marriage
proposal equally abrupt. Whereas *Rebecca*'s Fontaine was perplexed and
flustered by the sudden prospect of marriage, Lina in contrast is exhilarated because she, a near-spinster who reads books and lives with her parents, is to be the bride of the handsome and wild Johnnie Aysgarth.

The marriage. Lina and Johnnie elope. Their honeymoon is shown as
a montage of hotels: the Riviera, Monte Carlo, Venice, Paris, Naples, Capri.
On returning Lina is delighted with the house Johnnie has leased, though
she questions whether he can afford it. Financial troubles begin to surface
when Johnnie asks her for the thousand pounds he borrowed for the honeymoon. If he couldn't afford it, Lina asks him, why did he take such an
"extravagant house"?

> JOHNNIE: I didn't think you'd want to live in a shack. Girl like you is going
> to come into plenty of money someday.

> LINA: Johnnie. I'm just beginning to understand you. You're a baby. Oh, I know you didn't marry me for my money. You could have done much better elsewhere. But my income will never pay for all this. Never.

He suggests she ask her father for money. She suggests he go to work. He calls her a "dreamer" and tells her to be practical. A wedding present from Lina's parents arrives: two museum-quality antique chairs that entirely delight Lina and entirely disappoint Johnnie. Johnnie produces a letter from his cousin, Captain Melbeck, offering him a job.

Some time later, Johnnie's old friend Beaky Thwaite (Nigel Bruce) shows up and tells Lina he ran into Johnnie betting at the racetrack. But that can't be, Lina says, Johnnie's given up betting and would have been at work. Lina notices that the antique chairs are missing. Johnnie says he sold them to an "American" who liked the chairs for "a hundred apiece." Later Lina sees the chairs in the window of an antique store. Upset, she returns home. Suddenly Johnnie shows up with extravagant presents for everyone, including the antique chairs. He claims he won the money at the races, but promises to stop betting. A toast is proposed and Johnnie warns Beaky about his reaction to brandy, but Beaky has a drink anyway which results in a serious coughing fit. "One of these days it will kill him," Johnnie says.

Lina has a chance meeting with an acquaintance on the street who with evident malice tells her she's seen Johnnie at the races. But Johnnie was working, Lina tells her. She goes into the offices of Captain Melbeck (Leo G. Carroll) on an impromptu visit (and to prove to herself that her husband really *is* working). She is astonished to discover that Johnnie has been "discharged."

> LINA: What on earth are you talking about?
>
> MELBECK: How does he get away with it? What reason did he give you why I discharged him?
>
> LINA: When did you discharge him?
>
> MELBECK: Six weeks ago…. We had an unexpected audit six weeks ago, and the account showed a deficit of two thousand pounds. And when I looked into Johnnie's records … I'm terribly sorry Mrs. Aysgarth. He should have told you.

Melbeck says he won't prosecute if Johnnie returns the money. Lina tells Johnnie she knows that he lost his job. He asks whether she knows why. "No," she lies. Johnnie tells her that he and Melbeck just didn't get along.

Johnnie and Beaky make plans for a land deal using Beaky's money though the company will be in Johnnie's name. Lina sees that Beaky doesn't understand the deal. Johnnie, quite angry with Lina, tells her to keep out of his business. But the next day Johnnie tells Lina he is calling off the real estate plan: the soil isn't right, he says. He proposes taking Beaky to the land the next day to see for himself. That evening the three are playing anagrams with letter tiles, and Lina spells out "MURDER" with hers. She has a vision of Johnnie pushing Beaky over the cliffs and faints (Hitchcock emphasizes the vividness of her vision by superimposing images of Beaky falling over Lina's face). But Beaky not only survives, he tells Lina how he almost backed over the cliff and fell to his death until Johnnie jumped in the car and grabbed the brakes at great risk to himself.

Their business venture through, Beaky has to cancel financial arrangements, and invites Johnnie to go with him to Paris. Johnnie tells him he will drive with him as far as London where they can have an evening out. The next afternoon the police arrive and show Lina a newspaper article which tells how one Gordon Cochran Thwaite "met with a mysterious end in a house in Paris." It seems Mr. Thwaite was accompanied to this "house" by an Englishman who poured Beaky a very full glass of brandy, and disappeared before Beaky drank it and died. "According to the waiter, who has a slight understanding of English, his name would appear to be 'Allbeam' or 'Holebean'." Might Lina know who this other Englishman is? She tells the police only that Beaky went to Paris to dissolve the real estate corporation, though her apprehension is visible. After the police leave, she calls Johnnie's London club which tells her he didn't spend last night there. Lina is left alone, and in twilight the windows throw "spider web" shadows on the walls.

Johnnie returns. He's heard about Beaky's death. "The police were here." Johnnie looks worried and asks what she told them. Only that Beaky went to Paris to dissolve the corporation. He says he wishes she'd have let him handle it. Lina hears him tell the police on the telephone that he spent last night in London. Her suspicions that Johnnie is a murderer increase when Lina pays a visit to Isobel Sedbusk (Auriol Lee), a mystery writer, who mentions that Johnnie borrowed *The Trial of Richard Palmer*, a book about a man who poisoned someone with a large quantity of brandy. And Lina begins to fear that Johnnie is planning to murder *her* when she comes upon a letter from an insurance company denying Johnnie a loan against her insurance, and telling him that any insurance settlement is payable only on his wife's death.

Later, Lina and Johnnie are dining with Isobel, and have a conversation about murder that is on its surface light-hearted. Johnnie asks whether there is an undetectable poison. Isobel admits that there is and that it is commonly available, but declines to say more. Isobel comments to Johnnie,

"You couldn't commit a murder if you tried for a hundred years," though Lina is seriously interested in this opinion because the subject has become serious for her. The looks exchanged between Lina and her husband after Isobel's pronouncement seem fraught with meaning though *which* meaning is left unspecified.

Lina's suspicions bring her to shivers and emotional collapse in her bedroom. Her marriage appears to be unraveling as she asks Johnnie to sleep in his own room. When she awakens, Johnnie and Isobel hover protectively over her. Johnnie leaves the room and Isobel says that Johnnie is trying to worm her murder mystery secrets out of her—in particular, about the undetectable poison. "Is whatever it is painful?" Lina asks. "Not in the least. In fact I should think it would be a most pleasant death." Later, Johnnie and Lina are alone in the house. Johnnie walks upstairs with a glass of milk on a tray. "Goodnight Lina," Johnnie says. He puts the milk on her nightstand, kisses her, and leaves the room. Lina looks apprehensively at the glass. The shot ends.

Morning. We see the glass of milk untouched. There is tension between the couple, and Lina is packing to go to her mother's. Johnnie insists on driving her. While passing the cliffs near the sea (where Beaky nearly met his death) another near-death is enacted. The car speeds up, its tires squeal. Lina's door flies open and Johnnie's hand shoots out: a dizzying camera angle, and then the car comes to a stop. "You almost killed us both back there," Johnnie angrily tells her. "Because you had to pull away even when I was reaching over to save you from falling out of the car. Well, you don't have to put up with me any more." Suddenly Lina thinks she understands why Johnnie asked Isobel about the untraceable poison: he wanted to use it on himself rather than face prison for embezzlement. Johnnie agrees and tells Lina that he actually went to Liverpool when Beaky was in Paris to try to borrow against his wife's insurance to pay his debt to Melbeck. Lina gives a glad cry of relief, and begs him to turn the car around. "It's as much my fault as yours," she says. "People don't change overnight," he tells Lina, "I'm no good." But then the final scene, a long shot, shows the car turning around, away from Lina's mother and back to their marriage.

* * *

Suspicion was a popular success on its initial release. It was even nominated for Best Picture, losing to *How Green Was My Valley* (other losers that year included *Citizen Kane* and *The Maltese Falcon*). Joan Fontaine won Best Actress for 1941. The film's ending, however, was always problematic. Bosley Crowther, reviewing it for *The New York Times*, wrote that "the ending was not up to Hitchcock's usual style."[3] Leonard Maltin's *Movie*

Lina (Joan Fontaine) suspects her husband (Cary Grant) of contemplating murder. Her suspicions are evident after she discovers a letter from an insurance company denying Johnnie a loan against her insurance, and telling him that any insurance settlement is payable only on his wife's death. *Suspicion* (1941).

Guide says that its "finale (imposed by the Production Code) leaves viewer flat" (though the *Guide* still awards it three and a half out of four stars).[4] More serious critics, too, have reservations. Tania Modleski tells us that "Lina begins to suspect her husband of plotting her murder — a suspicion that the film, in a highly unsatisfactory ending, proves to be unfounded."[5] Those who find the end unsatisfactory must think that the film establishes Johnnie Aysgarth as a murderer — and then takes this back in its final scene. But is the ending of *Suspicion* happy? More specifically, is the correct understanding of what takes place near the cliffs by the sea, that Johnnie has offered true explanations for his seemingly murderous behavior, explanations that impute harm to himself but to no one else, and explanations that Lina with good reason believes, thereby relinquishing her wrongly held suspicions and continuing her marriage on a truthful foundation?

How *Suspicion* came to have the ending it did has a famously tangled history. The novel on which the film is based, *Before the Fact* (1932) by Francis Iles, tells the story of a woman who discovers that her husband gambles, lies, steals her jewelry, forges her name to checks, and embezzles from his employer. In Iles's story Lina also has good reason to believe that Johnnie caused her father's death (through overexertion) and inveigled Beaky Thwaite into his death-by-brandy in Paris. Johnnie takes out a large life insurance policy on her life, and discusses the "undetectable poison" with Isabel Sedbusk. Lina, convinced Johnnie is going to murder her, and finding herself pregnant, drinks the milk her husband offers, which she believes poisoned (and it is), so that he will not "reproduce himself." She thinks of herself as an "accessory before the fact" to her own murder, hence the novel's title.

What ending did Hitchcock have in mind? Donald Spoto alludes to a memo to RKO in which Hitchcock "stated emphatically that he wanted to make a film about a woman's fantasy life."[6] This memo, however, was to allay studio jitters about casting Laurence Olivier as a murderer. Once the film was cast with Cary Grant, however, it seems Johnny's murder of Lina was back on: a memo from screenwriter Samson Raphaelson to "Hitch" suggests shortening the time it takes for the poison to work on Lina.[7] In the first filmed ending Johnnie *does* give Lina poisoned milk, though exactly what else went on is also in dispute. Spoto says that in this first version Lina is shown to have had "illicit meetings" with another man, and drinks the milk knowing it to have been poisoned, her suicide thereby made acceptable to the Hays office as "the tactic of a sinner" — but a sneak preview audience laughed at this version.[8] However, the suicide Spoto mentions is seemingly contradicted by Joan Fontaine who told an interviewer,

"[Cary Grant] did kill me in the original cut, but at the preview, the audience simply refused to accept him as the murderer."[9] In any case, the suicide/murder ending had to be redone, and scripts exist for three different endings besides the one actually released.[10] Some of these verge on the grotesque. In one, Lina drinks the milk Johnnie offers while believing it to be poisoned — but it *isn't* poisoned. Johnnie is aghast that she would think that he tried to kill her, but touched that she would drink poisoned milk for him. Ugh! In later years Hitchcock told François Truffaut that he was not pleased with the way *Suspicion* ends.

> The scene I wanted, but it was never shot, was for Cary Grant to bring her a glass of milk that's been poisoned and Joan Fontaine has just finished a letter to her mother: 'Dear Mother, I'm desperately in love with him, but I don't want to live because he's a killer. Though I'd rather die, I think society should be protected from him.' Then, Cary Grant comes in with the fatal glass and she says, 'Will you mail this letter to Mother for me, dear?' She drinks the milk and dies. Fade out and fade in on one short shot: Cary Grant, whistling cheerfully, walks over to the mailbox and pops the letter in.[11]

This ending, Hitchcock said, was nixed by the studio. "Cary Grant could not be a murderer."[12]

So it may well be that Hitchcock made a film that piles up evidence that Johnnie Aysgarth has gambled, lied, embezzled money, murdered an old friend, and attempted to kill his wife — but then in the final scene, under the studio's gun, appends an explanation *ex machina* that Johnnie is innocent (of murder and attempted murder, anyway) after all. Thought of this way, the film that was released is like a muscular statue that has at the last moment been given an epicene head. One could regard the released version as an unfortunate result of studio interference, and analyze instead the film that Hitchcock intended. And there one would find a woman at the low end of self-esteem, willing to take the poison her husband feeds her because she loves him, a woman who would rather die than lose her husband's love (though one who would posthumously punish him — a martyr who takes revenge).

However, I don't think that *Suspicion* as released is a fatally flawed film. In fact I find its ending as released *more* satisfying than the other endings Hitchcock and his screen writers considered, even if Hitchcock didn't quite plan on having his film end this way. Necessity may in this case be the mother of inspiration. The released version sums up Lina's psychology. Even Hitchcock's preferred ending would have given us only the *frisson* of death and retaliation.

Suppose, though, we begin by assuming that the "happy" (i.e. non-murderous) ending is the correct reading — the final fictional truth in this movie that trumps all that's gone before. This, I think, is how casual movie goers understand the story line — and not only the casual movie goer but the sophisticated critic as well. Truffaut describes the plot line as one in which a wife suspects her husband to be a killer "though, in fact, subsequent events will prove she's wrong..."[13] Leslie Brill places *Suspicion* on a list of films whose protagonists "scramble to happy endings,"[14] though Brill also sees that not all is well with the Aysgarths. He calls theirs a "a remarriage without laughter."[15] If the film's ending is "happy," we have a story of a woman who suspected her husband of murdering his best friend and of attempting to murder her; but whose suspicions in the end prove entirely baseless and wrong. She comes, suddenly, to know that she is not married to a murderer; and then she, just as suddenly, comes to believe that her marriage can continue happily (though there is still the little matter of the embezzled funds to pay back).

If Lina's suspicions prove baseless, we may further wonder why she entertained them at all. We might even arrive at the conclusion that her suspicions are not simply baseless but are the products of mental illness. And indeed, some critics treat the narrative after the marriage but before the final scene as driven by or filtered through Lina's hyper-emotional psychology. Donald Spoto describes the ending as revealing that Lina's suspicions were only "based on her own neurosis."[16] Robin Wood takes the film to have a "therapeutic theme," wherein Lina is "cured" when her suspicions "are eventually forced into the open" with their "fallacy exposed" and "a new start made."[17] David Sterritt places Lina among those Hitchcock characters who act on "a sense of intuition that carries much emotional weight even though it is not connected with logical thought." Ultimately Lina's intuition proves "ironically mistaken."[18] Critics who take the line that Lina is neurotic or acting emotionally interpret the "spider web" shadows on the walls cast by the skylight as externalizations of Lina's suspicions, as if Lina entangled herself in her own unfounded distrust.

All this, however, founders on the fact that Lina's suspicions are based on evidence — not "intuition" — that *would* justify suspicions of murder in a rational (i.e., non-neurotic) observer. It's not as if Lina took her husband's enthusiasm for murder mysteries as in itself sufficient grounds to suspect him of trying to poison her, or worse, simply had on no factual basis at all but merely an "intuition" that he was out to kill her. Lina, to take the film's title seriously, *suspects* her husband of being a murderer. The view that the evidence Lina has is somehow a product of her neurotic fantasies or generated by emotional intuition would have to explain away what we're shown. But unless we are to read much of the film as akin to a dream sequence or hallucination — for example, that Lina merely imagines that the police tell her that an Englishman named "Allbeam" gave Beaky the brandy, that she has only fantasized a letter from the insurance company, that she has but dreamt that Johnnie is quizzing Isobel about an undetectable poison, and so on — Lina has *real* evidence for her suspicions of her husband's misdeeds.

Suspicion is shot in such a way as to bring about a nearly exact correspondence with the evidence available to Lina and the evidence shown to the film's audience. *Suspicion* thus falls into what George M. Wilson has called a "mode of nonomniscience" of cinematic narration, in which "the narration is conscientiously restricted" to one character's "epistemological position."[19] Lina is in nearly every scene. We know only what she knows and only when she comes to know it. We don't about Johnnie's dismissal from his job until Lina knows; we are not shown what happens to Johnnie and Beaky when they leave for London because the camera stays with Lina; we don't know about Johnnie's attempt to borrow money on Lina's insurance until she does; neither Lina nor the viewer know what if anything Johnnie put in the milk. The film is suspenseful for its audience, and the best explanation for audience suspense is *our* suspicions that Johnnie might well murder Lina. Hence the high drama of the walk upstairs with the possibly fatal glass of milk — the only scene in the film that the audience is shown and that Lina herself is not witness to. (This famous scene has no information in it; it is mainly designed as a cinematic tour de force to heighten audience suspicions — Lina is nearly prostrate with her own. Hitchcock cleverly emphasized the milk by putting a light *in* it as Cary Grant carries the tray upstairs.[20])

Even incidents that confuse Lina are shown to the audience ambiguously so that we get no clearer information than Lina. I have in mind the struggle on the hilltop during their courtship which we join in progress and which is shown in a long shot: Was Johnnie only trying to fix her hair? Kiss her? That scene is somewhat playful, but the later struggle in the car near the cliff may be attempted murder. Johnnie *says* he was trying to save Lina from falling out the door, though the visual images during the cliff sequence don't conclusively support his claim — indeed, if they are to establish suspense, these images should leave it open as to what exactly is going on.

Neither Lina nor the audience, at least until the final scenes, knows whether Johnnie is a murder though all suspect he is. Indeed, if Hitchcock's film is to produce suspense over Lina's fate — and it does — the viewer must entertain such suspicions. Viewers must take it to be at least likely that Johnnie will murder Lina and fear for her safety, suspense itself being but a species of fear that things may not go as we would want. Since the audience has all and only the evidence available to Lina, if Lina is neurotically suspicious then so is the audience. Does the audience too undergo a successful cure at the film's end?

What evidence is available to Lina? She knows that Johnnie lies: he's lied about his gambling, about the antique chairs, about why he was dismissed from Captain Melbeck's employ, about where he was on the night of Beaky's death. She knows that Johnnie needs two thousand pounds or he will face criminal prosecution. She knows that the real estate deal favors Johnnie: the company is in his name only, it is entirely financed by Beaky's money, Beaky doesn't really seem to understand the nature of the project, and suddenly Johnnie pulls out of the deal—"the land's no good." She knows that if Beaky were to be killed while the company is still in place, Johnnie would profit. She knows that Beaky died from an overdose of brandy, that Johnnie knew of and even researched Beaky's fatal sensitivity to brandy, that an Englishman whose name sounded like "Allbeam" or "Holebean" gave Beaky the fatal brandy, that Beaky used to call Johnnie "Old Bean," and that Beaky had gone to Paris to dissolve the real estate corporation. She knows that Johnnie has persistently asked an authority on murder about an undetectable poison. And now he serves her a glass of milk!

Of course, good evidence is intermingled in the story line with bad: a word randomly spelled out by letter tiles manages to put Lina into a faint, though in itself it is at most a scary coincidence that proves nothing (except that Lina already suspects Johnnie). And there is ambiguous evidence: the glass of milk (we never know if it's been poisoned or not), and the struggle in the car by the cliffs (does he try to kill her or save her?). But all told there is evidence sufficient to justify the suspicion that Johnnie Aysgarth is a murderer, even if Lina herself seems to base her suspicions on the good evidence together with the bad. Keep in mind that suspicion requires less evidence than belief.

But does Lina *merely* suspect that her husband is a murderer? Doesn't she come to believe — to take it to be almost certainly *true*— that her husband is a murderer? And isn't this going a bit over the top — perhaps a bit neurotic since the evidence available to her doesn't with near certainty establish her husband's guilt? Yet a wife might behave in similar ways whether she fully believed or just suspected that her husband is a murderer. Lina drives to the cliff where Johnnie and Beaky have gone. Couldn't this be motivated by suspicion? Lina suffers emotional collapse after dinner at Isobel's, though she may be driven to despair by suspicion as well as by belief. Lina does not drink the glass of milk. But wouldn't a rational person avoid milk she simply suspected to be poisoned? The person who but suspects that she is the target of a murder plot is caught in a sort of cognitive limbo, between believing this to be true and rejecting it as false. Suspicion seems, also, an inherently unstable state for it is natural to seek cognitive closure, to settle the matter to one's satisfaction one way or the other. Suspicion may strengthen and become very close to belief, or weaken and become tantamount to doubt. No wonder Lina is distraught.

Lina, though, is not entirely driven by evidence alone; few of us are. There *is* a sort of neurosis in Lina but it isn't because she entertains unsubstantiated fantasies that her husband is a murderer. Put simply, she lacks self-confidence. "I may seem provincial, but frankly I can't understand men like you — always give me the feeling that you're laughing at me," she tells Johnnie on the windy hilltop. Her parents inadvertently panic her with their remark that she will never marry. And suddenly Lina finds herself the object of attention from the "wild" and handsome Johnnie Aysgarth, who has a checkered past that scandalizes her very proper military father. Lina will cling to Johnnie despite her suspicions about his designs on her. Her neurosis is to need to think herself loved by her husband, literally for better or for worse.

If my connection of Fontaine's characters in *Suspicion* and *Rebecca* holds, then we might expect Lina to have problems believing in her husband's love. But in Lina's case her problems with belief are the reverse of the second Mrs. de Winter's. Lina falls in love with John Aysgarth out of an anxious desire not to be a spinster; *Rebecca*'s Fontaine falls in love with Maxim de Winter against an anxious desire to remain single (she insists she's not the sort of woman men marry). While Fontaine in *Rebecca* given half a chance takes all sorts of things as signs that Maxim de Winter does not love her and is still in love with Rebecca, Lina in *Suspicion* over and over denies any signs that Johnnie Aysgarth may not love her.

She reveals this most dramatically at the final scene in which her husband explains away the film's preceding evidence. Johnnie says he wasn't trying to push Lina out of the car but trying to keep her in the car. He wanted the undetectable poison because he faced prison for embezzlement from Captain Melbeck, and couldn't seem to raise the money any other way — and by the way he says he was in Liverpool, not London, on the night Beaky was killed, trying to borrow money on Lina's life insurance. Lina *allows* Johnnie's explanations to sweep away all the evidence that was available to her. I don't think Lina was neurotic (irrational) in suspecting her husband to be a murderer, though I do think she was neurotic in dropping her suspicions on his say-so alone. Far from being "cured" at this point, she reveals her anxious needs most clearly.

Surely there are lingering issues that a rational and objective observer would have addressed, though Lina does not. Was Johnnie really in Liverpool the night of Beaky's murder? He *says* he was though he might well have been in Paris (he's lied earlier — about gambling, his job, the antique chairs, being in London). He stands to gain by Beaky's murder — the corporation they had formed is still funded if Beaky died before dissolving it. Would Johnnie confess to Lina that he murdered Beaky, if he did murder Beaky, especially if he wants to murder Lina too? He stands to gain, too, from Lina's murder (her life insurance). Was the milk never poisoned? Johnnie implies as much but we don't really know. Did Johnnie ask about an undetectable poison to commit suicide? Perhaps, but he *didn't* commit suicide. And, to paraphrase something said at the inquest into Rebecca de Winter's death, John Aysgarth doesn't seem like the sort of person who would kill himself. Besides, why would he need an *undetectable* poison to do so? (It's difficult to read Cary Grant's acting as Johnnie explains away his suspicious acts to Lina. At one or two points he seems to portray Johnnie as making things up on the spot — watch his eyes. Still, Grant's performance doesn't *clearly* mark Johnnie as delivering a series of lies.)

Throughout the film the only counter-evidence against Lina's suspicions of Johnnie's murderous tendencies come from Johnnie himself. But Johnnie has a track record as a liar — this is even Beaky's characterization of him when Beaky first meets Lina. So Lina in effect abandons all her suspicions about Johnnie solely because he, a proven deceiver, asks her to. This is not far removed from the Lina who in Hitchcock's preferred ending would drink poison because her husband asked her to. And yet when Johnnie tells Lina that people don't change overnight and that he's no good, she disbelieves *those* words. It is as if she will not acknowledge anything that disputes Johnnie's love for her, as she earlier rejected out of hand the idea that he might have married her for her money when it's fairly clear that money was at least one reason he did marry her.

Lina has become her own deceiver. It's not that she comes to believe what's false — Johnnie *may* really be innocent of murder and murderous intent — but she acquires that belief on untrustworthy grounds: the words of a deceiver, even though the deceiver may have on this occasion spoken truly. Error comes from a misuse of the will, Descartes thought.

> Now when I do not perceive clearly and distinctly enough what the truth is, it is clear that if I abstain from judgment I do right and am not deceived. But if I assert or deny, I am using my free will wrongly; if the side I take is falsehood, then clearly I shall be in error; if I embrace the other side, I shall by chance fall upon the truth, but nevertheless this decision will be blameworthy; for it is obvious by the light of nature that

perception by the understanding should always come before the determination of the will.[21]

Rush to judgment — that is, assent to what is not clearly and distinctly perceived — and you risk being wrong. God's guarantee of the truth of clear and distinct ideas won't help you then. One might say that, as the final scene is played, Lina's thinking is *clarified* by what Johnnie tells her. *She* of course takes it that Johnnie's explanations clear up all confusions. But this shows that there is a problem Descartes never resolved. Can we trust clear and distinct perceptions if it isn't clear which perceptions are clear and distinct? In her tangled circumstances and distraught state of mind — she was almost, possibly, poisoned or thrown over a cliff — Lina should at this point remain skeptical. However what seems clear and distinct to Lina is what she *wants* to be true, which is that her Johnnie is a charmer, a schemer, and a thief but not a murderer.

Even if Lina turns out to be right about Johnnie, she can't *know* she's right, at least standing next to the car by the cliffs. She has used her will wrongly. Her will to believe that she is still in a happy marriage with the dashing Johnnie Aysgarth precedes her understanding. Fontaine's character in *Suspicion* gains no self-knowledge, and is left in a darker place than her character in *Rebecca*, even if Lina's Johnnie is the innocent she takes him to be.

Well, is Johnnie Aysgarth a murderer or not? We don't know. Peter Bogdanovich once asked Hitchcock, "But the way you filmed the ending of *Suspicion* implies something far more sinister than the script does. Was this conscious?" Hitchcock responded, "Hmm. He could have killed her when he got home. You leave it open, really.... I think it would have been better if I'd shown them both driving and he'd just look back over his shoulder regretfully — because he didn't push her over. Missed his chance."[22] Still, as released, *Suspicion* may portray a husband who murdered his best friend and who tried to murder his wife and may try again. Then again, *Suspicion* may portray a husband suspected of murder and attempted murder but who is at worst only a liar, gambler, and embezzler.[23] The "spider webs" cast by the windows may be mere suspicions (shadows of doubt) or they may represent the deadly trap Johnnie has set for his wife. Even the romantic swell of music that accompanies the couple's final reunion has a minor key undercurrent — in effect questioning whether the reunion is a happy one.

In truth, both Lina and the film's audience have good reason to discount Johnnie's explanations at the end. We know no more than she does about what really happened, or what Johnnie's intentions really are. It is instructive to contrast *Suspicion* with *Gaslight* (1944), another film about a putatively crazy wife. In *Gaslight* Charles Boyer's deceits are clearly revealed to the audience (though not to his wife). The audience is given independent evidence that Ingrid Bergman is not losing her mind and that her husband has designs against her. *Suspicion*, on the other hand, is like a murder mystery left unsolved.

Lina, it appears, believes Johnnie Aysgarth out of some deep need to keep her marriage going even if it is with someone who might have attempted to murder her — and who might do it again. Lina is, in this regard, sick. But there is a real puzzle why *audiences* believe Johnnie Aysgarth. Are they sick too? I think not. For one thing, the audience has nothing factually at stake if they're wrong in believing Johnnie's explanations, though Lina fictionally has everything to lose. Perhaps audiences yearn for happy endings and will grab the first one that comes around. Perhaps audiences to popular art can't accept ambiguity. Perhaps an audience takes as the (fictional) truth in a narrative the latest thing they see and hear. At the least, an audience's cognitive guard is down — after all, they're at the movies. But I think the principal reason most audience members accept the film's conclusion at face value is that they're charmed, as is Lina, by the handsome and debonair Cary Grant (whom, I'm convinced, Hitchcock hired precisely to play against type). And, to draw a Cartesian lesson, Hitchcock shows one way deceivers deceive. Though he marks Johnnie Aysgarth as untrustworthy, Hitchcock packages the character as the irresistible Cary Grant.

"'But if you are *certain*, isn't it that you are shutting your eyes in the face of doubt?' — They are shut." Lina at the film's end wills herself into something like Wittgensteinian certainty. She shuts her eyes in the face of doubt. Now Wittgenstein had in mind the sort of philosophical doubts that Descartes called "exaggerated" and "ridiculous" — for example, that all the books and other evidence on Napoleon are for all we know really products of sense-deception, forgery, and the like, and in truth Napoleon never really existed. It apparently has come to seem to Lina herself, in the light of day by the sea facing her handsome and contrite-sounding husband, that her suspicions about him are ridiculous doubts, worth shutting her eyes to. Yet we need not be extreme skeptics to see that these doubts are serious and should not simply be ignored. Wittgenstein also wrote, "For mightn't I be crazy and not doubting what I absolutely ought to doubt?" Lina may end up paying for her certainty with her life.

5

Vertigo

"Isn't dreaming precisely the state, whether one is asleep or awake, of taking something to be the real thing, when it is actually only a likeness?"
— Plato, *Republic*[1]

"It has to be admitted that the things that appear in sleep are like painted representations, which cannot have been formed except in the likeness of real things."
— Descartes, *Meditations*[2]

"Bad faith ... has in appearance the structure of falsehood. Only what changes everything is the fact that in bad faith it is from myself that I am hiding the truth.... It follows first that the one to whom the lie is told and the one who lies are one and the same person, which means that I must know in my capacity as deceiver the truth which is hidden from me in my capacity as the one deceived. Better yet I must know the truth very exactly *in order* to conceal it more carefully — and this not at two different moments, which at a pinch would allow us to reestablish a semblance of duality — but in the structure of a single project."
— Jean-Paul Sartre, *Being and Nothingness*[3]

Vertigo (1958) is based on *D'Entre les Morts* by Thomas Narcejac and Pierre Boileau (published in the United States as *The Living and the Dead*). Hitchcock not only changed the novel's story line significantly, he produced a masterpiece of cinematic tragedy from a piece of French pulp fiction. *Vertigo*, after a lukewarm popular and critical launch, holds second place (after *Citizen Kane*) in the 2002 *Sight and Sound* critics' poll of the world's ten greatest films.

I'll say that *Vertigo* divides into four segments: a prelude, part one, an interlude, and part two. In the prelude, Scottie, the police detective, chases a man over rooftops, a chase that ends with the death of a fellow officer. Part one begins after Scottie has voluntarily retired from the police force, and concludes with the death of the real Madeleine Elster. The interlude

47

begins with the inquest, peaks with Scottie's nightmare, and ends with his release from the sanitarium. The second part begins with Scottie's search for the dead Madeleine and ends with the death of Judy Barton.

A San Francisco police officer, John "Scottie" Ferguson (James Stewart), has retired from the force because he believes his vertigo resulted in the death of a fellow officer. He passes the time with Midge (Barbara Bel Geddes), his former fiancée. An old college friend, Gavin Elster (Tom Helmore), asks Scottie to shadow his wife, Madeleine (Kim Novak), who has begun to act strangely. Scottie follows Madeleine to a flower shop, where she buys a bouquet; to a cemetery where she lays the flowers at the grave of Carlotta Valdes; to a museum where she sits entranced by a portrait of Carlotta Valdes who holds an identical bouquet of flowers and wears her hair pulled back like Madeleine Elster; finally to an old hotel where the manageress at the desk tells him that Madeleine rents a room just to sit for a while, now and then.

A local historian (Konstantin Shayne) tells Scottie that the hotel where

The deceivers of *Vertigo* (1958) leaving Ernie's restaurant in San Francisco: Judy Barton (Kim Novak) pretending to be Madeleine Elster, with Gavin Elster (Tom Helmore).

Madeleine sits was once the house of Carlotta Valdes, built for her by her rich and powerful lover, and that Carlotta went mad after her husband left her and took their child, and eventually killed herself. Gavin Elster tells Scottie he believes Madeleine to be possessed by the spirit of Carlotta Valdes who was her great-grandmother.

Scottie follows Madeleine again, this time to the San Francisco Bay, where she jumps in the water, an apparent suicide attempt. He rescues her and brings her, unconscious, back to his apartment. She awakens unclothed in his bed. "What am I doing here? What happened?" Scottie tells her she "fell" into the Bay. On the telephone Gavin Elster tells Scottie that Carlotta Valdes committed suicide at twenty-six, Madeleine's age. Scottie finds Madeleine gone.

The next day Scottie follows Madeleine from her apartment to his where she leaves a thank-you note. They decide to "wander" together, driving first to a grove of redwoods, and then to the seacoast where Madeleine tells Scottie she fears she will soon die. The next day, distraught, Madeleine tells Scottie her dream about a bell tower in "an old Spanish village." Scottie recognizes the setting as a restored mission town, San Juan Bautista. He suggests visiting the mission as a way to "destroy" Madeleine's dream. In the stables Madeleine speaks of her childhood at the mission. Scottie and Madeleine kiss and exchange declarations of love, but Madeleine tears herself away. "Too late, too late... There's something I must do." She runs up the church stairs to the bell tower. Scottie, attempting to catch up, is slowed by his vertigo. He hears a scream, and through a window sees Madeleine plunge to her death. A subsequent inquest establishes that Madeleine "committed suicide while of unsound mind," but the coroner (Henry Jones) lays part of the blame for her death on Scottie's "weakness." Gavin Elster tells Scottie, "You and I know who killed Madeleine." Scottie falls into a deep depression and ends up in a sanitarium.

Back in the world after his recovery, Scottie visits places where he used to see Madeleine: Ernie's restaurant, the museum, her apartment building. He occasionally mistakes women of similar appearance for Madeleine. On the streets of San Francisco he spots a woman who bears a striking resemblance to Madeleine Elster, though this woman is brunette and has a somewhat coarse manner while Madeleine was blonde and refined. Scottie follows her to her hotel room where she tells him her name is Judy Barton (also played by Kim Novak), a salesgirl in a department store, originally from Kansas. He tells Judy she reminds him of someone. She guesses that it was a lost love and agrees to go to dinner with him in apparent sympathy.

When Scottie leaves her room, Judy recollects her role in Madeleine

Elster's murder, how she ran up the stairs to the top of the bell tower, and how Gavin Elster threw his already dead wife off the tower. She begins to pack, and writes Scottie a letter confessing her love for him and admitting her role in the murder of the real Madeleine Elster. "Dearest Scottie, And so you found me..." She, however, destroys the letter because she hopes Scottie will come to love her for herself.

Scottie, however, sees only the dead Madeleine in Judy. He wants to buy her a gray suit identical to the one Madeleine wore. Judy protests but finally agrees. Scottie even takes Judy to have her hair dyed and styled as Madeleine's. When she finally appears as Madeleine they kiss. Later, dressing for dinner, Judy puts on a necklace, which Scottie recognizes as an heirloom of Carlotta's that belonged to Madeleine. He now realizes that the woman he knew as Madeleine Elster and Judy Barton are the same person.

On the pretext of taking her to dinner, Scottie drives Judy to the mission at San Juan Bautista. Forcing her up the bell tower he interrogates her about her relationship with Gavin Elster. "I loved you so, Madeleine," Scottie tells Judy on the roof. "Oh, Scottie, please. You loved me. Now keep me safe. Please." "Too late. It's too late," he tells Judy. "There's no bringing her back." They kiss. A nun comes up to investigate. Her approaching shadow frightens the already distraught Judy who recoils and falls off the tower to her death. A distraught Scottie looks down.

***

Vertigo is ostensibly about Scottie's vertigo, showing the crippling effects a phobia can wreak on a man's life. However the title seems more designed to bring in the audience than to point to the film's true theme. For the film is more importantly about intense, obsessive love, which in Scottie's case ruins his life — twice. The film can be said to compare phobia and obsession: both narrow one's focus to one circumstance that one everywhere avoids or everywhere seeks. These similarities are emblematized in the title sequence in which the revolving spirals that stand for Scottie's vertigo become superimposed over the face of Kim Novak, an effect Martin Scorsese called a "whirlpool of obsession."[4] Scottie's attempt to restyle Judy into Madeleine can be seen as a metaphor for what men do to women in general — in Tania Modleski's words, "that femininity in our culture is largely a male construct."[5] Or more narrowly, what a film director does to an actress. Or more narrowly yet, a metaphor for the director of *Vertigo* himself, for what Scottie does is to turn plainly dressed, brunette Judy Barton into a stylish Hitchcock blonde.

The film is principally about deception. There is of course the deception of another, which connects *Vertigo* with *Rebecca* and *Suspicion*. Gavin

During location shooting of *Vertigo* (1958), Alfred Hitchcock shows Kim Novak (as Judy Barton) and several bit players the walk he wants.

Elster and Judy Barton's conspiracy of lies drives the plot until the murder of Madeleine. And even afterwards, Judy Barton, when chanced on by Scottie, continues to hide the truth from him; and when she betrays herself with the necklace, Scottie keeps his knowledge of the truth from her. *Vertigo*, however, explores another sort of deception, for it is Scottie Ferguson's predilection for *self*-deception that drives the plot after the murder. Deception hindered the self-realization of Joan Fontaine's character in *Rebecca*, and posed a danger to Lina Maclaidlaw's life in *Suspicion*. In *Vertigo* deception and self-deception are responsible for two deaths and the ruination of a man's life. This is deception raised to the level of Greek tragedy. And *Vertigo* truly is tragedy. It takes a noble man from happiness (or at least contentment) to misery. His fall comes about because of a tragic flaw: not his vertigo (this is a bit of a MacGuffin), but his romanticism, which is to say his capacity for accepting illusion though he knows it to be illusion — in brief, his self-deception.

The argument I shall make is rather complex, so let me first give an outline. I shall show that Hitchcock is mounting a critique of the romantic hero, and that he is doing this by replicating in *Vertigo* the essential elements of the medieval story of Tristan and Iseult. His critique consists of pointing to the romantic hero's willingness to accept illusion. In the first part Gavin Elster and Judy Barton in conspiracy present a fully developed illusory world to Scottie Ferguson. As Hitchcock films it, this illusory world is given the character of a dream. In part two Scottie wants to continue the dream and knowingly arranges things so that the illusion returns. His self-deception is cinematically presented as a lucid dream — a dream that the dreamer knows to be a dream. The thread of self-deception connects both parts. Scottie's police instincts should have allowed him to see through the illusion of part one; but he willingly suspends his disbelief: an indirect self-deception. In part two he intentionally sets out to continue the illusion of part one: a direct self-deception.

∗∗∗

The love of Scottie for Madeleine-Judy recalls the love of Tristan and Iseult (Isolt, Isolde): both are intense, adulterous, and tragic. In Richard Wagner's operatic version of the story, King Marke sets Tristan, his trusted nephew, on a journey to bring back Isolde, the woman Marke will marry. But a love potion brewed by a maidservant makes Tristan and Isolde fall passionately in love. They meet under cover of darkness, but are discovered. A knight, angered by Tristan's betrayal of King Marke, delivers to Tristan a fatal wound. Tristan, dying, returns to his ruined castle to await the arrival of Isolde, who he is sure will come. She arrives by ship, though too late to save Tristan, who dies in her arms, after which she also figuratively if not literally expires.

In *Vertigo*, a rich and powerful man sets his trusted college friend to guard his wife. Gavin Elster reveals, in his conversation with Scottie in the shipyard, a nostalgia for a past in which men had the "freedom and power" to do what they wished, which links him explicitly with the man who discarded Carlotta Valdes and implicitly with Wagner's King Marke, another man from the past exercising his freedom and power to work his will on an unwilling woman. Scottie falls in love with the woman he was to guard, thus violating his friend's trust, and the woman, we later find out, has fallen in love with him. There is no magic love potion in *Vertigo*, though Scottie's attraction is enhanced by Madeleine's trances and stories of the "sad Carlotta." The wound to Scottie is delivered by the coroner who during the inquest into Madeleine Elster's death calls him "an unfortunate choice" for the "role of watchdog and protector."

Scottie ends up not at a ruined castle but in a sanitarium. Tristan against all reason awaits Isolde's coming to Brittany, and Scottie against all reason searches San Francisco for the dead Madeleine. And astonishingly both Isolde and Madeleine show up! Wagner's lovers wait for the night: "O we were now / dedicated to night! / Spiteful day, / filled with envy, / could separate us with its deceit / but no longer cheat us with its lies!"[6] *Vertigo*'s lovers meet not at night but in dreams, on which more later.

Bernard Herrmann's score, his greatest, seems more integrated into *Vertigo* than in his other films with Hitchcock, moving this film towards opera. A *musical* resemblance between *Vertigo* and *Tristan*, however, ought not to be pushed too far. Dan Auiler finds in Herrmann's score an allusion to the "dark leitmotifs of Wagner's *Tristan und Isolde*."[7] Herrmann's score sometimes sounds like Wagner, but it also sometimes sounds like Tchaikovsky, sometimes like Dukas, and so on. To my ears the music recalls, when it's Wagnerian, the sound world of the *Ring*, not *Tristan*.

In the sources of the Tristan myth, there are two Iseults, a circumstance Wagner ignores. After their adultery is discovered, Tristan and Iseult are sentenced to death but escape, and after various hardships and adventures become separated. Iseult might have gone back to King Marke. But a second Iseult enters the story. In Denis de Rougemont's retelling, "Fresh adventures carry Tristan far away from Iseult, and he then comes to suppose that she no longer loves him. So he agrees to marry 'for her beauty and her name' another Iseult, Iseult 'of the White Hand.' And indeed this Iseult remains unstained, for after their marriage Tristan still sighs for 'Iseult the Fair.'"[8] Tristan, wounded, awaits the arrival of Iseult the Fair, who will signal her arrival by hoisting a white sail. But he is deceived by Iseult of the White Hand, who falsely tells him that that the sail is black. Tristan dies, and when Iseult the Fair does arrive, she dies also.

In the medieval version, Tristan seems to be making do with Iseult Two, who reminds him — with her beauty and name — of Iseult One. But this relation isn't entirely satisfactory to Tristan for this second Iseult remains "unstained." Scottie, too, isn't satisfied with Judy Barton, who strongly resembles Madeleine Elster. But unlike Tristan, Scottie sets out to remedy his dissatisfaction by remaking Judy into Madeleine, or at least creating for himself the convincing impression that Judy is Madeleine. *Vertigo* implies, after Judy is fully made-up as Madeleine, that she does not remain "unstained." But this relation is also doomed as Scottie's second Iseult is thrown down when a black veil appears in the form of a nun.

Hitchcock might have known of the sources of the Tristan legend from de Rougemont's book, which was well known in the 1940s, but almost surely became acquainted with the two Iseults from Victorian literature. For example, in "Tristram and Iseult" by Matthew Arnold, Tristram,

Alfred Hitchcock in his cameo appearance in *Vertigo* (1958) is carrying a hunting horn.

dying, longs for Iseult of Ireland, but is attended instead by Iseult of Brittany:

> *Tristram*: Soft — who is that, stands by the dying fire?
> *The Page*: Iseult.
> *Tristram*: Ah! not the Iseult I desire.[9]

The Tristan story was in the European air, so to speak, during the 1940s. In addition to de Rougemont's book, a French film of the Tristan story, *L'Éternel retour* (1943), directed by Jean Delannoy and written by Jean Cocteau, returns to the pre–Wagnerian "original" version, with two Iseults, the ethereal Nathalie *la blonde* and the earthy Nathalie *la brune*. As if in homage to the story's medieval roots, Hitchcock, strolling by Elster's shipyard in his cameo appearance, carries what appears to be a medieval hunting horn. (*Vertigo* isn't the only Hitchcock film to allude to Tristan and Iseult. In *The Birds* a recording of Wagner's *Tristan* is tucked into a shelf behind Annie Hayworth as she talks with Melanie about her failed romance with Mitch.)

But why insist on the Tristan legend as a source of *Vertigo*, when the film is based on *D'Entre les Morts*? The film departs from the novel in significant ways. In the novel, the discovery that Renée (who becomes "Judy" in Hitchcock's film) was really Madeleine is the surprise ending, which prompts Flavières ("Scottie") to strangle her in a rage, after which he is arrested. Hitchcock emphasized to Truffaut that he changed the timing of the discovery that Judy really was Madeleine (and not just a girl who looks like her) to induce suspense and not just surprise. "We followed the book up to a certain point. At first Stewart thinks Judy may be Madeleine; then he resigns himself to the fact that she isn't, on condition that Judy will agree to resemble Madeleine in every respect. But now we give the public the truth about the hoax so that our suspense will hinge around the question of how Stewart is going to react when he discovers that Judy and Madeleine are actually the same person."[10]

But more than this was changed. There is in *Vertigo* (but not the novel) the inquest, which delivers the nearly fatal wound to Scottie, who then, like Tristan, falls into a death-like state and longs for his beloved to return and heal him. Not only is there no inquest in *D'Entre les Morts*, Flavières flees the scene of Madeleine's "suicide," thus subjecting her husband to intense questioning by the police. (The husband is later killed, almost a suicide himself.) Scottie, like Wagner's Tristan, assumes responsibility for what has happened. *Vertigo*'s Midge Wood has no counterpart in *D'Entre les Morts*, though in the context of the Tristan story she plays the Kurwenal role, the faithful servant who understands but is barely acknowledged by the master. "I can give you one thing," Midge tells Scottie's psychiatrist, "He was in love with her.... He still is."

In Narcejac and Boileau's story, Flavières, who all but knows that Renée was Madeleine, spends his time torturing the truth out of her. In Hitchcock's film Scottie accepts Judy's story as "just a girl" from Kansas, but is driven by a need to have his beloved again, even in simulacra — which brings us very close to the second Iseult. Judy, unlike her literary counterpart Renée but like the second Iseult of legend, wants Scottie to love her for herself. "Couldn't you like me, just me, the way I am?" Flavières thinks Madeleine Gévigne still lives, having assumed a new identity as Renée Sourange. Scottie acknowledges that Madeleine Elster is dead, but constructs a fantasy in which she lives. And lastly in *Vertigo* (but not *D'Entre les Morts*) there is the nun who functions as the black sail of the Tristan legend, destroying both Scottie and Judy with her appearance.

Still, if Hitchcock is connecting *Vertigo* with the Tristan legend, why has he imported what seems an unsatisfactory element, the two Iseults? For those of us more familiar with Wagner's retelling, the introduction of the second Iseult seems to dilute the tragedy, not to mention being a bit far-fetched. Yet it is not uncommon, when a romantic relationship ends or fails, for the bereft lover to attempt to reproduce in a second partner the qualities of the first. *Vertigo* is not, of course, a slice of life. Scottie's attempt to reproduce Madeleine in Judy is more overt and extreme than what goes on in real life — but this limns Scottie's romanticism most clearly. The romantic man, like the hero, indulges in what appears to the ordinary observer as reckless or excessive behavior.[11] This is how we identify a man as a romantic, so long as his excessive behavior is aimed at a noble goal (if the goal is ignoble, we mark the man as demonic or mad).

***

The doubled character of Madeleine-Judy also gave Hitchcock an opportunity to indulge himself once again in one of his favorite formal devices. He had made prominent and successful use of doublings in *Shadow of a Doubt* (1943) and *Strangers on a Train* (1951). In these films, the doublings reinforced the similarities between the two Charlies of the earlier film, and between Guy and Bruno of the later (see chapters 8 and 9). In *Vertigo* Hitchcock's doublings have a more complex referential structure. They point to the sources of the Tristan legend, which link Scottie and Madeleine with one of the most enduring and tragic of love stories. The doublings are also self-referential, as they exhibit the downward movement of the narrative away from the possibility of happiness and towards misery. For Madeleine-Judy, while the most prominent double in *Vertigo*, isn't its only double.

Mirrors, dreams, pictures, and theater, each a mimetic device that doubles a subject, are prominent in the film: Midge's sketches, Scottie's rehearsal of his acrophobia, the portrait of Carlotta, the mirrors in Ernie's, Madeleine's vision of a hallway with fragmented mirrors, Judy's family photos, and Scottie's recognition of the Carlotta necklace in the mirror in Judy's room at the Empire Hotel. Even Scottie's nightmare in the interlude is an expressivist dramatization of the events of part one. Madeleine herself is not just doubled in Judy: she's quadrupled, in the other three women whom Scottie mistakes as her.

The film itself can be said to have a doubled structure in which part one is mirrored, darkly, in part two. In part one Scottie follows Madeleine with love and hope. In part two he retreads those paths with nearly hopeless despair. The romantic thrill of first seeing Madeleine, dressed in a magnificent gown, in Ernie's restaurant in part one devolves into the disappointment of eating a steak dinner with a girl, dressed in a simple dress, who looks like Madeleine. The interlude also mirrors the prelude, darkly. The prelude, which begets Scottie's guilt and disappointment in work, is *like* a nightmare. The interlude *is* a nightmare — an awful dream about Scottie's guilt and disappointment in love. Scottie is exonerated of blame for the officer's death in the prelude, but held culpable for Madeleine Elster's death in the interlude. Indeed, the pattern of doubles in *Vertigo* is such that the later double is a more distressing copy of the earlier.

The prelude ends with Scottie's voluntary retirement from the police force and an injury to his back. In the interlude Scottie is involuntarily committed to a sanitarium because of a far more serious injury to his psyche. The solemn museum portrait of Carlotta Valdes that fascinates Scotty is later spoofed by Midge, and Scottie is offended by her joke. In the first part Gavin Elster styles Judy Barton as Madeleine Elster to deceive Scottie Ferguson; in the second part Scottie styles Judy Barton as Madeleine Elster to deceive himself. Scottie's tender and concerned love for Madeleine in part one turns into his obsessive and dominating treatment of Judy in part two. Judy pretends to attempt suicide by jumping into the San Francisco Bay in part one; she really falls— or jumps— to her death in part two. Madeleine-Judy, the self-possessed beauty of part one who leads Scottie through *her* world of pretense, becomes the needy and passive shop girl of part two, pathetically following Scottie into *his* world of pretense. Ultimately Scottie, alone and independent at the film's opening, is left alone and despondent at its close.

Besides its doubles in which the second mirrors the first darkly, there is another way in which this film displays its march towards a tragic ending. In each segment someone falls from a high place. Although Scottie always assumes blame for the falls— he's a heroic type and expects more of himself than the ordinary man — his degree of responsibility is, from a more ordinary point of view, rather slight at the beginning but increases as the film progresses. In the prelude a fellow officer falls to his death, an accident for which Scottie blames himself, though in fact his responsibility is slight. "It wasn't your fault," Midge tells Scottie. "I know," Scottie responds unconvincingly. "That's what everybody tells me." Part one ends as the real Madeleine Elster is thrown off the mission tower by Gavin Elster. Again Scottie blames himself, and indeed his suspension of critical judgment, which allows him to be beguiled by Gavin Elster's ruse, does implicate Scottie, at least to some extent. In the interlude, Scottie dreams that he falls to his death, a dream prompted by his guilt over the fall of Madeleine Elster, and while he isn't killed by his dream fall, he ends up for a time catatonic. The second part ends as Judy Barton falls (or jumps) off the same tower, the death for which Scottie is most responsible. One assumes Scottie will hold himself fully accountable for *this* death, and his life will be unbearable.

***

Vertigo re-tells the Tristan story with modern embellishments. In particular, the role of deception, which through Descartes begins modern philosophy, plays a prominent role in Hitchcock's story. Tristan and Isolde deceived King Marke. In *Vertigo* it is Gavin Elster and Judy Barton who deceive Scottie. What mode does this deception take? Descartes' evil genius spins hallucinations, filling his victim's head with images of "sky, air, earth, colors, shapes, sounds and all external objects..." though in reality none of these things exist. Gavin Elster is not that powerful. Nor does he need to be, though he has a tough enough project on his hands. He must make Scottie think a shop girl is his wealthy and well-bred wife, and not just his wife but a woman who believes herself possessed by the spirit of a tragic and romantic figure of a century ago.

One might say that Elster has written a fictional play, which he introduces with the words, "I'm not making it up. I wouldn't know how." In his play Judy Barton convincingly portrays a certain Madeleine Elster, a beautiful, well-bred, and troubled woman given to trances and apparent possession by the spirit of the dead Carlotta Valdes. Elster's plot takes this woman from disquiet to suicide with various fanciful and grotesque episodes in between. We might say that Scottie is taken in because Judy Barton is a good actress and Gavin Elster a clever playwright, costumer, and director.

But there are differences between the experience Scottie is offered and a normal piece of theater. Theater asks for the voluntary cooperation of its audience: for the willing inactivation of their disbelief in the unreality of the events about to be staged. The spectators know from start to finish that they are present at a performance, yet they inactivate this knowledge so as to obey the conventions of theatrical presentation and thereby enjoy the play. Further, the players are normally behind the fourth wall, and the audience is not part of the performance.

The experience Gavin Elster creates for Scottie is not marked as a piece of theater; hence if Scottie is to inactivate his disbelief he must be tricked or charmed into it. Elster also breaks the fourth wall, and involves Scottie in the performance. He does this slowly. At first Scottie is an observer to Madeleine's comings and goings, hovering in the background. But then after Madeleine jumps into the bay, Scottie becomes an active character in Elster's story. He and Madeleine wander together, talk, kiss, and of course he follows her to her "suicide." But theatre now seems to be the wrong category for what Gavin Elster creates, because Scottie is put into an all-enveloping world — like the dreamer in a dream.

Hitchcock aids and abets this reading in how he portrays the Scottie-Madeleine moments of part one. Scottie's first introduction to Madeleine

Elster is done by a slow pan through the restaurant crowd. When he follows her through the streets of San Francisco, to the flower shop, the church, the art museum, the pace is the opposite of a chase. Scottie shadows Madeleine through languid tracking shots, accompanied by Bernard Herrmann's slow, wistful music. The script at points directs Madeleine to say certain lines "dreamily."[12] Hitchcock told Peter Bogdanovich he shot the Scottie-Madeleine scenes through a fog filter "in order to get this subtle quality of a dream-like nature."[13]

The Scottie-Madeleine moments of part one have not just the pace and look but also the structure of a dream. Strange things happen and ordinary things happen in strange ways. Madeleine enters the flower shop through a dark storage room into an explosion of color. She is seen entering a church, but then isn't there. She's found in the cemetery outside. She sits for a long time before a portrait of a woman whose hairstyle she mimics. She enters an old hotel, but then cannot be found in the room in which she was seen, and her car mysteriously vanishes.

The dream becomes erotic when Madeleine tears apart her floral bouquet over the waters of the San Francisco Bay. Suddenly she jumps and Scottie dives in to save her. Madeleine next wakes up naked in Scottie's bedroom without any memory of what has happened. She disappears from Scottie's apartment without a sound while Scottie is on the telephone trying to explain things to her husband. In the Muir Woods sequence she speaks as if she were someone else, and even vanishes for several moments while Scottie walks through the redwoods seeking her, bathed in a strange light. Madeleine tells Scottie she believes she will die soon, and later, at his, apartment, about a dream she recently had — about "an old whitewashed Spanish church with a cloister" near a "livery stable with red carriages lined up inside." At the mission Scottie's dream turns into nightmare as Madeleine pulls away and runs up the stairs of the bell tower, and in the fashion of nightmares Scottie desperately tries to catch up but cannot.

How odd that Elster chose a *police detective* as the target of his deception, a man whose profession it was to be suspicious, questioning, skeptical, and to uncover mystery. The film's official account — Elster knows of Scottie's vertigo — only explains why Scottie can't get himself up to the top of the mission tower. Indeed in their first encounter Scottie's skepticism reveals itself immediately. Gavin asks Scottie to follow his wife.

> GAVIN ELSTER: I'm afraid some harm may come to her.
>
> SCOTTIE: From whom?
>
> ELSTER: Someone dead. Scottie, do you believe that someone out of the past, someone dead, can enter and take possession of a living being?

SCOTTIE: No.

ELSTER: If I told you that I believe this has happened to my wife, what would you say?

SCOTTIE: Well, I'd say take her to the nearest psychiatrist or psychologist or neurologist or psychoan — Or maybe just the plain family doctor. I'd have him check on you too.

But Elster persists in "hiring" Scottie. Why is he so confident that Scottie will take the bait? Why does Scottie buy *any* of this?[14]

Scottie is a romantic hero (as was Tristan). Midge describes him as a "bright young lawyer" and he describes himself as a "man of independent means." Still, he became a police detective, a public servant in a dangerous job. But he has never married, and Midge, his former fiancée, has become his chum. He asks her about her love life, and they go out for beers together. As Tania Modleski remarks, Midge is "too prosaic for Scottie's romantic imagination."[15] And then there is Scottie's retirement. "I was sorry to read about that thing in the paper," Gavin Elster tells Scottie. "And you've quit the force." Might not Gavin Elster intuit that Scottie, disappointed with life and work, would welcome involvement with a beautiful woman enveloped in a sad yet romantic past?

Of course Scottie is not *literally* dreaming — or it put it another way, it is not a fictional truth of *Vertigo* that in part one Scottie is asleep and having dreams of flower shops, graveyards, old hotels, drowning women, and so on. However, like a dreamer and unlike a theatergoer, Scottie isn't aware that the scenes Madeleine presents to him are illusions. Most importantly, Scottie *submits* to his experience in the manner of dreamers.

What manner is this? Descartes, who worried about deception in dreams, compared dreamers to "lunatics, whose brains are so upset by persistent melancholy vapours that they firmly assert they are kings, when really they are miserably poor…. But then they are madmen, and I should appear no less mad if I took them as a precedent for my own case." Descartes continues, "A fine argument! As though I were not a man who habitually sleeps at night and has the same impressions (or even wilder ones) in sleep as these men do when awake! … As though I did not recall having been formerly deceived by just such reflections during sleep!"[16] Now to be deceived is to be brought to believe that what is false is true (or what is true is false).

But does the dreamer *believe* his wild impressions? Another famous dreamer, Samuel Taylor Coleridge, offered this hypothesis concerning dreaming.

Images and Thoughts possess a power in and of themselves, independent of that act of the Judgement or Understanding by which we affirm or deny the existence of a reality correspondent to them. Such is the ordinary state of the mind in Dreams. It is not strictly accurate to say, that we believe our dreams to be actual while we are dreaming. We neither believe it or disbelieve it — with the will the comparing power is suspended, and without the comparing power any act of Judgement, whether affirmation or denial, is impossible.[17]

There is a disagreement between Coleridge and Descartes on the matter of whether we believe our dreams. Since our "comparing power" is "suspended" in dreams, we're unable to perform "acts of judgment," and so, Coleridge concludes, the dreamer neither believes nor disbelieve his dreams. But Descartes sees, correctly I think, that because our ability to judge during dreams is impaired we almost cannot help but be taken in by them. The dreamer is cognitively crippled. He is unable, by and large, to say to himself, *This can't really be happening.*

Scottie is not cognitively crippled *exactly* in the manner of dreamers, but he voluntarily suspends his powers of critical judgment. Theatre requires the cooperation of its audience: it asks for their willing suspension (or inactivation) of disbelief in the unreality or fictionality of the events being staged. Gavin Elster, too, implicitly asks for Scottie's cooperation, and Scottie, after some initial resistance, gives in. He almost gladly disregards the sheer *preposterousness* of the whole Madeleine business. Better this sad and enchanting woman than beers with Midge and retirement.

All this sadness and enchantment leads to Madeleine's death — that is, the death of the real Madeleine Elster. During the inquest, while the coroner's remarks are not exactly on point, he does touch in Scottie a sensitive nerve, and Scottie, perhaps inchoately, realizes that he was somewhat complicit in Madeleine Elster's death. So in the interlude Scottie has a dream of horrible punishment. Flashing colors and an increasingly hysterical *habanera* from Bernard Herrmann accompany images of exploding flowers, a love triangle in which Gavin Elster embraces Carlotta Valdes with Scottie Ferguson as side-lined observer, Carlotta's necklace, and finally her open grave into which Scottie peers and begins to fall until his fall mimics Madeleine's fall as she fell to her death from the mission tower. His dream of punishment becomes true when Scottie is incarcerated in an institution in which he is forced to listen to the very Mozart that he at the beginning of part one asked Midge to turn off.

The second part is an enactment of Scottie's self-deception, which is the paradoxical condition of knowing the truth yet hiding it from oneself. After his recovery, Scottie re-visits places which Madeleine frequented:

her apartment building, the flower shop, Ernie's restaurant, the art museum. This is in part a natural expression of his sorrow: he is trying to maintain some sort of contact with the woman he loved through the places she's been. But Scottie seems to be going beyond this: he seems to *seek* Madeleine, actually expecting to run into her. Twice he thinks he's found her, though each time her look-alike looks less alike on closer inspection. The third time is a charm, when he sees Judy Barton on the street. He follows her into the Empire Hotel.

> SCOTTIE: Could I ask you a couple of questions?
>
> JUDY: What about?
>
> SCOTTIE: You.
>
> JUDY: Why?
>
> SCOTTIE: Because you remind me of somebody...
>
> JUDY: What do you want to know?
>
> SCOTTIE: I want to know your name —
>
> JUDY: Judy Barton.
>
> SCOTTIE: — who you are.
>
> JUDY: I'm just a girl. I work at Magnin's.
>
> SCOTTIE: How do you happen to be living here?
>
> JUDY: It's a place to live, that's all.
>
> SCOTTIE: But you haven't lived here long?
>
> JUDY: Yeah, about three years.
>
> SCOTTIE: Where did you live before?
>
> JUDY (exasperated): Salina, Kansas! Listen, what is this? What do you want?
>
> SCOTTIE: I just want to know who you are...

Scottie remains unconvinced during this dialogue, and only backs down when Judy produced a Kansas driver's license and family photos. If he's convinced that Madeleine Elster is dead, why should he demand proof from Judy Barton? If he's not convinced that Madeleine Elster is dead, why should he accept a driver's license as "proof" to the contrary? In fact Scottie tries to maintain himself in a state of hope, and so he must maintain the belief that the object of hope is attainable. A driver's license will do for now, though to the police detective it surely can't *prove* that Judy was not (and could not be) Madeleine.

Descartes wrote of the difficulty of maintaining his skeptical attitude in ordinary life. He even compares his inability to hold on to his skepticism to being asleep. Ordinary life without a skeptical attitude is like

"I'm just a girl from Salina, Kansas," Judy Barton (Kim Novak) insists to Scottie Ferguson (James Stewart), in *Vertigo* (1958).

dreaming. "I am like a prisoner who happens to enjoy an imaginary freedom during sleep, and then begins to suspect he is asleep; he is afraid to wake up, and connives at the agreeable illusion. So I willingly slip back into my old opinions, and dread waking up, in case peaceful rest should be followed by the toil of waking life, and I should henceforth have to live, not in the light, but amid the inextricable darkness of the problems I have raised just now."[18] And Scottie too connives at an agreeable illusion to avoid the inextricable darkness of his loss: Judy will *become* Madeleine. *Vertigo* is a film about the dangers *and* comforts of deception.

There is a phenomenon known as "lucid dreaming," which Descartes alludes to in the quote above. As described in a recent book, "Lucid dreams are those in which a person becomes aware that he is dreaming. As he realizes this the character of the dream changes, and as long as he remains aware of his state, he continues to be in a lucid dream."[19] Lucid dreamers sometimes have some control over the content of their dreams.[20] Descartes himself apparently had lucid dreams. In the third of his "Olympian Dreams," Descartes dreamt of a dictionary and a collection of poems. As recounted by Adrien Baillet, "It is a most remarkable thing that, wondering whether what he had seen was a dream or a vision, [Descartes] not only decided that it was a dream while he was still asleep but also interpreted it before he was fully awake. He judged that the *Dictionary* could only mean all the Sciences gathered together and that the anthology of the poets entitled the *Corpus Poetarum* represented in particular and in a more distinct way the union of Philosophy and Wisdom."[21]

When, after Scottie's detailed directives, Judy finally appears out of her bathroom in the Empire Hotel as fully Madeleine, she is bathed in an unearthly green light, a translucent dream woman. Scottie has gotten his dream going again. Now he can finally embrace Judy as Madeleine. Though he must be aware of the illusion — he himself after all has recreated it — he submits to it, again, as in a dream. As the camera circles the lovers, Judy's room at the Empire Hotel becomes the stables at the mission, and Scottie appears both surprised and pleased at the success of his illusion. This time around Scottie is dreaming *lucidly*. Has the pleasure and power of self-deception been any more vividly depicted?

But Scottie's dream becomes shattered with his recognition of the Carlotta necklace that Judy places around her neck. Robin Wood, who also treats the Madeleine-Scottie encounters of part one as dream-like, thinks that upon recognizing the necklace Scottie begins "extricating himself from the quicksands of illusion," and that in dragging Judy up the stairs in the mission tower "he wants to kill her."[22] In other words Wood thinks that Scottie snaps back to reality and becomes murderously angry. Yet this doesn't explain all that happens next. Why, for example, would Scottie take Judy to the mission? Why wouldn't he just, say, strangle her then and there in the Empire Hotel, as Flavières did to Reneé in *D'Entre les Morts*? And at the mission, why does he reenact the ascent of Madeleine Elster?

Scottie is at the least trying to cure himself of his obsession with Madeleine as he had tried to cure Madeleine of *her* obsession with *her* past. "I'm going to take you down there, to that mission this afternoon," he told Madeleine in part one. "And when you see it you'll remember when you saw it before, and it'll finish your dream. It'll destroy it, I promise you." In part two, Scottie tells Judy as they drive to the mission for the last time, "One final thing I have to do. And then I'll be free of the past." Once there Scottie assigns Judy a role. "I need you to be Madeleine for a while. And when it's done we'll both be free." Inside the mission: "One doesn't often get a second chance. I want to stop being haunted. You're my second chance, Judy. You're my second chance." Scottie's second chance at *what*? Surely not at saving Madeleine Elster. Getting to the top of the tower? But Scottie's acrophobia is the least of his worries at the moment. Rather, Judy offers him his second chance at making things right in another way. In part one Scottie tried to cure Madeleine by showing her that what she took to be a dream was only reality; in part two Scottie tries to cure himself by demonstrating that what he took to be reality was only a dream.

At the mission Scottie manhandles Judy up the stairs and forces her to admit her role in the murder of the real Madeleine Elster. At the top of the tower, Scottie tells Judy that she's unmasked herself. And then they have their *liebestod*:

> SCOTTIE: There's where you made your mistake, Judy. You shouldn't keep souvenirs of a killing. [Bitterly] You shouldn't — you shouldn't have been so sentimental. [Pauses, and then with great tenderness] I loved you so, Madeleine
>
> JUDY: Scottie ...when I saw you again, I couldn't run away. I loved you so. I walked into danger and let you change me because I loved you and I wanted you. Oh Scottie. Oh Scottie, please. You loved me. Now keep me safe. Please.
>
> SCOTTIE: Too late. It's too late. There's no bringing her back.
>
> JUDY: Please. [They kiss. A nun suddenly appears.] Oh, no. No! [She falls— or jumps?— and screams.]

Scottie now knows that the woman he knew as Madeleine Elster was a fictional character, a dream woman, and that the woman he loved never existed. This in part explains Scottie's anger and deep sorrow in these final scenes. It's not simply that Madeleine is no longer but that she never was. The best he can do is to tell the person who *portrayed* Madeleine Elster, "I loved you so, Madeleine," as if one were, hopelessly, to attempt communication with Hamlet by talking to Kenneth Branagh. And that, too, is why "There's no bringing her back." The dream world of part one requires a suspension of critical judgment, and Scottie can no longer do that. It is at this point that Judy Barton dovetails with the second Iseult of legend: Scottie does not want a substitute, regardless of her beauty.

Scottie's second chance meets with limited success: he cures himself of his obsession ("It's too late. There's no bringing her back.") as well as his acrophobia (he manages to look down without swooning from the top of the stairs). But in the contest between mental health and romantic illusion, mental health wins a Pyrrhic victory. Wagner's lovers expire, united in transcendental bliss, *höchste Lust*. Hitchcock's lovers separate forever, quarrelling and without reconciliation. Scottie is last seen standing on the ledge at the bell tower looking down in despair.

***

Appendix: the "tag ending." There is in the final script for *Vertigo* a small last scene after the death of Judy Barton, which had been filmed but not included in the American release. It is included on the Universal Studio's "Collector's Edition" DVD. Midge, in her apartment and wearing a bathrobe, sits listening to a radio. "Elster was last heard of living in Switzerland, but is now thought to be residing somewhere in the south of France. Captain Hansen states that he anticipates no trouble having Elster extradited, [pause] once he is found." Scottie enters. Midge hands him a drink. She sits down. Scottie goes to the window and stares out into the San Francisco night. End.

According to Dan Auiler, Hitchcock had never intended to include it in the American version, and shot it only to placate the censors[23] (who, one supposes, would object to Elster, a murderer, getting away with it). Hitchcock, however, included the tag end in the European release "under pressure from foreign distributors who insisted on a more conventional finale," according to the "Production Notes" on the Universal Studios DVD of the film. The Production Notes continue: "This brief final scene ties up many of the loose ends that have given *Vertigo* its incredible power. Although the scene adds little to the film, it does incontrovertibly reveal how much more powerful the director's instincts were than any commercial suppositions." But does the "power" of *Vertigo* derive from its "loose ends"? What "loose ends" are there, other than what became of Gavin Elster (and do we really care)? The film's standard ending frames Scottie's tragedy sublimely. The aesthetic error in including the tag ending is not that it removes ambiguities, but that it dislocates the viewer's attention away from Scottie's tragic plight — as if Wagner had, after the *liebestod*, tagged on a coda telling us what eventually happened to King Marke.

6

North by Northwest

"It follows that representation and truth are a considerable distance apart, and a representer is capable of making every product there is only because his contact with things is slight and is restricted to how they look. Consider what a painter does, for instance: we're saying that he doesn't have a clue about shoemaking or joinery, but he'll still paint pictures of artisans working at these and all other areas of expertise, and if he's good at painting he might paint a joiner, have people look at it from far away, and deceive them — if they're children or stupid adults — by making it look as though the joiner were real."
— Plato, *Republic*[1]

Vertigo was not a resounding commercial or critical success, and Hitchcock wanted to show he still could draw in audiences. For his next film he returned to a formula used in several of his earlier films: a man wrongly accused and pursued by the police. *North by Northwest* (1959) is at 136 minutes Hitchcock's longest work, and his second most financially successful film after *Psycho* (1960). Unfortunately the wittiness of its Ernest Lehman script is lost in plot summary.

Roger Thornhill (Cary Grant), a Madison Avenue executive mistaken for an American spy named George Kaplan, is kidnapped and brought to Phillip Vandamm (James Mason), a spy for a foreign power. Vandamm orders him killed but Thornhill escapes. The next day Thornhill brings in the police, but nothing remains to prove his story. Thornhill goes to the UN seeking the man who had him kidnapped, and finds himself holding the knife he pulls out of a diplomat who has been stabbed in the back.

Wanted for murder, his picture on the front-page of the newspapers, Thornhill takes a train to Chicago where he is seemingly aided by Eve Kendall (Eva Marie Saint). She tells him she's arranged a rendezvous with Mr. Kaplan, but when Thornhill takes a bus to the Illinois prairie stop, he is attacked by a crop-dusting plane and nearly killed. Back in Chicago, again trying to meet Mr. Kaplan, he bumps into Eve at her hotel. He follows her to an art auction where he finds her with Vandamm, her apparent lover. Vandamm orders his henchmen not to let Thornhill — still thought to be George Kaplan — leave alive. Thornhill stages a disturbance which brings the police, who instead take him to the airport.

There he meets the Professor (Leo G. Carroll). The Professor, working for the "United States Intelligence Agency," explains that Mr. Kaplan was but an imaginary agent created by the bureau as a decoy to lure suspicion away from Eve Kendall, who is a federal agent. But as she has at the auction revealed some feelings for Thornhill in front of Vandamm, he may now suspect her loyalty to him. The Professor plays on Thornhill's feelings for Eve and his patriotism to persuade Thornhill to go to Rapid City and act the part of George Kaplan. He agrees, and a plan is enacted in which Eve pretends to shoot Thornhill to reestablish her loyalty to Vandamm.

The Professor (Leo G. Carroll, right), working for the "United States Intelligence Agency," explains to Roger Thornhill (Cary Grant) that Mr. Kaplan was an imaginary agent created by the bureau as a decoy to lure suspicion away from federal agent Eve Kendall. *North by Northwest* (1959).

But Vandamm's secretary, Leonard (Martin Landau), discovers that her gun had fired blanks. About to board a plane, Vandamm tells Leonard that Eve is "best disposed of from a great height, over water." Eve bolts, and she and Thornhill are pursued around Mount Rushmore. As Eve and Thornhill dangle from a great height, the Professor has Leonard shot, which saves them. Eve and Thornhill are last seen, married, on a train heading into a tunnel.

⁎⁎⁎

Right from the opening credits, when to a jazzy fandango by Bernard Herrmann, abstract lines change into a glass-walled Madison Avenue office building reflecting the street below, *North by Northwest* is permeated with illusion and theatricality. It is replete with actors, acting, plays, audiences, theaters, and even critics. Roger Thornhill himself is an advertising man, whose job it is to promote "expedient exaggeration." However, the theatricality of this film is of a topsy-turvy sort. In nearly every scene of consequence, someone is either wrongly accused of role-playing, or someone really is playing a role though the role is either mistaken for reality or misunderstood in some other way. It is as if some of the audience to *Hamlet* did not know they were spectators to a fiction, while others took the lobby conversation during intermission to be the play.

Kidnapped before he can join his mother for an evening at the theater, Thornhill is brought to the Townsend residence in Glen Cove where he feels himself to be an unwilling actor in some sort of drama in which he is inadvertently playing a character named "George Kaplan." But it is Thornhill who is accused of pretense. "With such expert play-acting you make this very room a theater," Vandamm tells him, though Vandamm himself has prepared the room for a performance by drawing its curtains against the sun and turning on artificial light. The participants in this parlor drama are, however, in deadly earnest as they question and finally attempt to kill the man they take to be George Kaplan by staging a drunken automobile accident. In court for drunk driving, Thornhill's story draws raised eyebrows and bemused stares. Thornhill brings the police to the Glen Cove house, but it is as if an old stage set has been struck — books where there had been liquor bottles, a stain on the sofa gone — and a new melodrama is on the boards. This time the lady of the house tells the detectives that Roger had too much to drink last night. "What a performance!" Thornhill exclaims, not entirely ironically.

Thornhill, with his mother, thinks he's found Kaplan's hotel room and clothes. The maid and valet think Thornhill is Mr. Kaplan (because he's in Mr. Kaplan's room). Thornhill even begins answering the hotel phone as Mr. Kaplan. There is a sort of stand-up comedy bit on leaving the hotel

as Thornhill's mother (Jesse Royce Landis) jokes with Vandamm's thugs—
"You gentlemen aren't *really* trying to kill my son, are you?"—and the
audience in the elevator erupts into laughter. At the UN, Thornhill gives his
name as George Kaplan to talk to Mr. Townsend, who turns out to be a
diplomat bearing no resemblance to the kidnappers of the previous evening,
and who is promptly dispatched by a knife-throwing spy. Thornhill, photographed holding that knife, is thereby assigned his next role: assassin. On
the train to Chicago, Eve Kendall pretends to be an industrial designer roman-
tically taken with Thornhill (though her attraction is not entirely pretended),
and in Chicago Thornhill assumes the role of porter to elude the police.
Eve next appears in another role, as an accomplice of Vandamm, betray-
ing Thornhill and sending him to the Illinois cornfield. But this is also a
sort of pretense, as she is really working for the U.S. Intelligence Agency.

The elusive Mr. Kaplan is a fiction among fictions—a character who
doesn't even *fictionally* exist. Yet spies attempt to kill Kaplan, and Thornhill, desperate to meet him, is almost killed by a machine-gun toting plane
posing as a crop-duster (even mechanical objects have make-believe roles
in *North by Northwest*). After his narrow escape, Thornhill returns to
Chicago where he runs into Eve Kendall at her hotel, and plays another
role, this time of the returning lover who only wants to be with his beloved,
while she, too, plays a role as the solicitous girl friend who helps him out
of his dusty suit and has it cleaned. Each seems vaguely aware that the
other is playing a role though this awareness is kept to themselves.

At the auction house Thornhill calls Eve a "statue" and accuses her
of having no feelings to hurt, as if he were speaking to the character she's
portrayed. Vandamm, who's previously accused Thornhill of play-acting,
now accuses Thornhill of *bad* acting.

> VANDAMM: Has anyone ever told you that you overplay your various roles
> rather severely, Mr. Kaplan? First you're the outraged Madison Avenue
> man who claims he's been mistaken for someone else. Then you play a
> fugitive from justice, supposedly trying to clear his name of a crime he
> knows he didn't commit. And now you play the peevish lover, stung by
> jealousy and betrayal. Seems to me you fellows could stand a little less
> training from the FBI and a little more from the Actor's Studio.
>
> THORNHILL: Apparently the only performance that's going to satisfy you is
> when I play dead.
>
> VANDAMM: Your very next role. You'll be quite convincing, I assure you.

But playing dead isn't his very next role. When it becomes apparent that
Vandamm's men aren't going to let him leave, Thornhill feigns madness
(or drunkenness), creating a disturbance calculated to bring the police.

Thornhill loudly questions the authenticity of the art objects and makes crazy bids. Later, at Mount Rushmore, Vandamm will compliment Thornhill on his "colorful little exit from the auction gallery." In the police car, being driven away from the auction, Thornhill insists he's a "dangerous assassin" and a "mad killer on the loose"—Thornhill has begun to relish this role. But a radio call from the Professor to the police unmakes Thornhill's make-believe. "You ought to be ashamed of yourself," the police tell him.

"And now, what little drama are we here for today?" Vandamm asks Thornhill in the cafeteria at Mount Rushmore. It turns out to be a playlet in which Eve "shoots" Thornhill with blanks. But Vandamm and company take this to be real; thus Eve's loyalty is reestablished. Eve will later praise Thornhill's performance. At Vandamm's mountain lodge near Mount Rushmore, Leonard unmasks Eve's deception by "shooting" Vandamm with Eve's blank-loaded gun, a repeat of the earlier playlet in the cafeteria but one that uncovers rather than hides the truth. After Vandamm, Eve, and Leonard leave for the plane, the housekeeper catches sight of Thornhill's

One of many deceptions in *North by Northwest* (1959): Eve Kendall (Eva Marie Saint) shoots Roger Thornhill (Cary Grant) with blanks in the Mt. Rushmore cafeteria.

reflection in a television screen, and seamlessly assumes the role of house-keeper-who's-seen-nothing, only to return with a gun. She keeps Thornhill fixed at gunpoint, until he realizes it's a fake threat: the housekeeper is holding the gun loaded with blanks. It is fitting that the final chase takes place on a mammoth mimesis of four presidents' heads.

***

George Wilson comments that "the kidnapping has thrown Thornhill ... into a weird mélange of Alfred Hitchcock's films."[2] Certainly the film's prototype is *The 39 Steps* (1935). Hitchcock even described *North by Northwest* as "the American *39 Steps.*"[3] In that film, an innocent man, Richard Hannay (Robert Donat), is accused of murder — someone calling herself "Annabella Smith," a spy who's asked him for refuge, is found knifed in the back in his flat — and Hannay's picture ends up in the newspapers, a man wanted for murder. Pursued by both Annabella's killers, who are enemy spies, and the police, he links up — literally handcuffed — with a beautiful blonde (Madeleine Carroll) and manages to defeat the spies' plans by getting Mr. Memory (Wylie Watson) to correctly answer the question, "What are the 39 steps?" The secrets in *The 39 Steps* are in Mr. Memory's head; in *North by Northwest* they are in a little statue. There is a Professor in *The 39 Steps*, but he is the head of the enemy spy ring. Pamela, the beautiful blonde, while initially disbelieving Hannay's story and twice turning him over to the police, is later fully on the hero's side. *The 39 Steps*, which opens in the Music Hall and closes in the London Palladium, begins the play-acting continued in *North by Northwest*. Enemy spies lurking outside, Hannay escapes from his flat by dressing as the milkman. (The real milkman won't believe his true story about a murdered woman, so Hannay makes one up about a liaison with a married woman. Actually Hannay is better at improvisation than Roger Thornhill.) On the train to Scotland, he enters Pamela's compartment, and plays the role of her boyfriend; she declines to play his girlfriend. In Scotland Hannay pretends to be an auto mechanic in search of work. He survives being shot by the Professor when a hymnal in his breast pocket intercepts the bullet (an effect not unlike Eve Kendall's blanks). He escapes from the police by darting into a political meeting where he is taken to be the guest speaker and improvises a rousing speech in praise of a better world. "As long as I stand on this platform I'm delivered from the cares and anxieties which must always be the lot of a man in my position." (The wit in Charles Bennett's script gives Ernest Lehman's close competition.) At an inn, Hannay and Pamela, hiding their handcuffed hands, pretend to be married, and though the tension between them is apparent — he has threatened her with a gun (which is only his pipe) and she thinks he's a murderer — the innkeeper's wife takes them to "be so terribly in love with each other." There is a sort of chase in the London Palladium at the end — more a race against time as Hannay is about to be dragged off by Scotland Yard —from which he is rescued by a gunshot when the Professor shoots Mr. Memory.

There are also similarities with other Hitchcock films. When Dame May Whitty is nowhere to be found on the train in *The Lady Vanishes* (1938), the other passengers stage a bit of theater in which they deny ever having seen the old lady, and contend that the young heroine, who has befriended her, must be suffering delusions brought on by a conk on the head by a flowerpot. Cary Grant's drunken and almost fatal car ride in *North by Northwest* is reminiscent of his reckless driving near the cliffs in *Suspicion*, though in the earlier film it was Joan Fontaine who was endangered. And Grant's encounter with the crop duster was preceded by Joel McCrea who is nearly pulled into the gears of a windmill in *Foreign Correspondent* (1940). In that film a Dutch diplomat, carrying in memory a secret clause for an Allied treaty for his country, is abducted by enemy spies; in *North by Northwest* a statue stuffed with secret tapes is about to be taken out of the country.

In *Saboteur* (1942), Robert Cummings, falsely accused of sabotage, goes west to find the real saboteur. He is betrayed by a woman who eventually comes to be on his side. Returning east, he chases the real villain around the Statue of Liberty, another mammoth mimesis, from which the saboteur eventually dangles before plunging to his death. As he dangles, Cummings asks him to hold on. "I can't," he answers, just as Eva Marie Saint did on top of Mount Rushmore, though she did and he didn't. Ingrid Bergman in *Notorious* (1946) was enlisted to spy on Nazi agents in Brazil, and who is asked for the sake of the American cause to in effect prostitute herself by marrying Claude Rains. The Nazis come to distrust her and nearly succeed in poisoning her. Her handler in that film was of course Cary Grant, who expresses some bitterness towards Bergman for marrying Rains. In *North by Northwest* Grant is himself nearly poisoned by alcohol, and after expressing bitterness towards Evan Marie Saint for consorting with the Vandamm, becomes the spy who is handled.

What are we to make of all these similarities? It is probably true that there are only so many devices of suspense that they perforce have to be recycled: an innocent is accused of murder, the hero or heroine is in grave physical danger, spies steal secrets, the police give chase, and so on. Yet there is a self-consciousness about the use of these devices of suspense in *North by Northwest* that needs to be addressed. George Wilson thinks *North by Northwest* "the most self-referential of [Hitchcock's] films."[4] To say that Hitchcock is *referring* to his earlier films, or at least to their plot devices, must imply that Hitchcock is not simply re-using these devices, varying them somewhat, but *pointing to* and *saying* something about them. And if this is true, then we must ask why he is pointing to them and what is he saying about them.

Some critics take Hitchcock's title to refer to the main character of Shakespeare's *Hamlet* who told Polonius, "I am but mad north-north-west. When the wind is southerly I know a hawk from a handsaw." (II.ii) Stanley Cavell thinks Hitchcock is doing even more than this. According to Cavell, Hitchcock in *North by Northwest* is making reference to *Hamlet*, not to Shakespeare's play exactly, but to its sources. Cavell reminds us that the film opens with a man who identifies himself as a son. There is a "usurper" who has installed himself in the Townsend residence. The source for Shakespeare's play is Saxo Grammaticus's *Danish History* in which a beautiful woman is sent to seduce the hero — on which Cavell comments, "a peculiar prototype for Ophelia but ... near perfect for Eve Kendall." Ophelia has a brother, Laertes, a name Cavell thinks close enough to "Leonard" to establish an allusion. Thornhill's initials are "ROT," recalling Hamlet's something rotten. It is for Cavell further evidence that Hitchcock has gone back to Hamlet's source in that "north by northwest," which Cavell and other critics take to be at least an allusion to something Hamlet says, is not an exact quote from Shakespeare. Cavell concludes that "*North by Northwest* plays a special role in Hitchcock's oeuvre, a summary role. I take Hitchcock, as it were, to be saying something like the following. Granted that it is not necessary for anyone, let alone a filmmaker, to disclaim the intention of trying to compete with the quality and the importance of *Hamlet*, it is nevertheless my intention, as the filmmaker I am, to compete with Shakespeare in his handling of sources and in this way, or to this extent, to show myself to do whatever it is I do as well as Shakespeare does whatever it is he does."[5]

Even if we think there is some allusion in *North by Northwest* to the story of Hamlet, it is not necessary to appeal to Saxo Grammaticus to get a prototype for Eve Kendall. Shakespeare implies a sexual past between Hamlet and Ophelia, and let us not forget that Ophelia has been solicited by her father Polonius to find out what's up with Hamlet. That Hamlet feels Ophelia has thus betrayed him is a source of his later horrid treatment of her. Certainly Thornhill treats Eve in an Ophelia-like fashion: first he is sexually interested; later after her betrayal he refers to her as a "treacherous little tramp." On the other hand, it is a bit jarring to regard Leonard — whatever one makes of the similarities with the name "Laertes" — as a sort of brother to Eve Kendall: Leonard is jealous of Eve and informs against her, unlike Laertes who gives his life avenging his sister's death.

The Amleth of Saxo Grammaticus is far more focused on the "paramount duty of blood revenge" than Shakespeare's Hamlet, let alone Roger Thornhill.[6] While Thornhill spends much of the film wondering just what it is he is to do about his situation, he is not given Hamlet's central mission, which is to revenge his father's murder and reclaim what by birthright should have been his. What, after all, does Vandamm "usurp" other than a house in Glen Cove for a day or two? What does Thornhill reclaim?

The fact is that there is no evidence that Hitchcock intended to refer to Hamlet (let alone Saxo Grammaticus). Dan Auiler reprints several letters from a journalist, Otis Guernsey, which reiterate some ideas Guernsey discussed with Hitchcock "vaguely based on something which actually happened in the Middle East during World War II," in which a fictitious master spy is created as a decoy, and an American salesman is mistakenly saddled with this identity.[7] The ideas generated between Hitchcock and Guernsey eventually were handed to Ernest Lehman, whose first script was titled In a Northwesterly Direction. For a while the screenplay bore the name Breathless.[8] Through the second rewrite it was called The Man on Lincoln's Nose, because as Hitchcock told various interviewers, he wanted to have a scene in which Cary Grant hides in Lincoln's nostril on Mount Rushmore and has a sneezing fit.[9] North by Northwest, the title under which the film was shot, was suggested by an MGM story editor.[10] "It's a fantasy," Hitchcock told Peter Bogdanovich. "The whole film is epitomized in the title — there is no such thing as north-by-northwest on the compass."[11]

If Hitchcock is not alluding to Hamlet then he is not trying "to compete with Shakespeare in his handling of sources." Still, the sources of North by Northwest are evident to a moderately film-savvy audience, and these are Hitchcock's own films. Hitchcock returned to his sure-fire formulas to erase the semi-failure of his previous film, Vertigo, and to prove that he still could be commercially successful. In North by Northwest, his last great chase movie, Hitchcock takes the elements of suspense that he had successfully used earlier to new heights. Thornhill isn't simply accused of a crime he didn't commit; he's taken to be a master spy and sent on a chase from New York to South Dakota. A body isn't simply discovered in the hero's flat, he's photographed with the murder weapon in front of the whole world (well, the UN). Joel McCrea's encounter with the windmill is recreated as a classic of movie-making in the crop duster sequence; and the chase on Mount Rushmore is head-and-shoulders above a counterpart scene in Foreign Correspondent in which a trusted bodyguard tries to push Joel McCrea off Westminster Cathedral and ends up plunging to his own death. The auction house sequence of North by Northwest bests the political meeting of *The 39 Steps*, which was itself very fine. The spies don't simply have a hideout; they inhabit a house which appears to have been designed by Frank Lloyd Wright on top of a famous American monument. The relationship between Eve Kendall and Roger Thornhill is more complex than Hannay and Pamela's (which is comic and cute but not much more), and their conversation in the dining car is among the best instances of sophisticated flirting in film. I doubt that it can be said that *North by Northwest*'s treatment of the deceitful woman improves on *Vertigo*, and other plot devices are not so much improved on as spoofed in *North by Northwest*. Roger Thornhill's kidnapping is replete with witty lines and his drunken car ride is played for laughs; Cary Grant ludicrously disguised as a train porter has a comic shave in the men's room; the enemy spies of earlier Hitchcock are thuggish, while James Mason is urbane and droll; Thornhill and Eve banter as they dangle from Mount Rushmore ("My wives divorced me ... I think they said I led too dull a life").

And yet none of this accounts for a striking feature of this film. There is hardly an event in *North by Northwest* that does not involve some sort of ruse, guise, make-believe, or illusion. George Wilson comes closer to the mark: "*North by Northwest* presents us with a kind of wry apologia for the sort of illusionistic art — more specifically, for the sort of illusionistic cinema — that Hitchcock, paradigmatically, has always practiced. For this is a film in which the protagonist is both implicated in and thrown up against the fact that the contemporary world is a world that consistently generates and exploits the same varieties of illusionism that are directly characteristic of film itself."[12]

It is an odd sort of apologia that reiterates the very thing for which the apologia is given — as if one were to justify a claim by shouting it a second time even louder. And does the contemporary (real) world "consistently" generate illusions? I want, though, to take special exception to Wilson's assertion that *North by Northwest* exploits *the same* varieties of illusionism that are characteristic of film itself. The spectator who watches *North by Northwest* is at all times cognizant that it is a fiction, even if he does not at all times have this fact before his mind. Otherwise the spectator risks taking *North by Northwest* to be a documentary, or worse, taking Roger Thornhill to be really being chased by a crop-duster before the spectator's astonished eyes. Movie-goers are not ordinarily deceived into believing that what they're watching is real. We at some level always know it is a movie we're watching.

In contrast, the *characters* of *North by Northwest* are in nearly every scene mistaken or confused or uncertain whether it is make-believe or reality they are participants in or witnesses to. Plato worried because people mistakenly take mimetic art as reality. He never considered the opposite: that someone might mistakenly take reality to be make-believe. Roger Thornhill, a master of illusion as advertising man, is plunged into a web of illusion. In Glen Cove Phillip Vandamm takes Roger Thornhill to be play-acting, but he's not. On the train to Chicago Roger Thornhill thinks Eve Kendall is sexually interested in him, but she's play-acting — to some extent anyway. The auctioneer believes Thornhill to be mad (or drunk), but he's only acting — and he continues his act with the police, changing his role from madman/drunk to dangerous spy. Vandamm thinks Eve really shot Thornhill but she only make-believe shot him. The houskeeper catches sight of Thornhill's reflection on a television, a device that screens popular art, and keeps Thornhill at bay with what she thinks is a real gun. Leonard is shot and Vandamm wryly protests, "That wasn't very sporting, using real bullets," as if complaining that the film had violated one of its own conventions. *North by Northwest* is a metaphysical farce about illusion. The characters in *North by Northwest* sometimes behave like the proverbial yokel who jumps on stage to save the damsel from the clutches of the evil villain, sometimes like the (fictional) audience in *Pagliacci* who shout "Bravo!" not realizing that Canio has slipped out of his role as Pagliaccio to accuse his wife of actual, not make-believe, infidelity.

In the three films about deception we've considered earlier — *Rebecca, Suspicion,* and *Vertigo* — there is harm wrought by deception. Fontaine suffers through *Rebecca* due to a conspiracy of deceivers, though she rescues herself, so to speak, in the beach cottage as she comes to know what her role in her marriage to Maxim is and will be: a lifelong helpmate to an emotional invalid. *Suspicion* builds to a climax of deception in which Lina gives up, on little evidence, her suspicions about her husband's designs against her, and may well have sealed her own fate. The truth in *Vertigo* about who Judy Barton is and what her role in Madeleine Elster's death was, when revealed, brings about another tragedy both to her and to Scottie. By contrast, *North by Northwest,* a film in which nearly everyone is at one time or the other deceived, brings happiness, at least to its principal couple, once its truths come out. One shouldn't forget how much *fun* this movie is to watch. *North by Northwest* is Hitchcock's apologia, not for "illusionism" but for deception.

Descartes thought deceivers evil, and indisputably the deceivers in *Rebecca, Suspicion,* and *Vertigo* create harm. *North by Northwest* is a film in which deception permeates nearly every scene, but in which the principal deceiver is the Professor, who has acted with good intent (he's created George Kaplan to protect Eve Kendall, who is herself protecting America). And his deception, while it manages to create havoc in the lives of Roger Thornhill and Eve Kendall, brings good in its wake. It is, after all, deception that propels Roger Thornhill out of his "dull life," through his adventures, and ultimately to his marriage to Eve Kendall. After the cafeteria shoot-out, and with the sole exception of the housekeeper's gun-with-blanks, the film's characters are no longer confused about what's real and what's make-believe. *That* sort of deception, at least, is ended. Roger Thornhill, even if still thought to be George Kaplan, is in truth firmly with Eve and against Vandamm and company, who also now know that Eve, too, is not on their side and never was.

Certain films might be taken as illustrating the claim that love conquers all. But the problematic in *North by Northwest* is to discover what is truth and what is make-believe. As a general method of discovery, love has a pretty poor track record. The lover is usually thought to be blind or at the least to be wearing rose-colored glasses. It is not Eve and Thornhill's romance that somehow breaks through the make-believe. It is rather *Hitchcock* who stops the deceptions and confusions. I've earlier said that the Professor is the principal deceiver in this film. It is tempting to see the Professor as a stand-in for the Director: not only does the Professor create the fiction of George Kaplan, the source of confusion, but he is the only principal character never deceived about what's real and what's make-believe. When Thornhill meets the Professor at the airport, he is told all he needs to know to see through the various perplexities he's been facing. This meeting, too, enlightens the film's audience who share Roger Thornhill's epistemic position. It is the Professor who finally allows the lovers to be together, at least in the woods for a few moments, and the Professor who ultimately saves them from falling to their deaths. Perhaps Hitchcock *is* showing off his prowess: as a great manipulator of fictional characters and of real audiences. And perhaps Hitchcock is also saying that deceivers have their good sides.

II

MIND

7

On Knowing a Mind

"What then am I?" Descartes asked. "A conscious being. What is that? A being that doubts, understands, asserts, denies, is willing, is unwilling; further, that has sense and imagination. There are a good many properties—if only they all belong to me. But how can they fail to? ... Can any of them be called a separate thing from myself?"[1] In sum, there is nothing that could, so to speak, come between me and my thoughts—nothing that could deceive me about what I'm thinking—for, Descartes held, I *am* my thoughts.

If I am my thoughts, nothing—not even the evil genius—could come between me and my thoughts. If I am my thoughts, I can know them in a way no one else can. Philosophers call this the Cartesian thesis of "privileged access." Given the thesis of privileged access, *I* can't be wrong about what *I'm* thinking, sensing, or imagining. Philosophers call this the Cartesian thesis of "incorrigibility." I have no privileged access into another's mind; and I can be mistaken about what he is thinking—or even if he's thinking. Descartes tells us he "chanced ... to look out of the window, and see men walking in the street; now I say in ordinary language that I 'see' them ... but what can I 'see' besides hats and coats, which may cover automata?"[2] In other words while I know I have an inner awareness and intimate access to my thoughts, I have no access to the inner awareness of other "people" who may for all I know be automata: robots without spirit.

Thus for Descartes I cannot be wrong about what I'm thinking. Others can be wrong about what I'm thinking, and I can be wrong about what others are thinking.

In his *Philosophical Investigations* Ludwig Wittgenstein (1889–1951) denied the Cartesian theses of privileged access and incorrigibility, and thereby diminished Descartes' skepticism about knowing other minds. "'Only I know my thoughts.'—How do you know that? Experience did not teach you it." "To say 'He alone can know what he intends' is nonsense: to say 'He alone can know what he will do', wrong. For the prediction contained in my expression of intention (for example, 'When it strikes five I am going home') need not come true, and someone else may know what will really happen.... I can be as *certain* of someone else's sensations as of any fact." Wittgenstein also said this: "We also say of some people that they are transparent to us. It is, however, important as regards this observation that one human being can be a complete enigma to another."[3] Two films in the book's second part show how one can know another's mind very well: they are in this sense Wittgensteinian and anti–Cartesian. The two Charlies of *Shadow of a Doubt* (Teresa Wright, Joseph Cotten) and Guy and Bruno of *Strangers of a Train* (Farley Granger, Robert Walker) seem to know each other's thoughts so well that young Charlie is tempted to think of it as telepathy; and Bruno seems to know what Guy wants better than Guy himself. The Charlies are transparent to each other, as Guy is to Bruno (and to some extent Bruno to Guy). But just so: these characters are a complete enigma to others. Neither Bruno's mother nor Guy's wife Miriam nor Uncle Charlie's family suspect the evil that lurks in these men.

The other three films—*Psycho, Marnie,* and *Spellbound*—enact Wittgensteinian denials of privileged access and incorrigibility. These films portray people who have become disconnected with themselves. The principals of *Marnie* and *Spellbound* have lost a memory, which leads them to behave in ways that mystify not only others around them but themselves as well. John Ballantine (Gregory Peck) thinks himself first to be Dr. Edwardes, then to have killed Dr. Edwardes. Marnie (Tippi Hedren) knows that she lies and steals, but does not know why. Her "frigidity" with men is both painful and perplexing to her. Constance Peterson (Ingrid Bergman) enlists the aid of her own analyst to discover what's going on with Ballantine. Mark Rutland (Sean Connery), at first Marnie's captor, becomes a sort of detective, trying to discover the source of his wife's confusions and anxieties. Marnie's reluctance — in *Spellbound* it would have been called "resistance"— is matched by Mark's doggedness. A kind of committee — Mark, Marnie's mother (Louise Latham), and a private detective — are enlisted to find Marnie's memory. Not only do Marnie and Ballantine not have "*privileged* access" to the contents of their minds; they seem in a *worse* epistemic position than the others trying to help. Ultimately a memory is recovered in both films, though the memory is as much a surprise to Marnie and Ballantine as it is to their analysts.

Psycho is also anti–Cartesian though in a different sense. Descartes emphasized the inseparability of thought and the self. How can my thoughts fail to be part of me? "Can any of them be called a separate thing from myself?" But Marion Crane (Janet Leigh) and Norman Bates (Anthony Perkins) are not themselves, though they doubt, understand, assert, and so on. Marion has taken on the persona of a disloyal employee and a thief. Norman now and again takes on the persona of his demanding mother. The "I" of these unfortunate characters has been dislocated. Marion Crane tries to relocate her self, though her plan is cut short. By the end of the picture Norman Bates, too, has lost his "I" for good, and thoughts float through his head (the audience hears them) that are not his.

8

Shadow of a Doubt

"We also say of some people that they are transparent to us. It is, however, important as regards this observation that one human being can be a complete enigma to another."
— Ludwig Wittgenstein, *Philosophical Investigations*[1]

"What do you know, really?"
— Uncle Charlie

It was the heroines of *Rebecca* and *Suspicion* who were deceived. In *Shadow of a Doubt* (1943) it is nearly everyone *but* the heroine who is deceived. Fontaine's characters react mostly as passive victims of circumstance. Young Charlie Newton (Teresa Wright's character) takes much greater charge of her life, even at one point countering a death threat with a death threat. The second Mrs. de Winter and Lina Aysgarth remained devoted to their husbands despite what they come to know or suspect about them. Young Charlie, initially infatuated with her Uncle Charlie Oakley (Joseph Cotten), abruptly distances herself from him when she learns the truth about her uncle. Paradoxically, Hitchcock pairs what is perhaps his strongest female character — a young woman who refuses to be a victim — with one of his worst woman haters. Among Hitchcock's murderers, discounting his saboteurs and birds, Uncle Charlie's body count, three rich widows, is topped only by *Psycho*'s Norman Bates (six) and *Frenzy*'s Bob Rusk (four). But Norman Bates is not himself as the forensic psychiatrist tells us at the end, and Bob Rusk is more obviously demented than Uncle Charlie, who exhibits far more charm, intelligence, and self-control than Bates or Rusk (Uncle Charlie even has a sort of philosophy underpinning his murders).

Not everybody finds Young Charlie a strong character. "Charlie is a typical Hitchcock female," Tania Modleski writes, "both because her close relationship to her mother arouses in her a longing for a different kind of life than the one her father offers them and because she seems to possess special, incriminating knowledge about men."[2] I'm not sure what the "typical" Hitchcock female is, though Young Charlie stands head and shoulders above the self-doubting wives of *Rebecca* and *Suspicion*, the alcoholic and self-sacrificing Alicia Huberman of *Notorious*, the destructive Madeleine and passive Judy of *Vertigo*, and the loopy Melanie Daniels of *The Birds*. Furthermore, there is no evidence in *Shadow of a Doubt* of an especially close relationship between Young Charlie and her mother (nor do the female characters have an especially close relationship with their mothers in the other films I've just mentioned). Charlie seems to me straightforwardly bored with life in a small town. Meg Wolitzer's sense of Young Charlie is more consonant with mine: "For once Hitchcock not only approximates a realistic interpretation of what it means to be a woman, but actually manages an unexpected protean turn as an adolescent girl."[3]

***

The narrative can be divided into ten segments. (1) *Philadelphia*. After the titles, superimposed over an elegant ball with people waltzing, we see Joseph Cotten lying in bed looking moody. There is money carelessly strewn about which disturbs the landlady who enters to tell Cotten that two men have been asking about him. Cotten gives the men the slip, and sends a telegram to his sister's family in Santa Rosa, California. He is coming to visit and signs it with "a kiss to little Charlie from her Uncle Charlie." (2) *Happy family reunion*. Young Charlie is shown lying moodily on the bed. She thinks her family "has just gone to pieces ... we just sort of go along and nothing happens," and decides to send a telegram to Uncle Charlie inviting him to visit — and by remarkable coincidence Uncle Charlie has already sent a telegram announcing his visit. At dinner, Uncle Charlie has presents for the family — and a special present for his niece, an emerald ring. In the privacy of the kitchen away from the rest of the family, he puts the ring on her finger. Young Charlie notices something engraved on the band, "TS from BM." The opening waltz tune and visual recur, and Young Charlie comes back to the drawing room humming the waltz. She can't get it out of her head, and begins to guess what it is, "The Merry..." — but she's interrupted when Uncle Charlie spills his glass of water and her father's friend, Herbert Hawkins (Hume Cronyn) enters holding some *True Crime Stories* magazines.

(3) *The newspaper*. Reading the evening newspaper, Uncle Charlie is disturbed by something he sees. He insists on showing his younger niece and nephew how to make a house from folded newspaper. Young Charlie guesses there was something in the paper he didn't want the family to see. She finds the "lost" pages. "It's none of your business," Uncle Charlie angrily tells her, grabbing her wrist and snatching the pages from her. He

"But we're sort of like twins, don't you see," young Charlie Newton (Teresa Wright) tells her Uncle Charlie Oakley (Joseph Cotten), in *Shadow of a Doubt* (1943).

immediately apologizes and says it was just gossip about some people he knows. (4) *The "survey."* Young Charlie's mother, Emma Newton (Patricia Collinge), tells her brother that two men from "some kind of institute" want to interview "a representative American family." "It's called the National Public Survey," and pictures are to be taken. Uncle Charlie wants his sister to slam the door in the men's faces. "I've never been photographed in my life and I don't want to be." But Mrs. Newton says she couldn't do that, and allows that Uncle Charlie need not be part of the interview if he doesn't want to be. Uncle Charlie goes to the bank at which his brother-in-law Joe Newton (Henry Travers) works to deposit $40,000 in cash (making loud jokes about embezzlement). He also engages in a brief flirtation with the recently widowed Mrs. Potter. Back at the Newton's house, the two "surveyors" arrive. Uncle Charlie slips down the back stairs, but they manage to photograph him anyway.

(5) *First revelation about Uncle Charlie.* One of the "surveyors," Jack Graham (Macdonald Carey), takes Young Charlie to look around the town. Charlie guesses who he is. "I know what you are, really. You're a detective.

There's something the matter and you're a detective... You lied to us... You just wanted to get in our house... What are you doing around here, lying to us?" Graham tells Charlie that he is looking for a man who may be her uncle, though there is another man in the east they are hunting too. He asks Young Charlie not to say anything to her uncle, and she agrees. (6) *The library*. Charlie, home, sneaks out the back stairs to the library, which is closed and she has to beg her way in. She finds the newspaper headlined, "Where is the Merry Widow Murderer? Nation-wide Search Under Way for Strangler of Three Rich Women." The latest victim was Mrs. Bruce Matthewson, a musical comedy star formerly known as "the beautiful Thelma Schenley."

(7) *Uncle Charlie's revelations*. Young Charlie — her mother says "she doesn't look quite herself" — sleeps nearly all the next day, appearing only at dinner. She demands her mother stop humming the *Merry Widow* tune. During dinner, Young Charlie says she had "perfect nightmares" in which she dreamt Uncle Charlie was on a train running away from something. "When I saw you on the train I felt terribly happy." Young Charlie tells the family they have to face the fact that Uncle Charlie has to leave some-time, and tells Uncle Charlie that he doesn't have to play games with the newspaper tonight. Mrs. Newton asks her brother to lecture to her woman's club. This is Uncle Charlie's response (the script is by Thorton Wilder):

> Women keep busy in towns like this. In cities it's different. The cities are full of women, middle-aged widows, husbands dead, husbands who've spent their lives making fortunes, working and working. Then they die and leave their money to their wives, their silly wives. And what do the wives do, these useless women? You see them in the hotels, the best hotels, everyday by the thousands, drinking the money, eating the money, losing the money at bridge, playing all day and all night, smelling of money. Proud of their jewelry but of nothing else. Horrible, faded, fat, greedy women.

Young Charlie is aghast. "They're alive! They're human beings!" "Are they? Are they, Charlie?" her uncle responds. Mrs. Newton only asks her brother not to talk like that in front of her club. Herb drops by, and he and Joe talk of murder, upsetting Young Charlie, who leaves the house. Uncle Charlie goes after her. He drags her into a downtown cocktail bar. "How could you do such things? ...We thought you were the most wonderful man in the world." "Charlie, what do you know?" She produces the ring, and Uncle Charlie gives his second speech:

> You think you know something, don't you? You think you're the clever little girl who knows something. There's so much you don't know. So

much. What do you know, really? You're just an ordinary little girl living
in an ordinary little town. You wake up every morning of your life and
you know perfectly well that there's nothing in the world to trouble you.
You go through your ordinary little day, and at night you sleep your
untroubled, ordinary little sleep, filled with peaceful, stupid dreams. And
I brought you nightmares. Or did I? Or was it a silly, inexpert little lie?
You live in a dream. You're a sleepwalker, blind. How do you know what
the world is like? Do you know the world is a foul sty? Do you know if
you ripped the fronts off houses you'd find swine? The world's a hell.
What does it matter what happens in it? Wake up Charlie. Use your wits.
Learn something.

He asks her to help him. "Same blood flows through our veins... Charlie,
give me this last chance." "Take your chance," Young Charlie tells him.
"Go... See that you get away from here."

Uncle Charlie (Joseph Cotten) about to take his niece, also named Charlie (Teresa
Wright), into the 'Til Two Bar to ask that she not tell the detectives about him: "Same
blood flows through our veins... Charlie, give me this last chance." *Shadow of a
Doubt* (1943).

(8) *Uncle Charlie's apparent exoneration.* Detective Saunders (Wallace Ford) asks Young Charlie to tell them what she knows, but she will only tell them when her uncle leaves town. Herb tells Joe that the "noon broadcast" reports that "they caught that other feller, the one they call the Merry Widow murderer," who was not exactly caught but killed, chopped up by an airplane propeller in Maine. They were able to identify him by the initials on his shirt: "C.O'H." "I guess that closes that case," Herb comments. Young Charlie, unconvinced, stares at her uncle. Later Graham tells her, "Well, we got a wire from Maine so we can call off the job." Young Charlie says she is relieved and would like to "pretend the whole dreadful thing never happened." In the garage, Graham tells her he loves her and hints at a marriage proposal. Young Charlie says she'd like them to be friends.

(9) *Death threats.* As Young Charlie comes down the back stairs, a stair breaks and she almost falls (we see Uncle Charlie lurking nearby). Later, in the dark at the top of those stairs, she demands, "When are you leaving, Uncle Charlie?" Uncle Charlie responds that he's not going. He wants to settle down, open a business, and be part of the family. "I don't want you here, Uncle Charlie. I don't want you to touch my mother. Go away or I'll kill you myself. See, that's the way I feel about you." The family is to attend a lecture Uncle Charlie is giving to Emma's club. During the confusion about who is to ride in which car, Young Charlie goes to the garage. The family car's engine is running, but there is no key in the ignition to turn it off. The garage door suddenly shuts trapping Young Charlie. Saved by Herb who has heard someone pounding on the door, Young Charlie begs off from attending the lecture. She locates the emerald ring, which had gone missing, in Uncle Charlie's room. While guests assemble in the parlor after the lecture, Young Charlie descends the stairs making sure her uncle sees the ring on her hand. Uncle Charlie suddenly announces he must leave Santa Rosa, "but not forever."

(10) *Uncle Charlie's demise.* The Newton children board the train with Uncle Charlie (the widow Potter is there too). As the train pulls away the two youngest disembark, but her uncle holds Young Charlie back. "Have to do this, Charlie, so long as you know what you do about me." He tries to throw her off but after a struggle she pushes him into the path of an oncoming train (the waltz and ball images are superimposed again).[4] At the town funeral we hear the eulogy, "Santa Rosa has gained and lost a son, a son that she could be proud of..." Young Charlie tells Graham that she knew about her uncle, whom Graham calls "crazy."

***

A persistent motif in *Shadow of a Doubt* is the double. There are two Charlies, uncle and niece, each introduced by a series of camera shots, first through Philadelphia and then through Santa Rosa, then up to their bedroom windows, and finally each is shown lying pensively in bed. In Philadelphia there are two men lurking outside Uncle Charlie's room, and in Santa Rosa two women. There are two murder suspects, one in the east and one in the west, the latter pursued by two detectives. There are two brother-sister pairs, and two men who play games planning the perfect murder. On his way to the bank, Uncle Charlie is introduced to two young female friends of Young Charlie, and a bit later to two older women. Twice Young Charlie avoids her uncle by going down the backstairs, and twice she has an encounter with the town traffic cop. There are two family dinners each interrupted by the next door neighbor, two scenes in a garage, two scenes on a train, and in the end two trains. It is as if Hitchcock (or Wilder) couldn't stop. Uncle Charlie drags his niece into the 'Til-Two bar through double doors each of which has an image of a clock showing two o'clock; inside Uncle Charlie orders two double brandies from a waitress who has worked there for two weeks.

Sometimes one of the doubles is less substantial than — a shadow of — the other. The two ladies outside Uncle Charlie's room in the Newton's house are far less threatening than the two men outside his Philadelphia room. The plans for murder Joe Newton and Herb conjure up are but harmless mimeses of Uncle Charlie's real murders. Young Charlie is nearly hit by a car as she rushes across the street on her way to the library; Uncle Charlie was hit by a streetcar as a child when his bicycle skidded on the ice. "We thought he was going to die," Emma Newton says. Some of the doubles carry different emotional tones. The first Newton family dinner is happy and loving, with presents for everyone; the second anxious, passive aggressive, and downright nasty (Ann for unexplained reasons doesn't want to sit next to her uncle, Young Charlie makes a point about not playing games with the newspaper, Uncle Charlie makes his speech about "horrible, faded, fat, greedy women"). The family garage is first the scene of attempted murder, next a marriage proposal. And of course Uncle Charlie's arrival is revitalizing to Young Charlie, his departure nearly fatal.

Then there are the coincidences and remarkable occurrences. First, the coincidence of telegrams, his sent, hers planned. "Now what made her think to do that?" Mrs. Newton wonders about her daughter's plan to send a telegram. A card player (Hitchcock) on the train carrying Uncle Charlie to Santa Rosa holds all thirteen spades. And the most remarkable coincidence of all: After Uncle Charlie gives his niece the ring in the kitchen, she enters the dining room with a tune running through her head, the *Merry Widow Waltz*. Young Charlie tries to think of the name of the tune when a man named "Herbert" enters the room (Victor Herbert is the composer of the *Merry Widow* operetta).

The film also contains a fair amount of superstition (which is another form of the double in which one thing is feared to foreshadow or bring about something similar). The number of Uncle Charlie's rooming house in the city is "13," an address Mrs. Newton refuses to tell her daughter. Uncle Charlie is warned by Joe against putting his hat on the bed, but does it anyway when he's left alone. "Sing at the table and you'll marry a crazy husband," Ann (Edna May Wonacott) tells Young Charlie who is humming the waltz tune; and Ann later chants, "Step on a crack, break your mother's back." The train into Santa Rosa arrives belching black smoke. François Truffaut said to Hitchcock, "The black smoke implies that the devil was coming to town." "Exactly," Hitchcock responds.[5] (And perhaps the thirteen spades held by passenger Hitchcock on the train signify the devil, though this particular bit with the cards puzzles me. The train porter has just said that the passenger disembarking — Uncle Charlie — has been in his compartment ill for the whole trip. No one has seen him since the train left Philadelphia. "You don't look very well either," one of the card players comments to Hitchcock. But if the game is bridge, as it appears to be, thirteen spades is lay-down for grand slam, not a hand to look sick over.) But I doubt whether Hitchcock intended that, literally, Uncle Charlie be the devil, in the way that Peter Cook's character in Stanley Donen's *Bedazzled* (1967), a comic retelling of the Faust legend, is the devil. Uncle Charlie may be devilish but he is not a supernatural being.

***

Shadow of a Doubt revolves around the relationship between the two Charlies who are the principal doubles in the film. It is the formal role of the other doubles to echo (or shadow) their similarities. Just how similar are they? For starters, they're both quick and clever. Uncle Charlie understands immediately that the two "friends" who talked to his Philadelphia landlady are police. He easily eludes them and masks himself as ill on the train to Santa Rosa. He knocks over a glass of water before his niece can guess the name of the tune she finds herself humming. He rapidly turns a disturbing newspaper story into a children's game. He surmises that the "surveyors" who visit Emma Newton are police too, and tries his best to dodge them.

Young Charlie grasps almost immediately that her uncle's newspaper house is really an attempt to hide some page of the newspaper from the family. She guesses soon enough that the "surveyors" are detectives (no one else in the family — or town — seems to have a clue about the intentions of these two men who simply turn up one day). She connects the initials on the ring with the newspaper story of the Merry Widow Murderer. She knows that the broken stairs and closed garage door are not random accidents.

Her mother can only stammer, "I just don't understand it. First the stairs, then…" After her near-asphyxiation she quickly concocts a plan to stay home and hunt for the missing ring which she uses to blackmail Uncle Charlie into leaving Santa Rosa. Both Charlies know, and each knows that the other knows, that the suspect who is killed in Maine is not the real murderer.

The two Charlies are also determined, deceptive, and ruthless when necessary. Uncle Charlie, of course, must have deceived and disarmed those rich widows with his charm, which is a false front because he in fact loathed them. His charming demeanor slips off several times in front of Young Charlie (when she finds the newspaper pages he's tried to hide, in the 'Til Two Bar, and of course on the train at the end). Uncle Charlie has managed to fool nearly everyone in Santa Rosa into thinking him a dapper businessman from the east who eccentrically keeps his funds in cash. As he begins to understand that his niece has turned against him, he makes plans for her demise, and very nearly succeeds. Young Charlie has no need of charm, but does present another kind of false front to her family and the detectives. She fails to share her knowledge and evidence about Uncle Charlie's crimes with anyone (though she rationalizes this as concern for her mother's feelings). She is determined to find the newspaper story her uncle managed to hide from her. (Uncle Charlie, too, thinks people should "face facts," as he says to Young Charlie during the second family dinner.) Young Charlie matches Uncle Charlie's death threats with one of her own, and in the film's climax she kills him before he can kill her. I would like to point out one detail of this brief and violent sequence. Young Charlie's eyes are shown darting back and forth: she is—very quickly—planning how to push her uncle off the train. I emphasize this because some critics misdescribe what's going on. Robin Wood writes, "When Uncle Charlie *falls* in front of the oncoming train, his death is ambiguously accident and 'killing in self defense': it is staged and shot in a way that exonerates Young Charlie from all moral responsibility."[6] Uncle Charlie's "fall" is no accident, though killing in self defense exonerates Young Charlie from moral blame.

Not only are the two Charlies the film's principal doubles, their relationship is the film's principal conundrum. They clearly understand one another better than any other character understands either of them. It is as if they know one another's minds. Do they?

Young Charlie thinks it telepathy when the coincidence of the telegrams occurs. She asks the woman at the telegram office if she believes in mental telepathy, and walking home says to herself, "He heard me, he heard me." She explains the *Merry Widow Waltz* running through her mind by saying that she thinks tunes sometimes "jump from head to head." Robin Wood finds a "telepathy motif" in the film,[7] and Hitchcock told Truffaut that there is "telepathy between Uncle Charlie and his niece."[8] However, Hitchcock also spoke of Uncle Charlie as the devil, and surely he meant this figuratively. It is also worth pointing out that earlier in the interview Hitchcock said that *Shadow of a Doubt* is a picture "that our friends, the plausibles and logicians, cannot complain about ... the psychologists as well!"[9] Do Young Charlie and Uncle Charlie literally read each other's minds in a "telepathic" way? If the film is to appeal to the plausibles, logicians, and psychologists, then telepathy cannot be a fictional feature of *Shadow of a Doubt*. Hitchcock had also told Truffaut that he wanted Thorton Wilder to do the script because "he had written a wonderful play called *Our Town*... Before the writing, Wilder and I went to great pains to be realistic about the town, the people, and the decor."[10] Would Hitchcock then introduce the irrealism of telepathy?

If there were such a thing as mental telepathy, you could give me direct access to your thoughts in the way that you have direct access to them. I would share your thoughts, not in the way we might share secrets, whispering them to one another, but in the way that I know my own thoughts, though of course your thoughts would somehow have to be marked as yours. If I thought your thought mine, I would not recognize it as a telepathic communiqué. While telepathy is a staple in science fiction and horror stories, there are confusions with the very concept. How will I identify a thought in *my* head as *your* thought? Can you mark it as yours before you "transmit" it? What are the causal processes whereby thoughts can be transmitted? Are they modulated into waves of some sort? How? How are they demodulated by the recipient back into thoughts? None of this need concern science fiction and horror writers, who can construct narratives in which it is a fictional truth of *Star Trek* that Dr. Spock reads minds or a fictional truth of *Dracula* that Count Dracula gives telepathic orders to Renfrew, without solving the conceptual and mechanical problems raised. But these problems strongly suggest that telepathy is not casually possible in the actual world, and that a filmmaker who claims "plausibility" and "logic" for his film would not incorporate telepathy.

"I thus clearly recognise that nothing is more easily or manifestly perceptible to me than my own mind," Descartes wrote at the end of his Second Meditation.[11] The claim that we can know *all* the contents of our mind "easily" will strike the post–Freudian reader as naïve. Still, Descartes does put his finger on the situation with respect to occurrent, conscious thoughts, which is that they occur to us noninferentially. We simply know what many of our feelings, intentions, and desires are; we don't gather evidence and infer what they probably are. What now of knowing other minds? I do not know another's thoughts directly, in the way I know my own. What philosophers call the problem of other minds is this: Given that I have no direct access to another's mind, what can I know about his inner life and how can I know it?[12] I can read another's expressions of inner states— his face, body language, tone of voice — though not all inner states will or even can be expressed, and some might be hidden or disguised with a false front. I can rely on another's testimony as to his inner states, but perhaps some of the other's inner life will be withheld from me or he will tell untruths about his thoughts.

Or I can try to derive my knowledge of another's thoughts and feelings from considerations of my own thoughts and feelings— if I and the other are similar enough, that is. When two things, X and Y, are similar in certain respects, it is frequently the case that they are similar in other respects as well. This is analogical reasoning. In his *Dialogues Concerning Natural Religion* David Hume discusses its limits:

> The exact similarity of the cases gives us a perfect assurance of a similar event; and a stronger evidence is never desired nor sought after. But wherever you depart, in the least, from the similarity of the cases, you diminish proportionably the evidence; and may at last bring it to a very weak *analogy*, which is confessedly liable to error and uncertainty. After having experienced the circulation of the blood in human creatures, we make no doubt that it takes place in Titius and Maevius: But from its circulation in frogs and fishes, it is only a presumption, though a strong one, from analogy, that it takes place in men and other animals. The analogical reasoning is much weaker, when we infer the circulation of the sap in vegetables from our experience that the blood circulates in animals; and those, who hastily followed that imperfect analogy, are found, by more accurate experiments, to have been mistaken.[13]

Hume's concern in the *Dialogues* is to what extent the universe is like a machine (which is a product of intelligent design, and if the machine and universe are similar enough, the universe, too, is likely a product of intelligent design). Our concern here is other minds. If two people, A and B, were sufficiently alike, then A could come to know B's inner life by simple introspection of A's own thoughts and feelings. If A dislikes J, he can be sure B does as well. If a certain kind of criticism will hurt A's feelings, then he will predict that it will offend B as well. To the extent that A and B are *un*alike, A's attempt to come to know B's likes and dislikes through introspection of his own is "liable to error and uncertainty."

What I want to argue can be provisionally stated this way: *Shadow of a Doubt* is largely about Young Charlie's coming to know the terrible truth about her uncle's inner life. The interpretive issue forced by the film is how she does it. Young Charlie initially takes herself to be a "twin" of her uncle. If she were, she could know his inner life by inspecting her own (and she makes an inference about Uncle Charlie in just this fashion). But the two Charlies aren't quite twins, something Young Charlie will eventually discover for herself. However, they're similar enough — the doubles in the film reinforce this impression. And while Young Charlie's inferences to her uncle's inner life are based on her own are thus "liable to error and uncertainty," she still knows him better than anyone else in the film knows him precisely because of their strong albeit imperfect similarity to one another. *Shadow of a Doubt* becomes, after Uncle Charlie's arrival, a sort of detective story in which the audience already knows who dunnit (such strong suspicion is cast on Uncle Charlie from the onset that we know he's done *something* terrible), and the question becomes when will Young Charlie know and how will she know it.

Young Charlie initially takes herself to be just like her uncle. She tells him just this in their conversation in the kitchen during the first family dinner.

> YOUNG CHARLIE: I'm glad that mother named me after you and that she thinks we're both alike. I think we are, too. I know it…. We're not just an uncle and a niece. It's something else. I know you. I know that you don't tell people a lot of things. I don't either. I have a feeling that inside you somewhere there's something nobody knows about.
>
> UNCLE CHARLIE: Something nobody knows?
>
> YOUNG CHARLIE: Something secret and wonderful and I'll find it out.
>
> UNCLE CHARLIE: Not good to find out too much, Charlie.
>
> YOUNG CHARLIE: But we're sort of like twins don't you see. We *have* to know.
>
> UNCLE CHARLIE: Give me your hand, Charlie.

And so Young Charlie reasons analogically from herself to her uncle. As *she* has a "wonderful secret" inside (she doesn't lay all her cards on the table even for her family), so she assumes her uncle does too. She turns out to be half right: he *does* have a secret, but it's not wonderful. However, coming up only half right means that the analogy is not perfect.

To think yourself exactly like another is a form of narcissism. I do not mean that Young Charlie has an excessively high opinion of herself, nor that she's seriously disturbed, but that she assumes, at least now and again, others to be like herself. She tells her father that the "family is going to pieces" when in fact it is only *she* who is at a loss for what to do in Santa

Rosa. Her narcissism, though, may be mixed with a sort of hero worship. She makes the telling remark to Jack Graham (this is before she guesses that he is a detective): "It's funny. When I try to think of how I feel I always come back to Uncle Charlie. Are you trying to tell me I shouldn't think he's so wonderful?" But this may be because she tries to mold herself on what she thinks her uncle to be like (worldly and clever).

But not even a narcissistic identification with her uncle or hero worship can explain what happens after Uncle Charlie gives Young Charlie the emerald ring, and after she sees the engraving inside the band. She ends up humming the *Merry Widow Waltz*. While this is gripping cinema, the film at this point threatens to burst the bonds of plausibility. If we avoid an appeal to telepathy, we need an explanation of why this tune, whose title names Uncle Charlie's secret, pops up in Young Charlie's head at this very point. It is even hard to push a telepathic explanation for the tune. We would have to say that Young Charlie only partly reads her uncle's mind. She "receives" a waltz tune — was he humming it to himself? — but not the criminal thought accompanying it. A garbled communication? Usually telepathy, at least in the movies, works perfectly. Certainly she doesn't (yet) know that the ring is from a *murdered* widow, let alone that her uncle is the murderer. "I like it this way," Young Charlie says on noticing the engraving. "Someone else was probably happy with this ring." Possibly then she has made a guess as to the meaning of the engraving — two past lovers, one now a widow — the latter suggesting to her a tune. (The plausibles may have grounds for complaint here.)

Does Young Charlie have grounds for thinking herself and her uncle "twins"? "Charlie, think," Jack Graham asks her. "How much do you know about your uncle?" She responds with a tautology, "Why, he's my mother's brother." In fact, she knows very little about him. Let's imagine some rudiments of the past uncle and niece have had together. Uncle Charlie was probably an infrequent visitor to the Newtons. He is several times introduced as being "from the east," which would be days by train from California. He says on his arrival to Ann, "Bet you don't remember me." "I remember you, sort of," she responds. And perhaps Young Charlie, who at the beginning of the film expresses some vague dissatisfaction with her life in small-town Santa Rosa, might have envied Uncle Charlie as someone who lives an exciting life in the big city. He's sent his niece a present from time to time (such as the dress she wears at the first family dinner); perhaps they've exchanged some letters. She in a girlish way loves him, though I strongly doubt that their relation is incestuous, as some critics have thought.

Robin Wood sees a "double incest theme" of Young/Uncle Charlie and Uncle Charlie/Emma.[14] Wood thinks the incest is shown symbolically: Uncle Charlie fondles his "phallic" cigar; he "comes erect" when he steps off the train and sees Young Charlie; in her bedroom he plucks a flower for his buttonhole ("deflowering"). I think this is one of the times a cigar is just a cigar. The *literal* evidence in the film for any incest is all but nonexistent. Young Charlie is delighted her uncle came to visit, because among other reasons, "Mother's so happy." Wood claims that at the station as Uncle Charlie is about to leave Santa Rosa, he takes his sister's hands in his with Young Charlie "glowering" at him. There is a cut to Young Charlie's face, but her expression, far from a glower, is sad over her mother's sorrow because her brother is leaving. It's true that giving a young woman a ring suggests a sexual interest, but in *Shadow of a Doubt* the emerald ring is positioned as the most valuable gift Uncle Charlie has. In any case, Young Charlie does not approach her uncle with the anxiety that a history of incest would surely generate, and Emma's nostalgia about hers and Charlie's happy childhood is not at all ambivalent or uneasy. Sadness enters her recollections but it is over Charlie's bicycle accident.

Young Charlie may have perceived a few common qualities they share, such as their apartness from those around them and their quick intelligence. She may even have molded herself to be like her uncle (or her perceptions of her uncle). But of course Young Charlie isn't exactly like her uncle. Hitchcock's camera work in *Shadow of a Doubt* rarely draws attention to itself, consonant with the *Our Town* placement of the story. However, in the library after Young Charlie connects the newspaper story with the initials in the ring, and realizes her uncle is the Merry Widow murderer, the camera, beginning with a close-up on the emerald ring in Young Charlie's hand pulls back and up, until we get a ceiling's-eye view of the library as Young Charlie gets up from the table and slowly walks towards the door. Perhaps the meaning of the shot is to disorient the viewer as Young Charlie has herself become disoriented. But various other shots could have done this: going out of focus (suggesting a faint), spinning (suggesting dizziness), etc. I want to read the shot as signaling an end to Young Charlie's narcissistic identification with her uncle. The camera sees her as she has suddenly begun to see herself: alone and separate.

Young Charlie will now begin to see the differences between herself and her uncle. Uncle Charlie, of course, is a multiple murderer and she isn't. He loathes the rich widows he murders; she tells him that they're human beings (still, she exhibits little concern for Mrs. Potter, the widowed president of the local women's club, who is trying to catch Uncle Charlie's eye). I think Uncle Charlie genuinely likes his sister, Emma, though I suspect he only pretends to like the rest of the family. Young

Charlie on the other hand is genuinely solicitous to her parents and siblings. It is unlikely Uncle Charlie ever had a loving relationship in his adult life. Young Charlie becomes engaged to marry Jack Graham (yet her affection for him is not much in evidence in the film — if *Shadow of a Doubt* has a love interest for Teresa Wright it is Joseph Cotten).

And she will learn that they disagree in their world outlooks. Uncle Charlie's speech in the 'Til-Two bar was perhaps intended to win his niece over to his side (he may think she's halfway there already). The "ordinary" perceptions and dreams that Young Charlie has in Uncle Charlie's eyes are "stupid," the perceptions of a "sleepwalker" or a "blind" person. In reality there are "swine" behind the "fronts of houses." In truth, "The world's a hell." Plato's philosopher in the *Republic* released from the prisoners in the cave to the reality of the Good shining in the world above. Uncle Charlie has as it were gone in the other direction. He thinks that it is the Good that is mere appearance, while reality lies in the netherworld where he has chosen to dwell.

Reasoning with an imperfect analogy is liable to error and uncertainty, though it is better than nothing. Young Charlie may not be a "twin" of her uncle, but she is more like him than any of the other characters in the story. This gives her an epistemic edge, and may explain why Uncle Charlie is not suspected by anyone save his niece and the two detectives. After all, here is a man who shows up at the very time the Merry Widow murderer is being sought. The fact that Uncle Charlie destroyed one copy of the newspaper does not hide that story from everyone. He carries tens of thousands of dollars in cash for which only the vaguest explanation is offered. (He says he's a "promoter. Done a little bit of everything.") There are two characters in the film whose hobby is true murder stories, and who evince a keen interest in the Merry Widow case. Uncle Charlie all but confesses during the second family dinner, and his sister's only response is not to talk like that in front of her woman's club.

Robin Wood writes that each member of the Newton family is "locked in a separate fantasy world: Emmy in the past, Joe in crime, Ann in books…"[15] But this implies more alienation from the world around them than is warranted by the film. Emma is nostalgic about her childhood, but she is also a woman of the present, baking cakes, tending to her family, and organizing lectures for her women's club. Joe and Herb play games about planning hypothetical murders, but Joe also works in a bank and functions as a bemused paterfamilias. Little Ann reads books, but she shares a bit of Young Charlie's intuitions about Uncle Charlie when at the second family dinner Ann asks not to be seated next to her uncle. Besides, one need not be locked in a fantasy world to fail to see a beloved family member as a strangler; and murder in the quiet town of Santa Rosa seems to happen only in *True Crime Stories* magazines.

Of course, Young Charlie has the key piece of material evidence, the engraved emerald ring. Still, only she knows that her uncle has made attempts against her life (the stairs, the garage) which everyone else takes to be unfortunate accidents. And even after her uncle is officially cleared of suspicion Young Charlie remains unpersuaded. She takes steps to drive him away, and of course kills him when that becomes necessary. Could it be that she finds within herself the resources for murder, and since she and her uncle are so similar, she infers that he too has the same resources?

If Young Charlie has made an epistemic mistake at the beginning, thinking herself and her uncle to be twins, she makes another at the end. With the public eulogy to Uncle Charlie rambling on in the background, Young Charlie begins to think of herself and her uncle as very *un*alike.

> YOUNG CHARLIE: He thought the world was a horrible place. He couldn't have been very happy, ever. He didn't trust people. He seemed to hate them. He hated the whole world. He said that people like us had no idea what the world was really like.
>
> GRAHAM: It's not quite as bad as that. But sometimes it needs a lot of watching. It seems to go crazy every now and then. Like your Uncle Charlie.

One reading of this little speech is that Young Charlie has a nice view of people and the world in opposition to her uncle's nasty notions; and of course she thinks *she's* right just as her uncle thought *he* was right. However, Young Charlie now knows a bit about the nasty side of the world. This may explain why the imputed romance between Young Charlie and Graham doesn't exactly catch fire. Each — the niece and the police detective — know a bit more about the evil people can do than the average citizen of Santa Rosa. But the world can be *both* nice and hellish (which Graham seems vaguely to agree with). And not only the world: people can have "dual natures" too. Young Charlie is both a nice small-town girl *and* cunning, deceptive, and ruthless when she needs to be — just like Uncle Charlie.

9

Strangers on a Train

> "To say 'He alone can know what he intends' is nonsense: to say 'He alone can know what he will do', wrong."
> — Ludwig Wittgenstein, *Philosophical Investigations*[1]
>
> "Oh we do talk the same language, don't we?"
> — Bruno Anthony

Strangers on a Train (1951), based on a novel by Patricia Highsmith, is easily the richest and most complex of Hitchcock's films to that date. Screen credit for the script is given to Raymond Chandler and Czenzi Ormonde, though Hitchcock told Truffaut that "the work [Chandler] did was no good and I ended up with Czenzi Ormonde, a woman writer who was one of Ben Hecht's assistants."[2] Chandler returned the compliment by calling the plot of *Strangers* "ludicrous in essence."[3] (See the end of the chapter for the differences between film and novel.)

Guy Haines (Farley Granger), an amateur tennis player of some renown, and Bruno Anthony (Robert Walker), the idle son of a wealthy man, meet by chance on a train between Washington and New York. Over lunch, Bruno describes his idea for a perfect murder. "Two fellows meet accidentally, like you and me. No connection between them at all, never saw each other before. Each one has somebody that he'd like to get rid of. So — they swap murders.... For example, your wife, my father. Crisscross." Guy appears not to take Bruno seriously, and, forgetting his cigarette lighter, gets off the train in Metcalf where he is to meet his wife, Miriam (Laura Elliott) to discuss their divorce. But Miriam, pregnant with another man's child, changes her mind: she will move to Washington to be with Guy.

Later Bruno takes the train to Metcalf and follows Miriam and two male friends to an amusement park. Miriam and her friends take a boat through the Tunnel of Love to an island, where Bruno strangles Miriam. Outside Guy's home in Washington Bruno calls to him out of the shadows and says he's brought Guy "a little present," which turns out to be Miriam's glasses. "Nothing for us to worry about. Nobody saw me," Bruno says. Guy is horrified, though Bruno tells him that if he goes to the police he will be arrested as an accessory. "We planned it on the train together."

But the police *are* suspicious, and want to know where Guy was at 9:30 on the night Miriam was murdered. As it happens, Guy was on the train back to Washington, and he spoke with a professor in the club car. However, the professor was too drunk to confirm Guy's story, and a police "guardian angel" is assigned to Guy. Guy continues to see Ann Morton (Ruth Roman), the daughter of Senator Morton (Leo G. Carroll), who has only sympathy for Guy's predicament. At home, Guy finds a note from Bruno: "Dear Guy, We must get together and make plans. My father will be going away soon. Call me. B." Bruno begins to stalk Guy, at one point confronting him with Ann in the National Gallery. Later, Guy receives a special delivery envelope containing a key and a map of Bruno's house showing his father's bedroom. Bruno shows up at a party given by the Senator. His playful demonstration of how to strangle someone turns serious when he sees Ann's sister, Barbara (Patricia Hitchcock), who, with her glasses, resembles Miriam. This prompts Ann to ask Guy, "He killed Miriam, didn't he?" "Yes," Guy answers, "He's a maniac." He tells Ann about the chance meeting on the train. "And now the lunatic wants me to kill his father."

Guy calls Bruno to tell him that he has "decided to do what you want" and he will do it that night. He lets himself into the Anthonys' house and makes his way to Mr. Anthony's bedroom. He thinks he is talking to Mr. Anthony about his son, but it is Bruno waiting for him in his father's bed. Guy tells Bruno he has no intention of going ahead with their "arrangement." "I don't like to be double-crossed," Bruno tells him, and says that he'll think of some way to get back at him. The next day Ann pays a call on Mrs. Anthony to tell her that her son was responsible for a woman's death, but Mrs. Anthony won't believe her. Bruno appears and tells Ann that Guy had tried to get him to go back to the island to retrieve the lighter he dropped there. "You see, all the police are waiting for is one piece of evidence to convict Guy of the murder."

Guy realizes that Bruno will take his revenge by going back to the scene of Miriam's murder and leaving the lighter for the police to find. He wants to stop Bruno but has a tennis match to play and can't risk alerting the police by canceling the match. The film cuts between Guy's tennis match and Bruno's journey to the amusement park. When it gets dark, Bruno waits for a boat back to the island, but the boat operator at the Tunnel of Love recognizes Bruno from the night of Miriam's murder.

On their initial meeting, Bruno Anthony (Robert Walker, right) already knows that the cigarette lighter is a present to Guy Haines (Farley Granger) from Ann Morton, a senator's daughter. *Strangers on a Train* (1951).

Bruno attempts to leave the park, but Guy appears and he and Bruno jump on a carousel. The police shoot at Guy but hit the carousel operator instead. In a cinematic tour de force, we're shown the struggle of Bruno and Guy as the carousel spins faster and faster. Finally, someone gets to the brakes on the carousel, which lurches to a halt and explodes. Bruno is crushed under the debris. Guy and the police hover over him. "Bruno, can you tell the chief you have my lighter?" Guy asks. "I haven't got it. It's on the island where you left it." But as Bruno dies, his hand opens to reveal Guy's lighter.

***

The film re-employs the patterns of doubles from *Shadow of a Doubt*, though in *Strangers on a Train* the doubles are at once more subtle and richly textured. Hitchcock opens with two pairs of legs each emerging from a separate cab. Bruno and Guy meet when their feet accidentally touch, and near the end as Guy is again taking the train to Metcalf, one stranger's foot accidentally brushes another's. On the first train from Washington to New York, Guy is on his way to play a doubles tournament in

Southampton, and Bruno asks the waiter for "Scotch and plain water, please. A pair. Doubles." There is one Mrs. Haines at present, and Bruno makes a toast "to the next Mrs. Haines." Guy's cigarette lighter sports two crossed tennis rackets, while Bruno's tie has pictures of two-clawed lobsters (!). Hitchcock in his cameo boards the train in Metcalf lugging his physical double: a big bass fiddle. Miriam is accompanied to the amusement park by two boyfriends. There are two powerful fathers (Senator Morton and the wealthy Mr. Anthony), two women who resemble each other and wear glasses (Miriam and Barbara), two women at the Senator's party who have a conversation with Bruno about murder, two policemen who follow Guy in Washington, and then another two in Metcalf. Ann Morton twice notices Bruno's "Bruno" tie clasp. During Ann Morton's visit, first Mrs. Anthony and then her son, Bruno, take their leave with the same walk and little wave. Bruno and Guy each have snags on their way to the amusement park at the end: Guy's tennis opponent turns, in the announcer's words, "a quick victory for Haines ... into a dog fight," and Bruno must spend time fishing for Guy's lighter which he's dropped down a storm drain.

Some of the doubles are cinematically crisscrossed. After Miriam has told him she won't agree to the divorce, Guy calls Ann in Washington. "I'd like to break her foul, useless little neck ... I said I could strangle her," and there is a cut to Bruno's hands making a strangling motion. After Bruno has strangled Miriam, he looks at his watch which reads 9:30, and there is a cut to Guy on the train back to Washington, who looks at *his* watch. And of course there are the cuts between Guy's demanding tennis match and Bruno's difficulties retrieving the lighter on his trip to the Metcalf amusement park.

Sometimes the doubles become crisscrossed because one is confounded with the other. After Guy tells Ann on the phone that he could strangle Miriam, there is a cut to Bruno's hands making a strangling motion — but it turns out that he is only inspecting his nails during a manicure. Miriam thinks Bruno has a sexual interest in her as he follows her through the amusement park, and she may be right, but of course he mainly wants to kill her. Miriam's scream coming out of the Tunnel of Love makes it sound like she's being murdered then and there, but it is only a shriek of delight. Bruno later confuses Barbara Morton with Miriam Haines. "He looked at me," Barbara says. "His hands were on her throat and he was strangling *me*." Guy takes the figure in the bed in the Anthonys' house to be Mr. Anthony, but it is really Bruno. The Tunnel of Love boat operator tells the police, "He's the one. He's the one who killed her," and he means Bruno, but the police take him to mean Guy. The police shoot at Guy as he boards the carousel, but hit the carousel operator instead. The camera shows Guy punching Bruno's face during their struggle on the carousel, and we hear a woman's voice off camera, "My little boy. My little boy." But in the next shot we see she meant *her* little boy riding a carousel horse.

More interestingly, some of the doubles are crisscrossed in another sense in which one of the doubles is a kind of moral opposite of the other. Miriam is devious and in Barbara Morton's description, a "tramp." Barbara, her physical doppelgänger, is honest and reputable. Senator Morton is wise and sympathetic; Mr. Anthony, at least what little we see of him, seems argumentative and domineering (he wants to have his son "put under restraint"—perhaps not a bad idea). Bruno and his mother are soul mates, and while Mrs. Anthony (Marion Lorne) seems harmlessly daffy (she paints a wildly expressionist portrait she says is of Saint Francis), her son has strangled a complete stranger as part of a conspiracy to have his father murdered. Bruno's play strangling at the Senator's party becomes a real strangling. The professor on the train, drunk, seems to be Guy's alibi, but the professor at the police station, sober, can't verify Guy's story. Bruno pops a little boy's balloon with his cigarette on his way to murder Miriam, but after the murder he helps a blind man cross the street. Guy's feet brush Bruno's at the beginning of the film, initiating a friendly conversation if not also sexual interest; at the end Bruno's feet kick at Guy's hands trying to dislodge him from the reeling carousel. Bruno's opening gambit, "I beg your pardon. Aren't you Guy Haines?" is repeated to Guy at the end of the film, this time by a clergyman in a white collar.

As with *Shadow of a Doubt* the principal doubles in *Strangers on a Train* are its two main characters, Guy Haines and Bruno Anthony; and understanding their relationship, as with the earlier film, is the principal challenge of the film. The formal role of the doubles in *Shadow of a Doubt* was to echo the similarities between the two Charlies. The role of *Strangers on a Train*'s more multifaceted doubles is to point up the complexity of the relationship between Bruno and Guy.

At first glance it might seem that Bruno and Guy are opposite-doubles: Bruno is homosexual, theatrical, talkative, leisured, clever, envious of Guy, mad, and actively murderous; Guy is heterosexual, staid, taciturn, athletic, a bit slow, self-satisfied, sane, but passively murderous. Hitchcock even brings a Hollywood western convention into the film. Bruno tends to dress in dark suits, and is frequently shown at night. Guy tends to dress in light suits and plays tennis in daylight dressed in white. But as with the two Charlies, who are more alike than unalike, the differences between Bruno and Guy tend to blur when we probe a little deeper.

The film is all but about Bruno and Guy. The most interesting female character, Miriam, is strangled half-way through the film. The other female characters seem more like props for Bruno and Guy than genuine participants: Mrs. Anthony delivers comic relief and her role is to be "too close" to her son, Ann is little more than a motive for Guy to murder his wife, and Barbara's role is to be confused with Miriam. Some critics read both Bruno and Guy as homosexual. Vito Russo puts Bruno and Guy in the category of "covert homosexual relationships in Hitchcock films," and Donald Spoto refers to "the Guy-Bruno homosexual courtship."[4] But it is a rather one-sided courtship (at most Bruno courts Guy). Russo even titles a still of Bruno and Guy lunching together, "Farley Granger is seduced by Robert Walker in Alfred Hitchcock's *Strangers on a Train*."[5] If Russo means that Bruno has charmed Guy (or possibly has gotten tacit agreement on his murder plot), then he is correct. If he means that Bruno has bedded Guy, then he is incorrect — at least there is no evidence in the film for it. When, for example, would they have done it?

Robin Wood is less certain that Bruno is gay, because the attribution is based on "popular heterosexual myths about gay men than on any actual evidence the film ... can provide."[6] But it is just these "myths" which a heterosexual film director in 1951 would have used to signal homosexuality to a 1950's audience otherwise clueless about gay men. Bruno in this historic context is best read as gay. He is a dapper dresser: black-and-white shoes and striped trousers on the first train to New York, later a robe of circles and swirls (one imagines it to be blue and gold). Bruno and his mother have tête-à-têtes during manicures. Bruno also speaks in italics: "My father. He *hates* me." "I've got a theory — that you should do *everything* before you die." "I've had a *strenuous* evening." He's followed the handsome Guy Haines's career in the sports pages and the society section. He knows that Guy's lighter with its inscription, "A to G," is a gift from Ann Morton, the Senator's daughter. During their initial meeting he carefully gauges his progress with Guy. "Oh, there I go again — too friendly." He invites Guy to his compartment for lunch, and later calls Guy in Southampton to see if Guy has gotten his divorce. "Ah, so she's double-crossed you. Are you going to see her again?" He tells Guy he strangled Miriam because "you wanted it." Bruno is solicitous. "Oh, you must be tired, Guy." He sometimes behaves like a lover who hasn't gotten enough attention. "You're *spoiling* everything," Bruno tells Guy at the National Gallery. "You're making me come out into the open."

Bruno only has eyes for Guy when at a tennis match he fixes his gaze on Haines seated on a bench while the other spectators turn their heads left and right. Bruno persists even as Guy abuses him. At Senator Morton's

party, when Bruno comes to, having fainted during the strangling demon-
stration, Guy says to him, "You mad, crazy maniac. You ought to be locked
up. Will you get out of here and let me alone." "But Guy," Bruno croons,
"I *like* you." And when Bruno feels betrayed, he, like Medea, vows an
extravagant revenge. "Don't worry. I'm not going to shoot you, Mr.
Haines... I'll think of something much better than that. Much better."
Barbara Morton might have inadvertently gotten it right when she says to
Guy and Ann, "I still think it'd be wonderful to have a man love you so
much he'd kill for you."

Guy's sexuality, on the other hand, is somewhat ambiguous. On the
surface, at least, Guy is straight. He is trying to get out of a marriage to
one woman in order to marry another. He seems partly to sense the import
of Bruno's advances and is not comfortable with them. When Bruno asks
him to have lunch in his compartment Guy declines, and accepts only
when he is told there is a twenty-minute wait for the dining car. And Guy
seems to be entirely sincere when he repeatedly tells Bruno, "I never saw
you before and never want to see you again," "Will you stop pestering
me," "Will you get out of here and leave me alone," and so on. Yet Guy is
not entirely immune to Bruno's charms. He allows Bruno to strike up a
conversation after their feet touch, he ultimately accepts Bruno's lunch
invitation, and he leaves behind his cigarette lighter. Guy, when properly
worked up, can also speak in italics: "I said I could *strangle* her!" "You *crazy*
fool!" In a private room at the Senator's party, where Bruno has been carried after his fainting spell, he tells Guy, "I like you," whereupon Guy
responds with homosexual panic and punches him in the nose — but then
he becomes gentle and concerned. "Come on, pull yourself together. Here
let me." He adjusts Bruno's tie. "Your car here?" Guy asks as he helps
Bruno out the door. In Mr. Anthony's bedroom, Guy with some concern
tells Bruno that he's "terribly sick" and suggests he seek "some kind of
treatment," though Guy is mainly trying to get Bruno off his back. After
Bruno has tried to kill Guy on the carousel, and has been half buried under
debris from the exploded carousel, Guy still worries about him. "Can't
you get that stuff off of him?" he asks the police, though again there is some
self-interest here: Guy needs Bruno for his own defense. Even at the end
Guy expresses a grudging, if not ironic, admiration. "Who was he, bud?"
the boat operator asks. "Bruno. Bruno Anthony. A very clever fellow." So
between Guy and Bruno there is some concern and sexual tension, and
possibly an undercurrent of mutual sexual desire. Hitchcock would later
claim that he wanted William Holden in the part "because he's stronger."[7]
Yet a "stronger" actor like William Holden would have probably seemed
all straight; the ambiguity that Granger brings to the role makes his

character more interesting (because it makes him more like Bruno). Would William Holden have punched Bruno after the line, "But Guy, I like you"? I think not.

It is true that Bruno is idle in the conventional sense (this is his father's complaint about him — "With all the money he's got he thinks that I ought to catch the A5 bus every morning, punch a time clock somewhere, and work my way up selling *paint* or something"), while Guy plays tennis. "People who do things are important," Bruno tells Guy when they first meet. "Me, I never seem to do anything." Yet it is Bruno who initiates the lunch with Guy, the lunch where he states his theory "that you should do everything before you die," and of course where he tells Guy his idea for "a perfect murder." Guy plays tennis as an amateur, a highly ranked amateur to be sure, but as an amateur he earns no money from his playing. Yet he moves in the highest social circles of Washington. Guy is famous from the sports and society pages, not the business or politics sections. He seems himself like the leisured son of a wealthy man, especially when he tells Detective Hennessey, "When I'm through with tennis I'm going into politics..." I say that he *seems* like a scion of wealth, but the film does not establish where Guy gets his money. For all we know, he lives off women: besides the two fathers (Morton and Anthony), the only character in the film shown to have a job is Miriam, and even Guy's "elegant" cigarette lighter is a gift from Ann.[8] It is Bruno who acts to murder Guy's wife, Bruno who nags at Guy to keep up his end of the bargain, and Bruno who undertakes his revenge by transporting Guy's lighter back to the scene of the crime. The plot of *Strangers on a Train* is in essence: Bruno acts, Guy reacts.

Action and reaction are carried to some heights in the film's final scenes. We tend to be impressed by Hitchcock's cross cuts between Guy's tennis match and Bruno's trip to the amusement park and dazzled by the out-of control carousel sequence, and we may overlook just what Guy and Bruno are doing. Each is pushing himself to his limits. The announcer for the tennis match tells us that Guy Haines, usually "a quiet, lackadaisical player," now "takes chances I've never seen him take." Bruno drops the cigarette lighter down the storm drain, and his first reaction is the rich man's demand to have someone else recover it. When he sees he can't rouse anyone fast enough, he must strain himself to retrieve it. Their fight on the carousel is fairly ferocious— noteworthy since it is unlikely either man was ever in a fist-fight in his life. Through all of these exploits, each has an audience. Guy, of course, has the obvious audience at Forest Hills, but Bruno too has his onlookers as he struggles to reach the lighter. Both are literally the center of attention on the carousel during their fight, with a circle of panicked people around them. Their behavior in these public contests shows them to have risen to each other's challenge; they've grown to be more substantial men, capable of extraordinary fortitude and tenacity.

There is madness in Bruno, this is undeniable. The goal of Bruno's actions—the murder of Guy's wife in exchange for the murder of his father—is mad (if only because it's so bad). Bruno irrationally confuses Barbara with Miriam while pretending to strangle Mrs. Cunningham. Still, on the whole, Bruno's actions are carried through rationally and methodically. He nearly gets away with Miriam's murder. He conjures up an argument he knows will convince Guy not to go to the police. "Why should I go to Metcalf to kill a total stranger unless it was part of the plan and you were in on it? You're the one who benefits, Guy. You're a free man, now. I didn't even know the girl." He finds ways to pressure Guy to kill his father. He realizes that Guy's nocturnal visit to his home will not be to kill Mr. Anthony. And Bruno thinks of a poetic revenge on what he sees as Guy's betrayal, which might have worked had it not been for the accident of being recognized by the boat operator at the Tunnel of Love.

I wonder, though, how much of what passes for Bruno's madness is really just his theatricality. His mother mentions her son's plot to blow up the White House, but both she and he find it amusing. "I was only fooling. Besides, what would the President say." At the Mortons' party, Bruno tells the Senator about his "idea for harnessing the life force. It'll make atomic power look like the horse and buggy. I'm already developing my faculty to see millions of miles. And Senator, can you imagine smelling a flower on the planet Mars?" But this is so over the top that Bruno may be performing for his own amusement, and possibly as a warning to Guy that he is capable of anything.

It is also undeniable that Bruno is murderous: he wants to murder his father and has murdered Miriam Haines (and almost murders poor Mrs. Cunningham at the Senator's party). But Guy is murderous, too, in the sense that he wants to murder Miriam. "I'd like to break her foul, useless little neck," Guy tells Ann on the telephone from Metcalf. Guy hides Bruno's murderous activity from everyone, though he is finally forced to reveal it to Ann. Now, Bruno argued that if Guy did go to the police he would have been arrested as an accessory: they planned the murder on the train, and why after all would he, Bruno, murder Miriam, a woman he's never met. That Guy is convinced by this argument — at least, he doesn't go to the police — might be thought to be a flaw in the narrative. Hitchcock was sensitive to this very objection. "Here we have one of those stories that automatically bring on that old complaint: 'But why didn't he tell the police all about it?' Don't forget that we've clearly established the reasons for which he can't go to the police."[9] But what are these reasons? Is it that Guy really thinks that Bruno can prove that he and Guy planned Miriam's murder in a private compartment on a train? Or is it rather that Guy feels not just mistakenly implicated in Miriam's murder but genuinely complicitous in it (a feeling Hitchcock reinforces visually when he shows Bruno and Guy behind the jail-like bars of a wrought-iron fence), and hence guilty enough to hide from the police? Peter Bogdanovich had asked Hitchcock, "Does Granger chase after Walker mainly to expiate his own feelings of guilt about the murder of his wife?" "Sure he does," Hitchcock answered, "he felt like killing her himself."[10]

Besides its doubles, *Strangers on a Train* incorporates mythic symbols of life and death. Bruno gives a surprising — almost preternatural — display of strength for Miriam at the amusement park when he alone is able to ring the bell at the "Test Your Strength" machine. "Why, he's broken the thing!" the concessionaire jokes. Bruno follows Miriam in a boat named "Pluto" through the dark Tunnel of Love, where passengers appear only as shadows— shades— on the walls, to the dark "Magic Isle." As Pluto took Persephone, Bruno abducts Miriam to the land of the dead. Filmed as a reflection in a pair of eyeglasses, her strangulation is shown as a kind of magical transformation. (And like Pluto, Hitchcock's lord of the underworld is quite put out when Miriam seems to return to the world of the living as Barbara.) There is, later, an arresting moment when Guy enters the Anthonys' house, and sees a growling Great Dane at the head of the stairs. He carefully mounts the stairs, and the dog licks his hand and lets him pass. Hesiod describes the dog who guards the underworld (does Hitchcock all but quote this passage?):

> There, in front, stand the echoing halls of the god of the lower-world, strong Hades, and of awful Persephone. A fearful hound guards the house in front, pitiless, and he has a cruel trick. On those who go in he fawns with his tail and both his ears, but suffers them not to go out back again, but keeps watch and devours whomsoever he catches going out of the gates of strong Hades and awful Persephone.[11]

Guy is not Orpheus charming the beast to rescue his beloved from Hades, for Guy has little charm, and in any case he is there to rescue himself from Bruno. Why does the dog allow him exit? Can it be that the dog recognizes in Guy some of the qualities of Bruno— that Bruno and Guy are each, at that moment, if not co-rulers of the kingdom of death, at least king and vice regent?

***

Descartes thought we knew our own minds better than we knew anything else, certainly with more certainty than we know another's mind.

Wrote the ancient Greek poet Hesiod: "A fearful hound guards the house in front, pitiless, and he has a cruel trick. On those who go in he fawns with his tail and both his ears, but suffers them not to go out back again, but keeps watch and devours whomsoever he catches going out of the gates of strong Hades." Bruno Anthony (Robert Walker, left), positioned as lord of the underworld, is furious that Guy Haines (Farley Granger) has not kept up his part of the bargain. *Strangers on a Train* (1951).

Strangers on a Train presents a case study that casts doubt on this. In *Shadow of a Doubt* Young Charlie must use the newspapers to put together the bits and pieces of evidence she has about her uncle. Bruno has already done his homework before *Strangers* begins. He knows Guy awfully well from the sports and society pages. He knows whom "A" on the lighter names, he knows Guy is seeking to divorce his wife for "A," and he knows Guy would like his wife out of the way. There is, too, the fact that Bruno senses a similarity between himself and Guy, which gives him, as it gave Young Charlie, an epistemic edge in understanding what Guy thinks and wants. Bruno suspects that Guy might be interested in a sexual liaison with him, and he may not be entirely wrong (though Guy would deny it). On the train to New York, Bruno guesses that Guy would not be unreceptive to an invitation to trade murders. "You do my murder and I do yours."

What does Guy think about Bruno's offer? What he *says* is "Swap murders? Oh, ha, ha, ha, ha." What he *doesn't* say is, "What a crazy, terrible idea. No, never." In fact Guy never really rejects Bruno's idea. There is even a kind of verbal handshake — two in fact — on the deal Bruno's offered:

> BRUNO: Oh we do talk the same language, don't we?
>
> GUY: Sure, Bruno, we talk the same language.

And just a bit later:

> BRUNO: Now you think my theory's okay? You like it?
>
> GUY: Sure, Bruno, sure. They're all okay.

Guy intones his remarks as the condescensions one might make to a child or a madman. But if Guy thinks Bruno is mad, he should also think that a madman might well go through with such a scheme, and do his best to nip it in the bud. When Bruno puts through the call to Southampton after Guy has seen Miriam in Metcalf to see how the divorce is proceeding, and is told that Miriam isn't going to give him the divorce, Guy hangs up on him, again avoiding the chance to disabuse Bruno of his idea of the perfect murder. The strong implication is that Guy covertly *wants* Bruno to kill Miriam, and further that Bruno knows this even though Guy won't acknowledge it explicitly to himself.

Bruno hits this nail on the head when, after the murder, he says to Guy in the shadows, "But Guy, you wanted it. We planned it on the train together, remember?" Clever Bruno sees that he and Guy aren't all that different, and at points knows Guy Haines's inner life better than Guy Haines knows it himself. Bruno has simply put Guy's motive into action. He becomes, in a sense, Guy's will. Or at least this is how Bruno would describe it. In his father's bedroom, he irritably tells Guy, "I don't like to be double-crossed. I have a murder on my conscience. But it's not my murder, Mr. Haines. It's *yours*. And since you're the one to profit by it, I think you should be the one to pay for it." To which Guy replies, "Well I guess it's no use, Bruno. We seem to have nothing further to discuss." It's a bit surprising that Bruno should think he has a conscience — he may mention it mainly to make Guy feel guilty — but it's not surprising that he should think of Miriam's murder as Guy's. On Bruno's logic, if Guy had murdered Mr. Anthony, *that* would have been *Bruno's* murder. If Bruno can murder Miriam with Guy's motive, and Guy hasn't exactly discouraged Bruno from acting, then it is to some extent Guy's murder too. I don't mean, of course, that Bruno's logic is correct: the murder of Miriam isn't *only* Guy's murder. Certainly, Guy is not as morally culpable for Miriam's murder as Bruno. Bruno tries to shrug off all of his moral responsibility for Miriam's murder, which is wrong of him, but it is also wrong for Guy to refuse to share any of it.[12]

After Miriam's murder Guy will typically describe Bruno in terms of folk psychiatry: "You maniac," "You crazy fool," "You mad, crazy maniac," and so on (Guy doesn't have the largest vocabulary). It's not that Bruno isn't mad, but thinking of someone *only* as a madman screens out anything else he might have to say. What is it that Guy feels he must screen out? Just this: that Bruno is right about Guy's murderous desires, and partly right about his moral responsibility for Miriam's death (and just possibly right about Guy's sexuality), though Guy doesn't want to acknowledge any of this. Guy must battle Bruno on the out-of-control carousel — itself a machine gone mad — to wrest from him the lighter that would tie Guy to his wife's murder. The fact that Guy succeeds promotes a kind of falsehood. But at least it satisfies the police.

***

The pairs of twins, Young Charlie and Uncle Charlie, Guy and Bruno, the first related by family, the second strangers, exemplify some connection between good and evil. But what, exactly? On one reading, *Shadow of a Doubt* and *Strangers on a Train* are like David Lynch's *Blue Velvet* (1986): each portrays evil beneath the calm, good surface of everyday, bourgeois life. Good and evil are thus aspects of distinct social realities. Stay on the ordinary, everyday surface you find good, probe deeper and you find evil. This is essentially Robin Wood's take on *Shadow of a Doubt* (though he does not have a high opinion of the Lynch film).[13] The problem with the social (or Lynchian) interpretation is that it separates good from evil — as if middle-class society were like a house made of good timber but with a rotten foundation. Hitchcock, though, in *Shadow* and *Strangers* isn't particularly interested in social psychology. He is interested in character, and it is important in this context to reaffirm the similarities of the two Charlies and of Guy and Bruno. They are not moral opposites, one good, the other bad.

Certainly, the two Charlies are not moral equals: Uncle Charlie is a woman-hater and murderer. However, he has his virtues too: he is charming, intelligent, and clever. Young Charlie shares some of her uncle's virtues, along with some of her own: in particular, she, unlike her uncle, is capable of concern for the well-being of her family (though not really beyond her family). But Young Charlie also embodies some of what makes her uncle demonic: his capacity for duplicity, his ruthlessness, even his inner resources for killing. In *Shadow of a Doubt* Hitchcock demarcates good from evil at the level of motive. Young Charlie uses her "demonic" resources to protect her family, even including her uncle, though in the end she feels forced to destroy him. We are, I think, meant to regard these as good (or at least defensible) motives. Uncle Charlie preys on vulnerable widows to satisfy some terrible need that is left incomprehensible to the audience (he doesn't kill them for their money exactly, since he lives in a shabby rooming house and treats his plunder, tens of thousands of dollars, cavalierly, without much concern for keeping it secure). A childhood bicycle accident is mentioned, but this is so underdeveloped one might as well try to explain Uncle Charlie's behavior as caused by the phases of the moon. (Robin Wood understands the bicycle accident as "elementary Freudian metaphor for the trauma of premature sexual awakening," which provides the "clue" to the later widow murders.[14] But even if we grant the accident-as-metaphor, to connect the "accident" and the murders, Wood has to posit the "smothering sexual/possessive devotion of a doting older sister," for which there is no evidence whatsoever in the film.)

Guy and Bruno are even closer twins than the two Charlies. Each lives off of someone else's money; each harbors murderous desires; each seems self-absorbed; each rises to the demands of the other at the end. Though strangers, Bruno establishes an instant intimacy with Guy, to the point that he begins to function as Guy's will, acting on Guy's true desires. At the tennis match at Forest Hills, the camera shows in the upper frame a portion of Kipling's poem inscribed on the building: "And treat those two imposters just the same,"[15] which may be a comment on Bruno and Guy, each of whom pretend no moral responsibility for Miriam's death. Guy and Bruno are near moral equals with regard to motives (that is, each harbors murderous intent). Bruno, of course, actually commits murder and Guy does not. Bruno actively encourages Guy to kill Mr. Anthony and Guy refuses. Still Bruno takes Guy, with some justification, to have acquiesced to his scheme. The moral difference between Bruno and Guy comes at the moment of Bruno's actions. But I think it is incorrect to say that Bruno becomes bad when he kills Miriam. He was already morally culpable, Hitchcock implies, but no more than Guy himself.

***

Film and novel. Hitchcock's film departs from Patricia Highsmith's 1950 novel in several notable respects. In the novel Guy is a well-known architect, not a tennis player (oddly it is Bruno who has a tennis racket on the train). I like to think that Hitchcock made Guy an amateur tennis player to reinforce his similarity with the unemployed Bruno. Guy leaves behind on the train a copy of Plato, not a cigarette lighter, though the book allows a detective to establish that Bruno and Guy met on the train before Miriam's murder (they both said they'd only met months later). Highsmith's Bruno— actually "Charles Anthony Bruno"— is repellent and careless, unlike the suave, clever character portrayed by Robert Walker. The homosexual bond that develops between Bruno and Guy is a bit more obvious in Highsmith's novel: Bruno fantasizes about holding Guy's hand and runs his fingers over Guy's pipes in their rack; Guy accepts a present from Bruno and thinks to himself that he feels like Bruno's lover. Anne is from a wealthy family, but not a Senator's daughter; she owns a small design studio. The most striking plot departure is that Highsmith's Guy really does kill Bruno's father — Bruno hounds him into it. In the end, Bruno, drunk, drowns in a boating accident, and Guy writes a letter confessing his role in the murders.

The film's allusions to Pluto and the underworld are inventions of the scriptwriters (or Hitchcock), as are the final race to the amusement park and Bruno's and Guy's fight to the death on the carousel. The character of Barbara, Anne's sister, who doubles for Miriam, also has no counterpart in Highsmith's novel. Donald Spoto says that the film's doublings "had no precedent in the novel," and that Hitchcock dictated "the series of doubles ... in rapid and inspired profusion to Czenzi Ormonde and Barbara Keon during the last days of script preparation..."[16] It isn't entirely true that the novel has no doublings. Highsmith's Guy Haines speaks of a "duality penetrating nature" and of the "doubleness of everything," and at one point Guy muses on himself and Bruno: "Each was what the other had not chosen to be, the cast-off self, what he thought he hated but perhaps in reality loved."[17] Still, Hitchcock added doubles of far greater resonance. "Isn't it a fascinating design?" Hitchcock later said to Truffaut "One could study it forever."[18]

10

Psycho

"Now were Dr. Jekyll and Mr. Hyde two persons or were they the
same person who merely changed? We can say whichever we like."
— Ludwig Wittgenstein, *The Blue Book*[1]

"Mother. My mother. What is the phrase? She isn't quite herself
today."
— Norman Bates

Coming after the lavish production of *North by Northwest*, *Psycho*
(1960) has a B-movie look and deliberately so. "How would it be if somebody *good* did one of these low budget movies?" Hitchcock asked screenwriter Joseph Stefano.[2] The dazzling orchestral colors of Bernard
Herrmann's score for *North by Northwest* dull to strings-only in *Psycho*,
yet his music plays the more significant role in the latter film. Imagine the
shower murder without Herrmann's shrill strings. A hit from opening day,
Psycho turned out to be Hitchcock's most successful film financially, and
is probably still his best-known work. *North by Northwest* recapitulated
Hitchcock's devices of suspense. *Psycho*, on the other hand, was something
quite different, not only in Hitchcock's oeuvre but in movie history. For
better or worse, *Psycho* spawned a new film genre, the "slasher film," which
grew to include *Play Misty for Me* (1971), *The Texas Chainsaw Massacre*
(1974), *Halloween* (1978), and so on (and on and on).

Psycho is divided into two halves with the shower murder as a bridge
passage between them. The first half tells of the cheerless plight of Marion Crane (Janet Leigh), a secretary at the Lowery Real Estate office in
Phoenix, whom we first meet having a lunch hour tryst with Sam Loomis
(John Gavin), a man who says he can't marry her because most of his
money goes to his dead father's debts and alimony to his ex-wife. "I pay
too," Marion retorts. "They also pay who meet in hotel rooms." She suggests that they meet "respectably" next time. Back at her desk, Marion
endures the flirtations of a rich and inebriated client, Tom Cassidy (Frank

"You know what I do about unhappiness? I buy it off," Jack Cassidy (Frank Albertson) tells Marion Crane (Janet Leigh), who then takes his advice. *Psycho* (1960).

Albertson), who is buying a house as a wedding present for his daughter — paying for it in cash, forty thousand dollars. Marion takes the money to deposit in the bank, but instead stops at her house to change and pack. She is about to steal Cassidy's money.

Marion Crane has a guilt-ridden drive out of Phoenix. At a traffic light, her boss and his client cross in front of her car. She pulls off the road to sleep and is awakened by a highway patrolman staring at her through the window. "Is there anything wrong?" he asks her. "Of course not. Am I acting as if there's something wrong?" "Frankly, yes." At a used car dealer Marion wants to trade her car; the salesman is suspicious of her haste. Driving, she hears conversations in her mind's ear: the highway patrolman asking, "She look like a wrong one to you?" and the used car salesman responding, "Acted like one"; Mr. Lowery buzzing his other assistant to ask whether Marion is in yet; Mr. Lowery talking to her sister on the phone; and Mr. Cassidy vowing to get his money back. And then as it gets dark and begins to rain, Marion Crane wanders off the main highway and chances across the Bates Motel.

The shy, polite young proprietor, Norman Bates (Anthony Perkins), shows her to Cabin One — "It's closer in case you want anything. It's right next to the main office" — and invites her to have sandwiches and milk. In her room, changing, Marion hears an unpleasant, strident woman's voice, "I won't have you bringing strange young girls in for supper." Marion and Norman eat in a parlor behind his office, and Norman apologizes for his mother. She notices Norman's stuffed birds. Taxidermy, it turns out, is his hobby. They seem to find common ground when he remarks that "we're all in our private traps." Marion's suggestion that perhaps Norman should put his mother "someplace" arouses anger in the young man who explains that his mother isn't "a maniac, a raving thing. She just goes a little mad sometimes. We all go a little mad sometimes. Haven't you?" Marion agrees and says that tomorrow she's going to take a long drive back to Phoenix.

Marion returns to her room. Norman goes into the motel office, removes a picture from the wall, and peeps through a hole as Marion undresses. Norman leaves the office. As Marion showers, a female figure comes into the bathroom with a raised knife and brutally slashes and stabs her to death. Norman cries from the house, "Mother! Oh God, what —? Blood, blood! Mother!" He rushes to the motel, nearly retches from the sight, but pulls himself together and cleans up the blood, wraps Marion Crane's body in the shower curtain, puts it in the trunk of her car along with her other belongings (including the stolen money, which he's never noticed). Then he sinks the car in a swamp.

In the second half, Lila Crane (Vera Miles), Marion's sister, pays a visit to Sam Loomis in his hardware store in Fairvale and tells him Marion is missing. A private investigator named Arbogast (Martin Balsam) arrives and tells Sam that his girlfriend stole forty thousand dollars and that he's convinced she's somewhere in town. "Where there's a boyfriend..." Arbogast, canvassing motels in the area, makes inquires of Norman Bates who tells him, "No one's stopped here for a couple of weeks." But Bates lets slip that a couple was here last week, and Arbogast, now suspicious, asks to see the room register which shows the name "Marie Samuels." Then Bates admits that he does remember her, and Arbogast wants to search the cabins. Now the investigator notices a woman in the window of the house and asks to talk to her. Bates refuses, and Arbogast makes a call from a pay phone to Lila Crane, telling her that Marion spent last Saturday at the Bates Motel and that he's going back. There, he walks up to the old house, climbs its stairs, and is suddenly set upon by "Mother" wielding a knife, who stabs and slashes him to death.

Sam and Lila wonder what's happened to Arbogast. Sam drives out to the Bates Motel but doesn't see anything except a "sick old lady unable to answer the door — or unwilling." They go to the sheriff (John McIntire), who tells them that Arbogast couldn't have questioned Norman Bates's mother as she's been dead for ten years. Mrs. Bates, it seems, poisoned herself and her lover when she found out he was married. Back at the Bates house, Norman carries his mother to the fruit cellar. Sam and Lila turn up at the motel pretending to be married and take a room. Sam decides he will keep Norman occupied while Lila questions the mother. When Norman realizes Lila is gone, he rushes up to the house. Lila, hiding from Norman, goes into the basement where she sees what appears to be Mrs. Bates. What she discovers is the dried corpse of an old woman, stuffed and dressed. A figure in a wig and dress enters. It is Norman Bates with a knife, and Sam Loomis comes in time to struggle with Norman and wrestle him to the ground.

At the courthouse, a criminal psychiatrist, Dr. Richmond (Simon Oakland), tells the gathered police and reporters, "I got the whole story, but not from Norman. I got it from his mother. Norman Bates no longer exists." As "Mother" Norman Bates killed Marion Crane, Arbogast, and probably two other women who are missing. Norman killed his mother and her lover ten years ago, but stole her corpse before it was buried. He preserved it, and began to speak and act like her. If he felt a strong attraction to another woman, "the mother side of him would go wild." Now the mother personality has completely taken over Norman Bates, whom we last see staring straight ahead as "Mother's" voice talks in his head.

***

The dominant images of *Psycho* are eyes and wounds. *Psycho*'s characters try to figure one another out by looking, but are rarely correct. The film's characters are, in Wittgenstein's words, enigmas to one another. Mr. Lowery does a double-take as he crosses the street in front of Marion Crane's car, wondering what *she's* doing *there*. The highway cop stares at Marion as she sleeps and, waking, panics, trying to ascertain what this woman is doing alone in her car by a highway. Marion stares in her rearview mirror at the cop following her, wondering what *his* intentions are. Arbogast spies through the door of Sam Loomis's hardware store as Sam and Lila converse, seeking clues as to the whereabouts of forty thousand dollars. Later Arbogast studies Norman Bates's face to see what he might know that he isn't telling.

Indeed not only do eyes in *Psycho* yield no information, they inflict damage. Norman's peeping triggers his murderous rampage; Arbogast's wanting to have a look inside the Bates house brings about his death; Lila's search in fruit cellar creeps her out and almost kills her. Norman Bates himself has suffered from being watched. "Have you ever seen the inside of one of those places?" Norman asks Marion who's suggested he put his mother "someplace." "The laughing and the tears, and the cruel eyes study-ing you." This "studying" did not, we may safely assume, bring about understanding. That vision in *Psycho* is impaired as a tool for discovering truths about other minds is emphasized in another set of images about eyes, which are literally unseeing: the eyes of Norman's stuffed birds, Mar-ion's unblinking eye as she lies on the bathroom floor, Mrs. Bates's eyeless skull in the fruit cellar, Norman Bates's visionless stare in his prison cell. Such eyes have lost their epistemic function entirely.

Wounds, mental and bodily, form another set of images in this dis-concerting film. In the beginning Marion is wounded with shame from having sex in hotel rooms; after the theft she endures feelings of guilt, panic, and disorientation; Marion and then Arbogast are slashed to death (in Arbogast's case, the attacker seems to aim for his eyes); next, the pain, anger, and helpless frustration of Sam and Lila who have lost someone dear to them; and finally a psyche is displayed to us, one so damaged it has ceased to serve one of its primary functions, which is to present a series of thoughts as a unified self to a self. Taken together, the eye and wound images suggest a theme of epistemological impoverishment and the fragility or malleability of self.

***

It is clear that the two Charlies of *Shadow of a Doubt* and Bruno and Guy of *Strangers on a Train* are intended to be similar. The persistent dou-bling throughout both films emphasizes and exemplifies their alikeness. It would seem that Marion Crane and Norman Bates are as different as two people could be. And yet they are similar. Each assumes, at least for a while and for different purposes, another (additional) personality. *Psy-cho* thus continues, subtly and darkly, the theatricality that permeates *North by Northwest*. In the earlier film people are comically mistaken as being someone else; but no one thinks *himself* to be someone else. In *Psycho* peo-ple take on different personalities with dire consequences for themselves and others. The personae Marion Crane and Norman Bates adopt take them over; each loses sight of who he or she is.

Marion Crane assumes her role after her conversation with Tom Cas-sidy in the Lowery Real Estate Office. Cassidy is tipsy, amoral, flirtatious, and rich — a chubby old devil from Texas. "Hot as fresh milk," he com-ments on the weather as he enters the office.

> CASSIDY: You know what I do about unhappiness? I buy it off. Are, uh, you unhappy?
>
> MARION: Uh, not inordinately.
>
> CASSIDY: I'm buying this house for my baby's wedding present. Forty

It would seem that Marion Crane (Janet Leigh) and Norman Bates (Anthony Perkins) are as different as two people could be. And yet they are similar. Each assumes, at least for a while, another (additional) personality. *Psycho* (1960).

thousand dollars in cash. Now that's not buying happiness. That's just buying off unhappiness. [Chuckles.] I never carry more than I can afford to lose. [Hands Marion a wad of bills.] Count 'em.

CAROLINE (Lowery's other clerk): I declare —

CASSIDY: I don't. That's how I get to keep it.

Cassidy, unwittingly, has suggested a Faustian gambit to Marion Crane — Faustian in that she must subvert her real personality and act like someone she is not to carry it off. The personality Marion assumes is Cassidy's. She takes money that is not hers to take (as Cassidy keeps money that is not his to keep). She will use it to buy off her unhappiness. She changes costume for her new role, from white bra and slip to black. She acknowledges her debt to her teacher as she delivers a wry smile during her drive imagining Cassidy fuming over his lost funds. She even flirts a bit with Norman Bates as she stands in the doorway of her motel room.

Still, she can't quite pull off Cassidy's amorality. Marion is initially presented to us as a decent person who wants to legitimize her sexual relationship with Sam through marriage. She was a dependable employee. "A girl works for you for ten years," Lowery tells Cassidy. "You trust her." Marion is beset with guilt from the moment she spies Mr. Lowery crossing in front of her car in Phoenix. She knows she is behaving "like a wrong one" in front of the highway patrolman and the used car salesman, and even in front of Norman Bates. She is having trouble keeping to her role as immoralist. The court psychiatrist says near the end, "You see, when the mind houses two personalities, there's always a conflict, a battle." He was speaking of Norman Bates, but his general remark also applies to Marion Crane.

Marion discards her Cassidy-persona and returns to what we're meant to think of as her real self during her supper conversation with Norman Bates, of all people.

NORMAN: Where are you going?

MARION: I'm looking for a private island.

NORMAN: What are you running away from?

MARION: Why do you ask that?

NORMAN: No. People never run away from anything.... You know what I think? I think that we're all in our private traps, clamped in them, and none of us can ever get out. We scratch and claw, but only at the air, only at each other. And for all of it, we never budge an inch.

MARION: Sometimes we deliberately step into those traps.

NORMAN: I was born in mine. I don't mind it any more.

MARION: Oh, but you should. You should mind it.

NORMAN: Oh, I do. But I say I don't. [Laughs nervously.]

Marion eventually acknowledges that she's gone "a little mad." She is restored to herself by considering Norman's plight — or what she takes to be Norman's plight — and seeing some of herself in him. What she sees is not a man who has also, though more diabolically, taken on an alter-ego, but a man whose life has been badly damaged by his mother — and he's allowed this to happen to him. But Marion will not allow herself to damage her life, and she plans to return to Phoenix the next day to return the stolen cash. Unfortunately, she has come back to herself too late. Her fate is to be made a thing literally without self: a body stuffed into a car trunk, comically sunk into a swamp.

What of Norman Bates? The murder of Marion Crane only half-way through the picture was a shocker when the film was released. Hitchcock once said, "I purposely killed the star so as to make the killing even more unexpected."[3] Actually, the film has *two* stars: Janet Leigh and Anthony Perkins. The first half of the film tells Marion Crane's story, the second tells Norman Bates's. The audience is given a close relationship with Marion Crane. For starters, our information in the narrative is limited to her epistemic position. Even conversations that take place after she has left Phoenix are "heard" as her inner thoughts — the camera stays with Marion. (Norman isn't the only one who hears other voices in his head.) But during Marion's supper in the parlor of the Bates Motel, the film's epistemic point of view shifts — to Norman Bates. As Marion leaves the motel office, telling Norman she will be getting an early start the next morning for her long drive, the camera stays with Norman. We watch as Norman Bates struggles with himself, and finally removes the picture covering his peephole. Our view of Marion undressing is now *his* view.

It isn't only that the film's epistemic anchor unexpectedly drops out of the picture; she was the principal object of our concern in that narrative. After her abrupt murder, we're left with Norman Bates to care about. Hitchcock, Anthony Perkins, and Joseph Stefano collaborated to produce in Norman Bates a sympathetic young man, capable of holding the audience's empathy during the film's second half — at least until the appearance of Lila Crane and Sam Loomis, after which Norman begins to seem creepier than we thought. The Norman Bates of Robert Bloch's novel, a middle-aged, fat man with spectacles, socially clumsy and charmless, becomes in Hitchcock's film a young, handsome man of shy charm and some penetrating insight. Stefano also toned down the violence of Bloch's Bates.[4] We *want* to sympathize with Tony Perkins's Norman Bates—

because of his loneliness, his boyish good looks, the burden he has in caring for a destructive mother, the fact that he seems his mother's victim, and most of all because he seems to have been deprived of a real life. We pity him for being an outcast. We would even like to *understand* him. So would the other characters in the film.

The two Charlies of *Shadow of a Doubt* and Bruno and Guy of *Strangers on a Train* had what I called an "epistemic edge," special access into one another's minds because of their similarities. Not so in *Psycho*, whose characters don't even have regular epistemic entrée to Norman Bates's mind. We "read" others—form little theories about their motivation—based on our stock of experience with people. Marion thinks Norman is a shy young man, nearly broken in spirit by his mother, a person who really needs to get out on his own. She even feels a kinship with him, as both are in their "private traps." This turns out to be at once tragically true and wildly wrong, as Norman's private trap is not the one Marion imagines it to be. Arbogast suspects Norman has bedded Marion and is being paid to hide her in his house. Wrong. Lila Crane thinks Norman was after Marion's money to get out of an obviously failing business and build a new motel somewhere else. Wrong again.

The mistake the other characters make in trying to understand Norman Bates is to think of him as motivated by normal needs: filial devotion or sex or money. But Norman isn't like other people (to understate the matter). He kills Marion Crane and the private investigator Arbogast, in two of the most memorable murder sequences on film. We find out at the end that he probably killed two other women — missing persons. It isn't simply that Norman Bates kills these people; he does it violently and in a sort of amnesiac state, as his mother. Come back to himself, he doesn't recall the murders, as shown by his retching at the sight of Marion Crane, dead, in the bathroom.

One would think that the authoritative explanation of Norman Bates is delivered by the psychiatrist, Dr. Richmond (Simon Oakland), who at the courthouse, tells the gathered police and reporters, "I got the whole story, but not from Norman. I got it from his mother." It turns out that Norman killed his mother and her lover ten years ago, but stole her corpse before it was buried. He preserved it, and to assuage his guilt, as Dr. Richmond's narrative has it, "began to think and speak" for his mother, "give her half his life, so to speak. At times he could be both personalities, carry on a conversation. At other times, the mother half took over completely... He would walk around the house, sit in her chair, speak in her voice." And sometimes dress up like her. If he felt a strong attraction to another woman, "the mother side of him would go wild." Now, alone in his prison cell,

"Norman Bates no longer exists. He only half existed to begin with." We last see Norman Bates sitting while "Mother's" voice runs through his head.

Does the expert, the psychiatrist, understand Norman Bates? Not fully. He's heard the story from Norman Bates's mother, he tells us; Norman Bates no longer exists. This, taken literally (which may not be how Dr. Richmond meant it), would imply that *Psycho* is a back-from-the-dead or spirit-possession film. Somehow, against the laws of nature, Mrs. Bates's consciousness survived bodily death and has returned to reside in her son, eventually winning a psychic battle by extinguishing *his* mind. On such a reading, Norman Bates's body has incorporated his mother's consciousness and ultimately lost his own, a grotesque iteration of Locke's puzzle case: "For should the soul of a prince, carrying with it the consciousness of the prince's past life, enter and inform the body of a cobbler, as soon as deserted by his own soul, every one sees he would be the same *person* with the prince, accountable only for the prince's action..."[5]

But either the psychiatrist has got part of it wrong or he was speaking hyperbolically. Norman Bates isn't literally possessed by his mother. Nothing in *Psycho* signals that the afterlife is somehow involved. Compare *Psycho* with *The Possession of Joel Delaney* (1972), a film in which it is clearly a fictional truth that Joel Delaney is possessed by the spirit of a recently deceased Hispanic friend (Delaney suddenly begins to speak Spanish, for one thing). Norman Bates, on the contrary, is delusional. He *thinks* himself, now and then, to be his mother, which is not the same as *being* his mother. However, there is a sense in which Norman Bates no longer exists. His personality — his desires, values, world outlook, and possibly memory — are apparently no longer operative. He no longer thinks and behaves like the shy young man of some charm we first encountered in the Bates Motel. He has ten years ago assumed a role, which was to be his shrill, possessive, demanding mother, and has assumed it so thoroughly that he can't back out. This is the "private trap" he's hinted at during his supper with Marion Crane in the parlor of the motel.

In Dr. Richmond's explanation, read naturalistically, Norman Bates assumes the role of his mother, complete with her taunts and demands, to assuage his guilt over his matricide. There is no one to deliver a diagnosis of Marion Crane, but simply put Marion Crane assumes the role of thief and liar to assuage her guilt over her illicit sexual episodes. One difference between them of course is that Norman has managed to think himself into the role of Mother so thoroughly that he can't back out; Marion finally tires of her role though for reasons beyond her control *she* can't back out either. *Psycho* is a film about the dangers of *becoming* another mind.

***

Psycho has an unsettling effect on its audiences that is not, I think, fully explained by the suddenness and violence of the two murders, nor even by the air of Grand Guignol — wigs, preserved corpses, and so on — that surrounds Norman Bates's madness. Its unsettling effect is brought about in part through Hitchcock's manipulation of his audience's concern.

We initially sympathize with Marion's frustration with her romantic predicament, by which I mean we understand it and wish her a good outcome. Our sympathy is compromised when Marion steals Cassidy's money. Now the outcome we wish for her is ambivalent. We at once want her to get away with it, and to come back to her senses. In other words, we sympathize with her Marion-persona *and* her Cassidy-persona. Now if this is so, we too are "split" into two personae, one siding with conventional goodness, the other with amorality. Our relief that she is about to return the money must be accompanied by a bit of disappointment that she isn't going through with it.

Suddenly Marion is horribly done away with. Now we have Norman Bates as the object of our concern. Already we feel sorry for his victimization at the hands of his mother, a bit hopeful that he can find a way out of his "trap," though we also understand that he has resigned himself to his situation and for this we pity him. When after Marion's murder it seems to us that his mother *is* a maniac and a raving thing whose crimes her son enables, our sympathy is similarly compromised. We still pity Norman, but now we realize that he is partly complicit in Marion's murder (legally, he would be an accessory after the fact). Our sympathies are turned around again when at the end we realize that Norman Bates was a seriously damaged young man, who had to adopt grotesque strategies to deal with himself and who murdered other people, even though he was not fully in control of his actions. We feel in the end tainted by the film which draws us into sympathy with someone who proves ultimately beyond sympathy.

11

Marnie, Spellbound

"'Tis evident, that whatever is present to the memory, striking upon
the mind with a vivacity, which resembles an immediate impression, must become of considerable moment in all the operations
of the mind, and must easily distinguish itself above the mere
fictions of the imagination. Of these ideas or impressions of memory we form a kind of system, comprehending whatever we remember to have been present, either to our internal perception or senses;
and every particular of that system, joined to the present impressions, we are pleas'd to call a *reality*."
　　　　　　　　　　　　— David Hume, *A Treatise of Human Nature*[1]

"Mother, mother I am ill.
Send for the doctor over the hill.
Call for the doctor, call for the nurse.
Call for the lady with the alligator purse.
Mumps said the doctor.
Measles said the nurse.
Nothing said the lady with the alligator purse."
　　　　　　　　　　　　　　　— Baltimore children's chant

Spellbound (1945) is Hitchcock's first "therapy film." *Marnie* (1964),
far better, is his second. Each is a film whose plot revolves around the
recovery of a memory. Each has as its principal characters a troubled individual implicated in crimes and someone who functions as an investigative psychiatrist. Each builds to the dramatic recollection of a childhood
incident whose recitation is aimed at a cure (though it only clearly works
in one case). *Spellbound* begins in an explicitly psychiatric setting (a mental
hospital). Its investigator is a psychoanalyst, Dr. Constance Peterson (Ingrid
Bergman), who takes as her patient a man (Gregory Peck) who believes
he has murdered another psychoanalyst and who can't recall much of anything else. *Marnie* takes place in ordinary surroundings: business offices,
cars, homes. Its investigator, Mark Rutland (Sean Connery), is not a real
psychiatrist — he runs a publishing business and his hobby is zoology —

but he functions like one. He takes on as his patient his wife, Marnie (Tippi Hedren), who is a serial thief, imposter, and liar, and who fears thunderstorms, the color red, and sexual contact with men. Both Peterson and Rutland press their patients into recovering the traumatic memory with the hope that this will head them towards mental health. Constance Peterson is in love with her patient, though she waits until he is cured to marry him. Mark Rutland is also in love with Marnie, but he marries her first, then sets out to cure her.

***

Spellbound tries to be simultaneously psychoanalytic inquiry, suspense thriller, and love story. It was advertised as if it were another *Suspicion*—"Will he kiss me or kill me?"—though its heroine is in jeopardy only briefly (she almost skis over a precipice). The publicity surrounding Salvador Dali's design of the dream sequence stirred interest in the film, though the dream's original shooting time of twenty minutes was cut to about two.[2] The film has its virtues: a warm and caring performance by Ingrid Bergman, Hitchcock's wonderfully atmospheric mise en scène and lighting, and Miklos Rozsa's score, which won the film's sole Academy Award and which established the Theremin as *the* Hollywood leitmotif of mental illness. The film's plot, despite a screenplay by Ben Hecht, is another story. Raymond Chandler found the situation in *Strangers on a Train* "ludicrous in essence." I wonder what he would have said about *Spellbound*.

The director of a psychiatric hospital, Green Manor, Dr. Murchison (Leo G. Carroll), has been forced into retirement (he apparently had some unexplained mental lapse earlier). His replacement, the eminent Dr. Anthony Edwardes (Peck), has written a book, *Labyrinth of the Guilt Complex*. It is clear that Dr. Edwardes and fellow analyst Dr. Constance Peterson (Bergman) are taken with one another, though she notices that he is strangely upset by parallel lines (on the tablecloth, on her robe, etc.). Later Constance discovers that the signature of the man calling himself "Dr. Edwardes" and the author's signature in *Labyrinth of the Guilt Complex* are not the same. She confronts Peck (as we'll now call him). "Who are you?" "I remember now," he answers. "Edwardes is dead. I killed him, and took his place. I'm someone else, I don't know who. I killed him." Later he will tell Constance, "I have no memory." Peck writes a note to Constance telling her that he is leaving for the Empire State Hotel in New York. She follows.

Trying to avoid the police (who want to question Peck about the disappearance of Dr. Edwardes), Constance and Peck take a train to Rochester to visit her old psychoanalyst, Alex Brulov (Michael Chekhov). Dr. Brulov guesses soon enough that the couple are not married as Constance had alleged, and that Peck is mentally disturbed. Both analysts try to interpret Peck's dream — the Dalí-designed dream sequence — in which he finds himself in a gambling house festooned with eyes, plays twenty-one with blank cards, is threatened by the head of the gambling house, slides down a roof, etc.

Noticing Peck's anxious reaction to sled tracks in the snow, Constance takes him skiing to jog his memory. Just as the two approach a precipice, Peck suddenly remembers that he accidentally killed his brother when he was a child (sliding down a balustrade, he impales the brother on a fence), and is now able to remember that the real Dr. Edwardes skied over that very precipice. (Edwardes was consulted by Peck who was suffering from "nerve shock" due to a plane crash during the war, and had invited Peck to go skiing — perhaps in homage to its Austrian origins, psychoanalysis in this film is with some regularity practiced on a ski slope.) Later the rest of Peck's lost memories tumble out (name, occupation, etc.). But Edwardes's death turns out to be no accident. The police later arrive at the

Noticing that her patient (Gregory Peck) has an anxious reaction to sled tracks in the snow, Constance Peterson (Ingrid Bergman) takes him skiing to jog his memory, in *Spellbound* (1945).

ski lodge with the information that the body of Dr. Edwardes was recovered with a bullet found in his back. Peck (now called John Ballantine) is convicted of murder.

Back at Green Manor, Dr. Murchison lets slip to Constance Peterson the admission that he knew Dr. Edwardes, which he had denied earlier. She now understands that Peck's dream points to Dr. Murchison as the killer of the real Dr. Edwardes. Murchison admits his guilt and shoots himself. John Ballantine — freed from prison, cured of his amnesia and guilt complex — and Constance Peterson marry.

***

While the inferior *Spellbound* proved very popular with audiences and critics on its release (and received six Academy Award nominations), *Marnie* was neither a popular nor a critical success. Universal Studios considered the film a disaster.[3] It's perhaps not hard to see why the film failed. It lacks a conventional Hollywood romance and a clearly happy ending. Coming after the thrills and chills of *Psycho* and *The Birds*, the suspense in *Marnie* is relatively low key, generated mainly by making the audience wonder what made Marnie so neurotic. (*Marnie* is in this respect like a whodunit, only it's a whodunit-to-her.) The film's expressionist elements — the reddening of the screen during Marnie's panic attacks, the camera zooming in and out as Marnie tries to steal Rutland's money — may have stricken some initial viewers as hokey (though no one seemed to be bothered in 1946 when Ingrid Bergman's poisoned delirium in *Notorious* was expressed with out of focus and "woozy" camera movements). Then there are what appear to be technical gaffes. The ship at the end of Mrs. Edgar's Baltimore block is conspicuously a painted backdrop — Hitchcock said he wanted "the effect of a ship on dry land. It didn't come off the way I wanted it to…"[4] The matte shots for Marnie's horseback ride, car travel, and especially the fox hunt seem, for 1964, irritatingly out-of-date — and perplexing after the polished technical achievements of its immediate predecessor, *The Birds*. Sometimes it is alleged that Marnie's panic attacks over the color red are inconsistent.[5] Red gladioli and a jockey's uniform bring them on, but not the red carpet in Rutland's home nor the red furniture in the Rutland offices. However, the trigger for her attacks is not simply red but red against a white background, exactly reminiscent of the sailor's blood-stained white undershirt. In this Hitchcock is consistent.

Tippi Hedren's performance, too, has dissatisfied some viewers. She sometimes appears to be trying too hard — her *acting* is sometimes evident. She appears "stiff," though her character has a lot to hold in. However, after several viewings I find her convincing as a very troubled young woman, living under a series of false identities, without human attachments (she seems comfortable only with her horse), and begging love from her unresponsive mother. In fact, some of the unpopularity of *Marnie* might be traced to Hedren's *success* at portraying a woman who shuns human relationships: her character puts off the audience as well. The male lead, Sean Connery, is not everyone's idea of a mainline Philadelphia gentleman, especially when his Scottish burr comes through ("South Amerrrica"), though he projects an aggressive sexuality that surely threatens the "frigid" Marnie. (Even his character's name, "Rutland," suggests rutting.) Despite its flaws, the film verges on greatness because of Hitchcock's overall direction, expert camera work, the many beautiful sequences of pure visual cinema, and Bernard Herrmann's doleful score, as much a part of *Marnie* as it was of *Vertigo* and *Psycho*.

***

A dark-haired woman carrying a large purse and a suitcase takes a train to New York City where in a hotel room she washes the dark rinse out of her hair, transfers a large amount of money from the purse to a suitcase, and switches one identification card for another. "Robbed. Cleaned out. $9,967," Mr. Strutt (Martin Gabel) of Strutt and Company tells the police. "And that girl did it. Marion Holland." Mark Rutland (Connery), a client, seems somewhat amused that there was a robbery "by a pretty girl with no references."

After her theft from Strutt, Margaret Edgar, called "Marnie" (Hedren), takes a train to Maryland, visits her horse, Forio, at Garrod's stables, and then her mother, Bernice Edgar (Louise Latham), in a waterfront neighborhood of Baltimore. Mrs. Edgar, who uses a cane after her "bad accident," thinks Marnie is "private secretary to a millionaire." "I can't take in the way you jump around all over the place like you do. Boston, Massachusetts. Elizabeth, New Jersey." Noticing Marnie's blond hair, her mother warns, "Men and a good name don't go together." Marnie agrees, "We don't need men, Mama." Red gladioli upset Marnie who replaces them with white chrysanthemums (and Marnie will be upset by more red-on-white: spilled ink, a jockey's uniform, etc.). Her mother pulls away when Marnie touches her. "Why don't you love me, Mama? I've always wondered why you don't." Upstairs, Marnie naps and some past trauma begins to surface as she talks in her sleep. "No. I don't want to, Mama, no... Don't make me move, Mama, it's cold."

In Philadelphia, Marnie, calling herself "Mrs. Taylor," applies for a job as payroll clerk at Rutland & Co., a publishing firm. But the job seems already filled as Marnie overhears Sam Ward (S. John Launer) tell Mark Rutland that the woman he's just interviewed "seems to have the exact qualifications." But Mark, who seems to recognize her, asks for Marnie to

Marnie Edgar (Tippi Hedren) as brunette "Marion Holland," changing identities in a hotel room after her theft from Strutt and Company. *Marnie* (1964).

be sent in. She claims to be a widow, taught accounting by her late husband. But she has no references. Rutland insists on hiring her anyway. "I don't get it," Sam Ward says. "You're not supposed to get it," Rutland retorts.

Rutland asks "Mrs. Taylor" to work overtime on a Saturday. She is to type his manuscript, "Arboreal Predators of the Brazilian Rain Forest." Rutland explains that he was going to be a zoologist before being drafted to head his family's publishing firm.

> MARNIE. Does zoology include people, Mr. Rutland?
>
> MARK. Well, in a way. It includes all the animal ancestors from whom man derived his instincts.
>
> MARNIE. Ladies' instincts, too?
>
> MARK. That paper deals with the instincts of predators. What you might call the criminal class of the animal world. Lady animals figure very largely as predators.

A thunderstorm terrifies Marnie who ends up in Mark's arms, and he kisses her.

Driving her home Mark notices that Marnie likes to listen to horse racing on the radio. He invites her to the Atlantic City track, where she tells a man who claims to recognize her as "Peggy Nicholson" that he is mistaken. In response to a question from Mark, Marnie denies she's had a tough childhood. "I think you did. I think you've had a hard, tough climb. But you're a smart girl, aren't you? The careful grammar, the quiet good manners. Where did you learn them?" "From my betters," Marnie coldly answers. Mark takes Marnie home to meet his father and horses.

After work one Friday, Marnie steals money from the Rutland safe. Mark finds her riding at Garrod's (he's traced her through some inquiries about horses). Marnie gives him what money she has. She's sent the rest to a New York post office box in a registered package. Mark demands the key and receipt. "This receipt and the unopened package are as good as a signed confession. You understand that?" Marnie nods. She concocts a story in which she and her mother, deserted by her father, move to Los Angeles; her mother dies, and Marnie is raised by a family friend, Mrs. Taylor. But Rutland knows that she had worked for Strutt. "I saw you there once…" "You mean you knew all about me when you hired me?" "No. I wasn't positive. But I thought it might be interesting to keep you around." Marnie explains that she had to get away from Rutland's. "Don't you understand. Things were — we were — " Mark announces they're to be married "before the week is out."

> MARNIE. What are you trying to pull?
>
> MARK. I'm trying to pull a proposal.
>
> MARNIE. But you know what I am … I'm a thief and a liar.
>
> MARK. It seems to be my misfortune to have fallen in love with a thief and a liar.
>
> MARNIE. Listen to me, Mark. I am not like other people. I know what I am!
>
> MARK. I doubt that you do, Marnie…. Somebody's got to take on the responsibility for you, Marnie. And it narrows down to a choice of me or the police, old girl.

A huge diamond ring, a "meager, furtive little wedding" as the Rutlands' banker cousin calls it, and Mark and Marnie are off on a cruise to the South Seas.

In their cabin, Mark tries to kiss his new wife who is almost frozen with terror. "I can't stand it! I'll die! If you touch me again, I'll die!" Mark gives her "his word" that "he won't," but some nights later he does, and Marnie tries to drown herself in the ship's pool. The couple return home early. Mark asks his wife to keep up the façade of marriage. He also tells her he's repaid Strutt anonymously, a remark overheard by Lil Mainwaring (Diane Baker), the sister of Mark's deceased wife. Mark brings home Forio to Marnie's obvious delight. Through Lil's eavesdropping, Mark discovers that Marnie has a mother in Baltimore, and hires a detective who not only finds the mother but also discovers that she was tried for murder some years ago. "I want to know," Mark asks the detective, "what happened to the little girl, the daughter."

At the party before the hunt, Lil has invited Mr. Strutt (whose entrance is shown in a tracking shot borrowed from *Notorious*). Strutt recognizes Marnie who panics and packs to run away. Mark suggests to Marnie that Strutt will not want to lose the Rutland account by prosecuting her. Marnie tells Mark that there were four other "jobs," which Mark proposes they repay while Marnie expresses regret and contrition. Forced to shoot her horse after an accident during the hunt, Marnie takes the keys to the Rutland office safe and tries to steal more money, but finds she can't.

Mark drives her to Baltimore and confronts her mother. "Marnie hasn't been very well. I don't believe she's been very well since you had 'your accident.'" "You don't know the whole story," Bernice Edgar says. "And nobody does but me." Marnie is brought to remember, and in flashback we are shown, how Bernice Edgar, then a prostitute, brought home a sailor (Bruce Dern), who in a struggle with Bernice, falls on her. Marnie picks up a fire poker and beats the sailor to death with it, his red blood staining his white shirt. Mrs. Edgar had told the police it was she who killed the sailor, but was acquitted on a claim of self-defense. In the film's closing shot, Marnie says to Mark she doesn't want to go to jail. "I'd rather stay with you."

* * *

In contrast with Young Charlie and Bruno Anthony, who seemed to have a more natural access into the inner lives of *their* targets, Uncle Charlie and Guy Haines, the investigative psychiatrists, both professional and amateur, of *Spellbound* and *Marnie* have the devil's own time figuring out what makes their subjects tick. This is in part because the genre of the "therapy film" demands it, but in part because their subjects act in ways that mark them as different from their investigators. The epistemological edge that Young Charlie and Bruno had in understanding their respective targets comes from their mutual similarities. There are fewer inter-personal similarities between Constance Peterson and "Dr. Edwardes," who can't remember who he is, who fears parallel lines, who believes he's killed an eminent psychoanalyst, and who sleepwalks carrying a straight razor; nor between Rutland and Marnie, who presents herself under various false identities, who lies and steals, and who fears the color red, thunderstorms, and sex. It is a bit like trying to understand the mental life of another species—and Rutland is an amateur zoologist as well as an amateur psychologist.

Both films present characters who are ill, though Peck exhibits all the suffering of a mild rash, while Marnie looks genuinely troubled—even the children playing outside her mother's house sing as she arrives, "Call for the doctor, call for the nurse, call for the lady with the alligator purse," which happens to be what Marnie is carrying. The idea advanced by both films is that their respective subject's odd behavior is caused by repressing the memory of a traumatic past event, and the plot of each film is aimed at recovering this memory. Dr. Peterson explicitly uses the techniques of psychoanalysis—*Spellbound* sometimes seems like an infomercial for psychoanalysis—urging Peck to say whatever comes into his mind, asking him what he remembers when aroused to anxiety by parallel lines, taking copious notes during his dream recitation, etc. Peck will be found to be suffering from a "guilt complex." "People often feel guilt over something they never did," Constance Peterson tells one of her patients while Peck listens. "It usually goes back to their childhood. The child often wishes something terrible would happen to someone, and if something does happen to that person, the child believes he has caused it. And he grows up with a guilt complex over a sin that was only a child's bad dream." Peck's guilt complex is ultimately revealed to be caused by his repressed memory of having accidentally (or so we are led to assume) killed his brother. When Peck recovers his memory of this accident he realizes that he hadn't really killed Dr. Edwardes after all. Constance Peterson explains, "That was the thing that set you off, the start of your own guilt complex that made you think you had killed him."

Rutland's psychiatry in *Marnie* is less explicitly theory-laden, but equally effective. After discovering Marnie's theft from his company, he intuits that something is wrong with her. "I know what I am!" Marnie insists. "I doubt that you do," he replies. After her admission that she can't stand to be touched, Mark Rutland slips into a therapist's role. "What happened to you?" he asks his wife, with the psychoanalytic notion that the past causes the present. "Nothing," she protests. "Nothing happened to me..." Marnie has nightmares, and Mark conducts a psychological investigation around one. "Who hurt her?" "What noises?" "Who makes them?" Marnie at first mocks these attempts—"You Freud, me Jane"—but word association on "death" and "red" brings her to collapse in Mark's arms. "Oh, help me. Oh, God, somebody help me." And Mark takes what he thinks is the next, right step: to Baltimore. "Your daughter needs help, Mrs. Edgar," Mark says to Marnie's mother. "You've got to tell her the truth. She has no memory of what happened that night." Mark provides a catalyst for Marnie's recollection by reproducing the tapping she hears in her dreams. "Remember, Marnie, how it all was." At the end, Mark will tell his wife, "When a child, a child of any age, Marnie, can't get love, it takes what it can get, anyway it can get it."

Both films rely on views traceable to Freud though by the time of *Marnie* they are no longer the arcana of psychoanalysis but have become part of folk psychiatry. The cure effected by the released memory relies on Freud's idea that knowledge brings relief. "Actually there is no lifting of the repression until the conscious idea, after the resistances have been overcome, has entered into connection with the unconscious memory-trace. It is only through the making conscious of the latter itself that success is achieved."[6] Mrs. Edgar, we may note, demurs from the Freudian view. She thinks that Marnie's lost memory of the sailor incident "was a sign of God's forgiveness."

In *Spellbound* Peck recalls in a brief cinematic flashback lasting perhaps five seconds how he accidentally pushed his brother onto a fence. In *Marnie* there is an extended flashback representing Marnie's act of recollection. Peck's memory is verified (as a true memory of what really happened) because it relieves his symptoms (amnesia). Peck's recovery, though, seems entirely too speedy — a cure ex machina. Mrs. Edgar, a witness to the events Marnie has forgotten and is brought to recollect, verifies her daughter's memory, but Marnie's cure is less obvious than Peck's. We know only that she wants to stay with Mark and not go to jail. Who wouldn't?

Coming to remember — to pull up something from memory — is, it would seem, a paradigm case of coming to know one's own mind, directly. But in the case of a repressed memory, the subject is barred from direct access to it — this is the point of departure for both films. Freud again: "Experience shows that we understand very well how to interpret in other people (that is, how to fit into their chain of mental events) the same acts which we refuse to acknowledge as being mental in ourselves. Here some special hindrance deflects our investigations from our own self and prevents our obtaining a true knowledge of it."[7] This "special hindrance" is repression, or more accurately, the resistance to the lifting of repression. The idea advanced by *Spellbound* and *Marnie*, consonant with Freud's suggestion, is that with respect to one person's repressed thoughts it may actually be easier for *another* person to come to know them. The persons who possess the memory, Peck and Marnie, are positioned as all but unable to know their own minds.

The external psychologists in these films, Constance Peterson and Mark Rutland, therefore drive the investigation, with their subjects sometimes reluctant accomplices. Constance Peterson has some idea of what's going on with her patient: she may not know the specific memory he's repressed, but she (not he) knows it bears on parallel tracks. Mark knows something happened to his wife connected with her mother's "accident," which Marnie denies. The pursuit of the repressed memory in *Spellbound* and *Marnie* is like the pursuit of the mysterious but vital fact that structures other Hitchcock films: What are the 39 steps? What's in the cellar of the Nazi spies (*Notorious*)? Who is Ambrose Chapel (*The Man Who Knew Too Much*)?

Indeed, the lost memory that is the object of everyone's attentions in *Spellbound* and *Marnie* is itself as if an external fact — like, for example, the uranium ore in Claude Rains's cellar in *Notorious*. It is noteworthy that to find the memory, the investigators have to take their subjects to the place it was lost — the ski slopes in *Spellbound*, Marnie's childhood house in Baltimore — and stage a simulation of the forgotten incident. Peck remembers his role in his brother's death, which involved sliding down a steep grade, as he himself is about to ski over the precipice where Dr. Edwardes met his death. Marnie's recitation is prompted by a struggle between Mark and her mother who wants him out of her house, and then by Mark who knocks three times. One suspects Peck's and Marnie's memories are more news to them than they are to Constance and Mark. It is not a figure of speech to say that Peck and Marnie, in recollecting their respective past traumas, come to know *another* mind.

The flashback sequence in *Marnie* is especially telling in this regard. From Marnie's anguished face, Hitchcock cuts to a sofa, then to a hallway as the camera moves towards Bernice Edgar's bedroom of a time past. The visual sequence is especially disorienting, perhaps suggesting the anxiety attendant on recollection. (Hitchcock used the same technique when James Stewart looks down the tower in *Vertigo*: the camera moves back and zooms forward at the same time.) During the flashback re-enactment, Hitchcock cuts back to Marnie's face several times, with Mark asking her what she sees, what happens next, and so on. Marnie's coming to remember is thus presented as a kind of cinematic screening which among the film's characters only Marnie observes.

Yet what, exactly, is it that Marnie "sees"? Mark's and Mrs. Edgar's version of what Marnie has come to know about herself is simply this: that as a child Marnie killed a sailor who was beating her mother. This is consonant with what Marnie reports verbally to Mark during her recollection — what she *tells* him she remembers. "He hit my mama! ... I hit him with a stick! I hurt him!" The adult Marnie views her recollection through a child's eyes — at least she reports them in a little girl's voice: the sailor is trying to kiss her, he is beating her mother, she must save her mother, etc. But she doesn't report all she sees, or at least doesn't report the event as it is "shown" to her (and to us) with all its nuances. In the flashback sequence the sailor is actually trying to comfort Marnie, who is already upset (and cold) because she had to leave her bed, and is further frightened by thunder and lightning. Bernice-past begins to beat the sailor with the fire poker for "touching" her daughter, and the sailor, confused, tries to fend her off. As both sailor and mother fall down entangled, little Marnie picks up the poker and with great force beats the sailor to death, his red blood literally drenching his white shirt. Bernice-past can't recognize that the sailor is attempting to be kind, probably because she already feels immense loathing for the men she services. Probably, too, the child Marnie is already traumatized by her mother's prostitution — as an adult she remembers with great anxiety that "them in the white suits" knock and then she feels cold. By the time of the killing, child-Marnie probably has already taken on her mother's loathing for men, hence the extreme violence of a little girl towards the sailor. The film's audience, privy to Marnie's cinema of the mind, knows more about what happened than she does. So much for Descartes's thought "that nothing is more easily or manifestly perceptible to me than my own mind."[8] (I wonder, though, what even the audience takes away from the flashback sequence. One critic says that Marnie's "neurosis was caused by an attempted rape when she was a child and her accidental killing of her prostitute mother's client."[9] Attempted *rape*? *Accidental* killing?)

In real-life therapy, such a traumatic childhood incident would be examined with great attention to detail and would be placed in the context of a larger picture of Marnie's psychology. *We* can connect Marnie's history with her present: she acts out her distrust of men by taking from them what makes them powerful: their money. But can Marnie herself make this connection? She has only Mark as her therapist, and he gives every indication that her therapy has been successfully concluded. The memory Peck recovers is instantly familiar to him: he comes to know, again, that he is John Ballantine, that he is a doctor, and so on. He truly re-connects with *himself*. Even Bernice Edgar, who also indulges in a bit of reminiscence, seems strangely comforted by her confession that Marnie was the outcome of her teenaged exchange of sex for a boy's basketball sweater. Marnie, however, is brought face-to-face with an alien self. Ballantine is obviously pleased to join his past with his present and call it reality; Bernice is less pleased but at least she acknowledges her foolish choice of years ago; Marnie appears stunned and bewildered by her recollection.

Why should Constance Peterson and Mark Rutland be so interested in the minds of their respective subjects? Both films position the investigator as in love with his or her patient. The love between Peck and Constance Peterson in *Spellbound* is quite genuine even if from the point of view of psychoanalytic practice unorthodox and probably unethical. It begins, for Constance, concurrently with her realization that Peck is possibly mentally ill (she notices his fear of lines, his puzzled reaction to her mention of a guilt complex), and seems to increase with her understanding of how acute his illness is. When Peck and Constance have their first screen kiss, Hitchcock inserts a wonderful shot showing a long corridor with a number of doors opening one after the other, making literal Constance Peterson's opening up to her feelings. (Peck has a different description of *his* feelings: "It was like lightning striking," though he means this in the good sense.) Peterson's and Peck's interaction with each other is as much pillow talk as psychoanalytic inquiry. Donald Spoto overlooks this in writing that in *Spellbound* Hitchcock "dealt with guilt incapacitating the reach toward love..."[10] On the contrary, the sole significant insight into human affairs in *Spellbound* is the similarities it reveals between therapy and a love affair. Both require an intimate sharing of one's past history and present feelings, though only therapy promises a cure. One hopes therapy to be terminable, a love affair to be interminable.

Her love interest is presumably what motivates Constance Peterson to take some unorthodox actions after Peck's startling claim that he killed Dr. Edwardes. She abandons her job to follow him to New York, she manipulates the hotel detective into revealing the number of Peck's hotel room, she takes Peck to Rochester to visit her old psychoanalyst and to avoid the police (with Constance Peterson's picture on the front page of the newspapers, the film takes on overtones of *The 39 Steps* and other chase films), she lies to her own psychoanalyst, she takes Peck to the ski slopes to jog his memory and nearly plunges to her death. Their sense of medical ethics, however, keeps the couple chaste during these adventures.

The easy intimacy between Peck and Constance Peterson is missing between Marnie and Mark. Rutland's love interest — if that's what it is — in *Marnie* is puzzling if not downright neurotic. Mark, as he admits, half recognizes Marnie to be the woman who stole from Strutt where he was a client, but hires her anyway (over another applicant with more obvious qualifications and references). Marnie is clearly physically attractive (Mark remembers her at Strutt's as "the brunette with the legs"). Constance Peterson may have been attracted to neurosis (a kind of weakness) in Peck. In contrast, Mark Rutland seems to be initially attracted to Marnie because of her apparent strengths: he describes Marnie after her theft from Strutt with some admiration as "resourceful," and tells her after her fright during the storm, "You know, I wouldn't have pegged you for a woman who'd be terrified of anything"? Yet Rutland first kisses Marnie after her extreme fright during the thunderstorm outside his office, which means he, too, is attracted by neurosis.

Marnie is physically attractive, resourceful, neurotic — and a criminal. Indeed, it is Marnie's criminality — her dangerousness — that also attracts Rutland, who is also attracted to jungle predators. (There is precedent for this in Hitchcock's films. Grace Kelly is turned on by Cary Grant's criminality in *To Catch a Thief*.) Hitchcock told Truffaut he thought of having a scene in which Mark secretly watches Marnie as she commits robbery. "Then, he would have taken her by force while pretending to be outraged. But you can't really put these things on the screen. The public would reject them."[11] Lil, the sane woman in the Rutland household, has marital designs on her brother-in-law, and knows not all is right with Marnie nor with Mark's interest in her. She is puzzled that the lord of the manor, in a sort of inversion of the Gothic romance, prefers the madwoman in the attic. Marnie herself wonders about her husband's motives.

> MARNIE. Why can't you just leave me alone?
>
> MARK. Because I think you're sick, old dear.
>
> MARNIE. *I'm* sick? Well, take a look at yourself, old dear. You're so hot to play Mental Health Week, what about you? Talk about dream worlds. You've got a pathological fix on a woman who's not only an admitted criminal but who screams if you come near her!

Mark Rutland seems a complex if not impossible character, a bad guy for some of the film, then finishing off as a good guy. To begin with, he is attracted to a woman whom he suspects to be a thief, and risks his firm's money by hiring her. After her theft, and even though she begs him to let her go, Mark blackmails Marnie into marrying him ("me or the police, old girl" — Maxim de Winter's offer, "me or Mrs. Van Hopper," is gentle by comparison). Knowing that Marnie is truly terrified (and not just being coy) about sex, he gives his word that he won't touch her, but later forces sex on her and thereby drives her to attempt suicide. (The rape scene in Hitchcock's first screen treatment was strongly resisted by Evan Hunter, the film's first screenwriter, on the grounds that "Mark is *not* that kind of person."[12] His replacement, Jay Presson Allen, in an interview published on the Universal Studios DVD of *Marnie*, said that she decided that what happens on board ship wasn't rape but rather "a trying marital situation.") After the disaster of the honeymoon, Mark wants Marnie to observe the "façade" of a marriage (just as Rebecca wanted her husband to do).

On his good side, Mark thinks, with some justification, "Somebody's got to take care of you and help you." He thinks of himself as taking on "responsibility" for Marnie and saving her from prison, which is where her compulsive thievery would probably have landed her. Mark is materially good to Marnie. He repays Strutt, and offers to pay the others from whom she stole — Marnie estimates her total take at $50,000 — although even here Mark's good deeds are mingled with blackmail: he threatens to take his business away from Strutt if he goes to the police. Mark buys Marnie a huge diamond ring, and takes her on what most would consider a romantic cruise to the South Seas. After the honeymoon doesn't work out, he brings her horse home to cheer her up. Mark may have a neurotic fascination with dangerous women, though he is otherwise pretty healthy. Unlike Maxim de Winter, who is haunted by his first marriage, Mark is not in the grip of his past. Marnie tells him she's sorry that the storm destroyed his wife's pre–Columbian art. "You said it was all you had left of your wife." Mark corrects her. "I said it was all I had left that had *belonged* to my wife."

In his most beneficent act, Mark becomes determined to find the cause of Marnie's neurosis. He devotes his life in the last third of the film to finding out the awful secret in her past. He becomes her de facto analyst. He hires a private investigator, makes Marnie pay close attention to her dreams, and brings her to Baltimore for the cathartic revelation that will begin her cure. He seems genuinely concerned for her well-being, at least after the shipboard rape. And he says he loves her. "It seems to be my misfortune to have fallen in love with a thief and a liar," which puts a positive spin on his fetish: he at least accepts her for what she is.

What is Mark Rutland about? He is hardly a great man with great flaws. In the early versions of the story's development, Mark sends Marnie to an analyst, Dr. Roman.[13] By the time of the filmed version, Dr. Roman has disappeared, his function taken over by Mark. Is Mark therefore another of the film's technical gaffes, a botched composite character? I tentatively advance the idea that Mark does not veer arbitrarily from bad to good. Rather Mark is trying, sometimes clumsily and sometimes destructively, to bring about the sort of intimacy that came so easily to Peck and Constance Peterson. He begins on the level of animal training (and we should remember that Marnie is herself a horse trainer). Rutland studied predatory animals in the Amazon, and in his office keeps what appears to be a picture of a cat:

MARK. And that's Sophie. She's a jaguarundi. South American. I trained her.

MARNIE. Oh. What did you train her to do?

MARK. To trust me.

MARNIE. That's all?

MARK. Well that's a great deal, for a jaguarundi.

Later, after her theft from Rutland's, Marnie complains that Mark thinks of her only as "some kind of animal you've trapped." "That's right, you are," he agrees. "And I've caught something really wild this time, haven't I? I've tracked you and caught you, and by God I'm gonna keep you." Later Marnie acts out Mark's animal metaphor by dressing as a "cat burglar" after Strutt recognizes her at the pre-hunt party.

Mark begins to train Marnie to trust him by being understanding with her, though when positive reinforcement fails to bring about the desired result, he forces his attentions on her. And when that doesn't work, he decides on therapy, which at least begins the conversation about her past which is the start of intimacy for the two of them. Mark will also have to contribute, of course. Mark has helped Marnie towards sexual intimacy, and she, with less fanfare and without deliberate intent, takes him from leering single man, to captor and rapist, and then to caring husband.

The audience is left with the vague impression that Mark and Marnie may one day settle into marital contentment.

MARK. Oh, Mrs. Edgar, I'll bring Marnie back. She's very tired. *(Mark and Marnie leave Mrs. Edgar's house.)*...

MARNIE. Oh, Mark, I don't want to go to jail. I'd rather stay with you.

MARK. Had you, love? *(MARK and MARNIE drive away.)*

Even so, the Greek chorus of children outside Mrs. Edgar's house continue to chant as Marnie and Mark drive off, "Mother, mother, I am ill..."

III

KNOWLEDGE

12

Problematic Knowledge

For most philosophers, the problem of knowledge is principally the attempt to justify claims to know in the face of skeptical doubts. Indeed, the plot, so to speak, of two-hundred years of European philosophy from Descartes through Kant is to bridge the epistemological gap between our "ideas" of the world and physical reality itself. There are those who think the gap can be bridged and that we can know the external world with certainty (Descartes), those who think the gap cannot be bridged and remain skeptics (Hume), and those who fall somewhere in between (Kant).

Few philosophers, however, question the value of knowledge itself. Indeed philosophers are characterized by Plato as people who want to know every truth — "sightseers of the truth" he calls them.[1] "Only two things are relevant to knowledge," Descartes wrote, "ourselves, the subjects of knowledge; and the objects to be known."[2] Only two things? Are there, then, no ethical constraints on knowledge? *Rear Window* (1954) raises that issue. Perhaps there are things it would be dangerous to know. *The Man Who Knew Too Much* (1934, 1956) is about dangerous knowledge.

Rear Window is a film about "peeping," a topic that engages all of the main characters at one time or another throughout the story. Some are for it, some against, some switch sides in the course of the story. Is a person's private life a fit subject for knowledge? Jeff and Lisa (James Stewart and Grace Kelly) of *Rear Window* strive after a clear understanding of what their neighbor has done; they pass from looking across the courtyard to telephoning him and finally breaking into his apartment. So far there is little of which Descartes would disapprove (well maybe the breaking-in part, though in Amsterdam Descartes attended dissections of the human body, an activity that was denounced by the Catholic Church and was illegal in various parts of Europe[3]). Kierkegaard, on the other hand, would place the behavior of Jeff and Lisa at the level of the "aesthetic" — a kind of pre-ethical childishness. *Rear Window* is a case study in peeping, complete with philosophical dialogues on its pros and cons. In a sense their peeping is ultimately justified, though they cannot have known that it would be: Lars Thorwald really has murdered his wife and will be punished for it. And yet their spying is not motivated by a desire to see the guilty punished but played as a kind of unseemly game.

In *The Man Who Knew Too Much* Ben and Jo MacKenna (James Stewart and Doris Day) are punished for knowing something they were not meant to know and didn't seek. They have to make the wrenching decision to risk a political assassination in order to save their child. This— or these, for *The Man Who Knew Too Much* was made twice — is Hitchcock's film on existential choice. If *Rear Window* is Hitchcock's Kierkegaardian film, *The Man Who Knew Too Much* is Sartrean.

Knowledge is problematic in *Rear Window* and *The Man Who Knew Too Much* for ethical reasons. Knowledge is problematic in *The Birds* (1963) for a rather different reason. Our experience of birds has shown us that they do not attack people, that different species of birds do not flock together, and that they are not intelligent enough to plan and launch coordinated assaults. But the birds of Hitchcock's films *do* attack people, crows and gulls *do* flock together, and they *do* launch coordinated assaults. And we never are told how or why. Indeed, the inability of the characters to figure out what's really happening is a major theme of the film.

This suggests that *The Birds* is a cinematic example of skepticism. The skepticism of *The Birds* is not of the Cartesian sort: deception by an evil genius or being now caught in a dream. It is skepticism about our knowledge of the uniformity of nature, first broached by David Hume. "All reasonings concerning matter of fact seem to be founded on the relation of Cause and Effect," Hume wrote.[4] But the relation of cause and effect is itself contingent.

> It implies no contradiction that the course of nature may change, and that an object, seemingly like those which we have experienced, may be attended with different or contrary effects. May I not clearly and distinctly conceive that a body, falling from the clouds, and which, in all other respects, resembles snow, has yet the taste of salt or feeling of fire? Is there any more intelligible proposition than to affirm, that all the trees will flourish in December and January, and decay in May and June?[5]

Hume's so-called "skeptical solution" to the problem advances "custom and habit" as the explanation for why we expect snow *not* to taste of salt or feel like fire. "After the constant conjunction of two objects — heat and flame, for instance, weight and solidity — we are determined by custom alone to expect the one from the appearance of the other."[6] The solution is skeptical because *our* customary expectations in themselves provide no basis for the uniformity *of nature*. The behavior of the birds in *The Birds* is like Hume's trees that flourish in December and decay in May. No wonder this was Federico Fellini's favorite Hitchcock film.[7]

13

Rear Window

All men by nature desire to know. An indication of this is the
delight we take in our senses; for even apart from their usefulness
they are loved for themselves, and above all others the sense of
sight. For not only with a view to action, but even when we are not
going to do anything, we prefer seeing (one might say) to everything else. The reason is that this, most of all the senses, makes us
know and brings to light many differences between things.
— Aristotle, *Metaphysics*[1]

Jeff, if you could only see yourself.... Sitting around looking out of
the window is one thing, but doing it the way you are, with binoculars and wild opinions about every little thing you see is diseased.
— Lisa Carol Fremont

In *Rear Window* (1954) L. B. "Jeff" Jeffries (James Stewart), a photojournalist who has broken his leg covering an auto race, is confined to a
wheelchair in his Manhattan apartment, and spends his days looking at
the activities of his neighbors whose windows face his across a courtyard.
There is the beautiful dancer "Miss Torso" (Georgine Darcy) who exercises and fends off suitors; a composer trying to complete a song (Ross Bogdasarian); a salesman (Raymond Burr) and his invalid wife (Irene
Winston) who nags and mocks him; a middle-aged married couple (Sara
Berner and Frank Cady) who sleep on the fire escape during the New York
heat and have a little dog; a single woman, "Miss Lonelyhearts" (Judith
Evelyn), who is desperate for male companionship; and a newly-wed couple (Rand Harper and Havis Davenport) who move in and promptly pull
down the blinds.

Stella (Thelma Ritter), a visiting nurse, describes the punishments in
store for Peeping Toms. Jeff tells Stella that his girlfriend, Lisa Fremont,
expects him to marry her, though he doesn't want to. Stella delivers a lecture on the virtue of quick marriage. Evening falls, and Lisa (Grace Kelly)
arrives beautifully dressed, with dinner from "21." She suggests that Jeff

might want to stop traveling and open a studio in New York; Jeff calls her idea "nonsense" and tells her about the rough life she would lead as the wife of a photojournalist. They quarrel. After Lisa leaves, a woman screams, "Don't!" and a glass shatters.

Later that night, during a rainstorm, Jeff sees the salesman leave and return three times with a suitcase. In the morning, through binoculars, Jeff sees the salesman wiping out his sample case, then refilling it with costume jewelry. Through his telephoto lens, Jeff sees the salesman wrapping up a saw and butcher knife in newspaper. Lisa arrives and Jeff tells her what he's seen. She belittles Jeff's suspicions, but then notices the salesman tying up a large wooden crate with rope. Lisa, now intrigued, gets the tenants' name off the mailbox: Mr. and Mrs. Lars Thorwald. Jeff calls an old friend, Detective Tom Doyle (Wendell Corey).

Doyle investigates and later reports that witnesses saw Thorwald leave his apartment with Mrs. Thorwald. He produces a postcard signed by Anna Thorwald and sent from the country town of Merritsville. Doyle

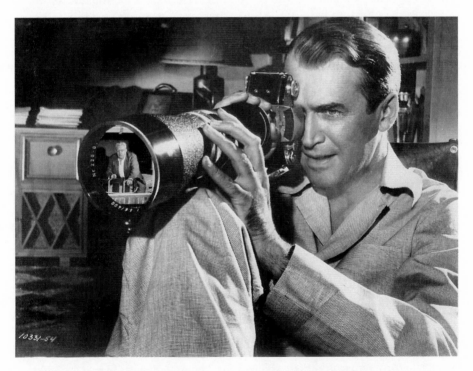

Photographer Jeff Jeffries (James Stewart) watches his neighbor across the courtyard, Lars Thorwald (Raymond Burr, reflected in camera lens), as he ties up a suitcase filled with his wife's clothes. *Rear Window* (1954).

leaves and Lisa arrives. She tells Jeff that a woman wouldn't leave without her favorite handbag and jewelry, and so the woman Thorwald left with was not his wife. "At least not yet." On another visit, Doyle tells Jeff that the Merritsville police inform him that Mrs. Anna Thorwald has picked up the trunk her husband shipped there. As far as he is concerned, there was no murder. Lisa and Jeff are visibly disappointed.

A woman screams. Her dog has been found strangled. Neighbors run to the window — all except Lars Thorwald, which makes Stella, Lisa, and Jeff suspect that Thorwald killed the dog, who had been sniffing around Thorwald's flower beds. Jeff writes a note, "Lars Thorwald, What have you done with her?" and Lisa slips it under Thorwald's door. Jeff then telephones Thorwald to arrange a "business meeting" at a hotel bar, hinting he knows Thorwald's wife is dead. After Thorwald leaves for the "meeting," Lisa and Stella dig at the flower bed, but find nothing. Lisa, however, climbs the fire escape into Thorwald's apartment to search Mrs. Thorwald's handbag. Thorwald returns and surprises Lisa. They struggle, but Jeff has called the police, who arrive and arrest Lisa for burglary. As she leaves she signals to Jeff that she is wearing Mrs. Thorwald's wedding ring. Suddenly Lars Thorwald knows that his neighbor across the courtyard knows the truth.

Heavy footsteps approach his apartment, and Jeff arms himself with flashbulbs. Thorwald enters Jeff's darkened apartment, and is blinded by flashes. He struggles with Jeff, who ends up falling out the window as the police arrive. Soon they report, "Thorwald's ready to take us on a tour of the East River." We last see Jeff in his wheelchair with two broken legs, Lisa beside him. She reads *Beyond the High Himalayas*, but then realizing Jeff is asleep, trades it for *Harper's Bazaar*.

***

The main plot of *Rear Window* involves a mystery or puzzle regarding the correct explanation of what we see in Lars Thorwald's apartment. I say what "we" see, though our epistemic point of view — our line of sight — is largely limited to that of L. B. Jeffries. We are given but one glimpse that Jeffries is not: Lars Thorwald is shown to us, but not to the sleeping Jeffries, leaving his apartment on the morning after his nocturnal suitcase adventures with a woman dressed in black. The mystery, put simply, is this: Has Lars Thorwald murdered his wife, cut up her body, carried body parts out in his sample suitcase, and later had a woman friend pose as his wife to mail postcards and pick up a trunk of clothes? Or have marital problems and illness split up the Thorwalds, with Mrs. Thorwald moving to the country, and Mr. Thorwald remaining by himself in the city? Jeff, then Lisa, and eventually Stella incline to the former; Doyle and the police to the latter. Ultimately, of course, Jeff and company are proved correct. Thorwald implies his guilt in the anonymous call Jeff makes to him, and explicitly confesses to the police at the end.

There is a dialectic of evidence and counter-evidence throughout the story. Jeff and Lisa's evidence, as Doyle points out, hardly *establishes* Thorwald as a murderer: Mrs. Thorwald nagged and denigrated her husband; he then makes three nocturnal trips with a suitcase which is later wiped clean, wraps a knife and saw in newspaper, and ties a trunk with rope; Mrs. Thorwald is no longer in the apartment but her jewelry and wedding ring remain. To counter this Doyle cites witnesses "that deep" who saw Mrs. Thorwald board a train to Merritsville and once there pick up a trunk of clothes addressed to her. And we ourselves have seen a woman leave the apartment with Lars Thorwald. Eventually Jeff tricks Thorwald into revealing his guilt through notes and phone calls.

At least one function of this dialectic is to keep the audience in suspense. It is made to seem as if Thorwald probably murdered his wife — and then this evidence is undermined by Detective Doyle. (*Rear Window* is Hitchcock reversed; usually his protagonists are *innocent* men against whom evidence mounts.) However, there is another function of the evidence-counter-evidence dialectic that moves through *Rear Window*, besides establishing suspense. The argument I will make can be prefigured this way. *Rear Window*'s two main protagonists, Jeff and Lisa, live aesthetic lives, by which I mean (a) that they thrive on looking and being looked at, and (b) that they avoid commitment especially of the marital sort. They follow their suspicions about Lars Thorwald not so much because of a desire to punish the guilty but because of the thrill of seeing what happens next. This puts them in approximately the same position as the film's audience, who also wants to know what happens next. But the film's audience is allowed their curiosity — they are, after all, at the movies — whereas actually poking around in people's lives to see what they will do remains an ethically questionable activity.

Rear Window is based on a short story by Cornell Woolrich.[2] The film follows the story's basic plot line: a man confined to his apartment watches a salesman engage in suspicious activities, the salesman's wife disappears, a policeman friend is involved, the policeman presents counter-evidence, but eventually the salesman is caught out. Hitchcock and screenwriter John Michael Hayes make Woolrich's protagonist into a photographer, amplify the slight character of Sam the houseman into the rich and comic character of Stella, and add the other colorful inhabitants of the apartment complex, Miss Torso, Miss Lonelyhearts, and the rest. Most importantly, Hitchcock and Hayes add Lisa Fremont. But Lisa is more than a love interest. She provides the circumstance for one of the two ethical situations presented in the film: whether Jeff should marry Lisa. The other ethical issue, the morality of looking in at one's neighbor's private lives—"rear window ethics," as Lisa calls it—is highlighted in *Rear Window* though it is an issue that barely ruffles Cornell Woolrich's storyline.

In fact, the film is as replete with views about the ethics of peeping and the value of marriage as it is with theories about the fate of Mrs. Anna Thorwald. Stella is an ethicist right from her entrance.

> STELLA: New York state sentence for a Peeping Tom is six months in the workhouse.... They got no windows in the workhouse. You know, in the old days, they used to put your eyes out with a red-hot poker. Any of those bikini bombshells you're always watchin' worth a red-hot poker? [Regretfully] Oh, dear. We've become a race of Peeping Toms. What people ought to do is get outside their own house and look in for a change. Yes, sir. How's that for a bit of homespun philosophy.
>
> JEFF: *Reader's Digest*, April 1939.
>
> STELLA: Well, I only quote from the best.

In other words, peeping, Stella thinks, is commonly acknowledged to be wrong and yet everyone does it though they'd be better off engaging in self-examination. (Can the "race of Peeping Toms" remark be an allusion to McCarthyism?[3])

Stella says she "can smell trouble right here in this apartment." Jeff thinks it will come with Lisa Fremont, who wants him to marry her, which provides the segue into the film's other ethical issue. Jeff thinks Lisa too beautiful, talented, and sophisticated for a "camera bum" like himself. "If she were only ordinary," he says.

> STELLA: Look, Mr. Jeffries, I'm not an educated woman, but I can tell you one thing: When a man and a woman see each other and like each other, they ought to come together—wham!—like a couple of taxis on Broadway, and not sit around analyzing each other like two specimens in a bottle.
>
> JEFF: There's an intelligent way to approach marriage—
>
> STELLA: Intelligence. Nothing has caused the human race so much trouble as intelligence. [Laughs.] Modern marriage.
>
> JEFF: We've progressed emotionally—
>
> STELLA: Once it was, see somebody, get excited, get married. Now it's read a lot of books, fence with a lot of four-syllable words, psychoanalyze each other, until you can't tell the difference between a petting party and a civil service exam.

JEFF: People have different emotional levels—

STELLA: Lisa's loaded to her fingertips with love for you. I got two words of advice for you. Marry her.

In other words, it is the right thing for two people who like each other to marry, though it is getting harder to do. Peeping is on the rise, marriage on the decline: not good in Stella's homespun philosophy.

Disputations about peeping and marriage percolate through the film. Jeff's editor tells him, "It's about time you got married before you turn into a lonesome and bitter old man." "Yeah," Jeff replies, "Can't you just see me. I'm rushing home to a hot apartment to listen to the dishwasher and ... the nagging wife." When Lisa hints that Jeff open a photographic studio in New York—an indirect marriage proposal—he calls her idea "nonsense." "Jeff, isn't it time you came home?" she responds. They quarrel about whether a person can change and about which person should change. Should she go with Jeff on his dangerous shoots or should he stay in New York? This ends in stalemate:

LISA: So that's it? You won't stay here, and I can't go with you?

JEFF: It would be the wrong thing.

LISA: You don't think either one of us could ever change?

JEFF: Right now, it doesn't seem so.

Later Lisa will show up with another proposal in the form of a Mark Cross overnight case. "I'll trade you," she says to Jeff, "my feminine intuition for a bed for the night."

Detective Doyle arrives and after telling them that witnesses saw Mrs. Thorwald get on the train to Merritsville and that Mrs. Thorwald collected the trunk of clothes addressed to her, delivers his opinion on peeping: "That's a secret, private world you're looking into out there. People do a lot of things in private they couldn't possibly explain in public." Later, after Doyle leaves, Jeff and Lisa watch as Miss Lonelyhearts brings home a young man, who nearly date-rapes her. They are embarrassed for being witnesses. "You know, much as I hate to give Thomas J. Doyle too much credit, he might have gotten a hold of something when he said that was pretty private stuff going on out there. I wonder if it's ethical to watch a man with binoculars and a long-focus lens. Do you—do you suppose it's ethical even if you prove that he *didn't* commit a crime?" Jeff asks Lisa. "I'm not much on rear window ethics," she replies. She notes that they're disappointed because a man *didn't* kill his wife. "We're two of the most frightening ghouls I've ever known."

Stella (Thelma Ritter, left) and Lisa Fremont (Grace Kelly), after some initial resistance, join Jeff (James Stewart) in "peeping" at a possible murderer. *Rear Window*
(1954).

The killing of the dog brings Thorwald's guilt — and Jeff's and Lisa's
enthusiasm — back into the picture. Even Stella joins in, looking through
Jeff's "portable keyhole," as she calls his camera, and helping Lisa dig up
the flower bed. Then Thorwald joins in the peeping when he is made aware
of Jeff across the courtyard. Things take a serious turn as Thorwald attacks
Lisa and then Jeff, who defends himself with an instrument of peeping,
the flash camera.

With all this worry over the ethical, do Lisa and Jeff manage to do the
right thing? Looking at the consequences, yes. Thorwald confesses, and
Lisa and Jeff seem poised for marital commitment. Yet if doing right
requires a certain intent, they fail. Lisa and Jeff are not motivated by a good
will, working to apprehend a murderer because that is the right thing to
do. Jeff begins watching Thorwald out of boredom, Lisa joins in because
it seems exciting (and possibly a way to tempt Jeff into marrying her), and
they pursue the affair to its conclusion because it seems the one project
that they can both take up without changing too much in their lives.

The Cartesian project of surmounting the possibility of deception and achieving genuine knowledge of the external world is given another dimension by Søren Kierkegaard, who inquired into our personal relation to the data stream that eventually constitutes knowledge. In *Either/Or* Kierkegaard described two types of relationships: the aesthetic and the ethical. The paradigm of the aesthetic man is the seducer, though Kierkegaard's seducer, Johannes, is not the sexual athlete one might expect. Johannes thinks the sex act somewhat *déclassé*: "Most men enjoy a young girl as they do a glass of champagne in a single frothing moment. Oh, yes, that is all right, and in the case of many young girls it is really the most one can manage to get; but here there is more." Johannes is really more of a voyeur, not exactly a Peeping Tom (though he has his moments), but rather a man who watches his Cordelia in a state of psychical distance from her, intervening occasionally to get her to react, and eventually managing things so that it is she who breaks off their engagement. "Last evening the aunt had a little party. I knew Cordelia would have her knitting-bag with her, so I had hidden a little note in it. She dropped it, picked it up, read it, and showed both embarrassment and wistfulness. One should never fail to take advantage of such opportunities." He even desires to observe her in her private moments. "If it were possible for me to stand behind Cordelia when she receives a letter from me, it might be very interesting. Then I could easily find out how far she has, in the most essential sense, appropriated the erotic to herself." Towards what point are his attentions directed, if not sex? "I am watching the birth of love within her. I am even almost invisibly present when I visibly sit by her side. My relation to her is that of an unseen partner in a dance which is danced by only one, when it should really be danced by two."[4] The aesthete's relation to others is like the relation of the voyeur to the objects of his sightings: each is excited and entertained by what he sees.

Now Jeff and Lisa are also aesthetes. Jeff is a photographer who makes his living by capturing images of other people. His work — disasters, glamour shots — are the result of viewing exciting events and beautiful women from behind a camera. Lisa herself is involved with fashion. She makes her entrance in the film turning on the lights in Jeff's apartment very theatrically, in a dress "right off the Paris plane." "If there's one thing I know," she tells Jeff, "it's how to wear the proper clothes." L. B. Jeffries knows how to look, Lisa Fremont knows how to have a look. Jeff (like Kierkegaard's seducer) seems to have little interest in sex. Yet despite their similarities Jeff and Lisa malign the other's profession. "What is it but traveling from one place to another, taking pictures?" Lisa says of Jeff's photojournalism. "It's like being a tourist on an endless vacation." Jeff mocks her interest in clothes, and accuses her of thinking only about "expensive restaurants," "a new dress," a "lobster dinner," and "the latest scandal."

Their relation to the denizens of the Greenwich Village apartments seen from Jeff's bedroom window is aesthetic. While Lisa *seems* initially disapproving — "Sitting around looking out of the window to kill time is one thing, but doing it the way you are, with binoculars and wild opinions about every little thing you see is diseased!" — she makes this remark out of pique for Jeff's lack of attention to *her*. Eventually she, too, takes up peeping. "Let's start from the beginning again, Jeff. Tell me everything you saw, and what you think it means." At this point Lisa begins her active involvement with the Thorwald affair, getting the name from the mailbox, and ultimately invading his apartment. Lisa and Jeff are entertained and excited by what they see. Indeed, they most fully come alive when viewing the comings and goings of Lars Thorwald. "Wasn't that close?" she breathlessly asks after shoving Jeff's note under Thorwald's door. "What was his reaction, I mean when he looked at the note?" ("If it were possible for me to stand behind Cordelia when she receives a letter from me, it might be very interesting.") A bit later, Lisa, exhilarated, waggles her finger wearing Anna Thorwald's wedding ring, and Jeff gushes like a schoolboy, "Gee, I'm proud of you."

An ethical interest in Thorwald would manifest itself as a desire to punish the guilty because it is a duty. It isn't, however, clear that Jeff and Lisa have such a desire; even if they do, it is not their primary motivation. They despair when it seems Thorwald *isn't* guilty, prompting Lisa to remark that they're "ghouls." Lars Thorwald himself wonders about Jeff's intentions: "What do you want from me? [*Pause*] Your friend, the girl, could've turned me in. Why didn't she? [*Pause*] What is it you want, a lot of money? I don't have any money. [*Pause*] Say something. Say something! Tell me what you want!" Here Thorwald is like the male heroes of *The 39 Steps*, *Foreign Correspondent*, *North by Northwest*, and other films, men who are caught up in circumstances they don't understand.[5] On Stewart's silence Hitchcock comments, "Stewart doesn't answer because, in fact, his actions are unjustified; they're motivated by sheer curiosity."[6] And, he might have added, motivated too by the thrill of the hunt.

The seducer was for Kierkegaard the paradigm of the aesthetic way of life, so conversely marriage was the paradigm of the ethical way of life. In an admonishing letter to the seducer, "Judge William" writes: "You were constantly clinging to a given immediacy as such, to an impulse implanted by nature, and did not dare to allow it to transform itself into a consciousness common to both of you; for this is what I meant by the expression sincerity and candor.... But for this a decisive step is required, and hence it requires courage, yet conjugal love sinks into nothing when this does not take place; for only by this does one show that one loves another and not oneself."[7]

Stella and Doyle represent the ethical attitude in the film: both frown on peeping, each is happily married, though each falls under the sway of the aesthetic (Doyle is attracted by Miss Torso; Stella, against her better judgment, gets involved with peeping at Thorwald). Three people try to steer Jeff towards marriage: Stella, Gunnison (Jeff's editor), and Lisa. Stella thinks people who are attracted should marry, wham: not quite Kierkegaard's idea of sincerity and candor but that may come later (as Stella implies it did in her marriage: "When I married Miles, we were both a couple of maladjusted misfits. We are still maladjusted misfits, and we have loved every minute of it."). Gunnison tells Jeff, "It's about time you got married, before you turn into a lonesome, bitter old man." While Lisa tries to steer Jeff towards marriage, she does it by tempting him with a position in New York's fashion industry. She spends extravagantly on him: a lobster dinner sent in from "21," an engraved silver cigarette case. Later she arrives with a more straight-forward temptation, a sexy nightgown, but this plan is derailed by Jeff's interest in Lars Thorwald.

Marriage is constantly on this film's mind. The first words spoken are by a radio announcer warning of a biological clock ticking away: "Men, are you over 40? When you wake up in the morning, do you feel tired and run down? Do you have that listless feeling?" Jeff threatens his editor to get him out of his two-room apartment or he's going to do something "drastic"—like get married. Right from the start Jeff is anti-marriage. "Can't you just see me," he tells his editor. "I'm rushing home to a hot apartment to listen to the automatic laundry and the electric dishwasher and the garbage disposal and the nagging wife." Jeff tells Stella Lisa is at once "too perfect" and "too Park Avenue," by which he means she is too involved in superficialities and he is not of her class. He wants life on the edge eating fish heads and rice; she wants him to wear a business suit and take society pictures. They argue over whether either can change or will change. Lisa, too, seems to court both romantic and sexual failure. She pursues a man who is manifestly uninterested in sleeping with, let alone, marrying her. Besides, what sexual activity does she think she can coax out of a man encased in a toe-to-hip cast?

And yet it *seems* that at the end they are on the road to marriage. After the capture of Lars Thorwald, Hitchcock places Jeff and Lisa's relationship among other by-and-large happy endings: Miss Torso's surprisingly short, plain boyfriend returns from the army (to her evident happiness); the middle-aged couple have a new puppy; Miss Lonelyhearts and the composer have linked up; the composer has finished his song, "But dream forever in your arms, oh Lisa"; but the newlyweds have begun to bicker (because he's quit his job).

Still, if the arc of this narrative is from the unlikelihood of a marriage between Jeff and Lisa to their impending wedding, there is some explaining to do. Hitchcock has earlier made explicit a symmetry between the unhappy Thorwalds and Jeff and Lisa. Both Jeff and Anna Thorwald have physical limitations that confine them to bed. Both are peevish with their respective partners. Lars and Lisa have served their respective partners a lovely dinner. Yet Anna Thorwald throws away the rose her husband brought her on the dinner tray, while across the courtyard Jeff in exasperation tells Lisa her dinner is "perfect. As always." Lars and Anna Thorwald have an unhappy marriage; Jeff and Lisa have an unhappy relationship. Both Anna Thorwald and Lisa Fremont are attractive blondes, and each makes demands on their respective partners who become annoyed. The Thorwalds bicker, though over what we do not hear (possibly a girlfriend is implicated); Lisa and Jeff bicker over whether one will change to suit the other. Jeff, when he's not avoiding Lisa's advances, makes passive-aggressive remarks about nagging wives and unhappy marriages, which shows him to be like Lars Thorwald: each man wants to be unmarried. In the end Jeff, like Anna Thorwald, is almost dispatched by Lars Thorwald. It is as if Hitchcock has placed a sort of curse, the curse of the Thorwalds, on Jeff and Lisa. Have they worked their way out of it?

The couple has drawn closer together during their spying exploits. "Gee, I'm proud of you," Jeff beams at Lisa. Hints are dropped that marital commitment may not be quite what the couple has achieved. We last see Lisa reading a book and wearing work clothes that bespeak an interest in Jeff's profession, yet she quickly turns back to her fashion world. Sitting by the window, Lisa seems to regard her new stage of life as a reason to change outfits. Has Jeff fallen in love with Lisa? Has he discarded his anti-marriage sentiments? When? He's not saying much as he sleeps by his window, ending this film as he began it. Their career issue is left unresolved. Will he stay in New York? Will she go to the High Himalayas? Or, put another way, has either changed? The romantic mood of the ending makes us think that *somehow* they've resolved all of this, but this is really just *our* emotions talking. I don't mean to imply that it is a *bad* thing that Jeff and Lisa haven't worked everything out. They've had some good times watching their neighbors, and may yet have some good times being married. The aesthetic way of life, as Kierkegaard himself recognized, is attractive, especially compared with the ethical "Judge William," who is quite the bore (as are Stella and Doyle when in lecturing mode). *Rear Window* after excitedly engaging with the aesthetic "either" seems to settle down in the ethical "or"—though Lisa still reads her fashion magazines and Jeff is still a photographer.

***

Critical opinion on *Rear Window* with a fair amount of consistency implicates the audience in Jeff's voyeurism, and sometimes makes voyeurism the constant condition of watching a movie. Robin Wood, for example, writes that "Hitchcock enables us to feel just that small amount of uneasiness necessary for us to question the morality of what he is doing—our own morality since we are spying with him, sharing his fascinated, compulsive 'Peeping-Tom-ism.'"[8] Robert Stam and Roberta Pearson put the point this way: "Jeffries is our specular reflection, our double. We do not merely watch him performing actions; we perform the identical action—looking." They side with Christian Metz, to whom they attribute the thought that "the mechanism of gratification in the cinema ... 'rests on our knowing that the object being looked at does not know it is being looked at.'" *Rear Window*, then, is a "reflexive film-about-film."[9] And John Fawell in a recent book on *Rear Window* writes, "Hitchcock, most critics agree, meant Jeff to be seen as a stand-in for the filmgoer. If the windows in *Rear Window* are mirrors of L. B. Jeffries, L. B. Jeffries is also a mirror of the filmgoer. When Lars Thorwald finally returns Jeff's gaze ... [he] has detected our voyeurism as well as Jeff's."[10]

There are, to be sure, similarities between the mise en scène of *Rear Window* and film in general (though the similarities are a bit stronger with live theatre). L. B. Jeffries fixed in one spot is like the audience. He has a view of apartment windows, which can be seen to be like little theaters, in which he glimpses small narratives: a composer trying to complete a song, a lonely woman trying to get a date, and most interestingly, a man who might have murdered his wife. He often uses the telephoto lens of a camera to spy on his neighbors, and he even begins directing the action a bit (sending the note to Thorwald, making the phone call). Yet to be a *reflexive* film-about-film, it seems necessary not simply to resemble viewing or making movies in certain respects, which lots of films do, but to be *about* film history or film making or film viewing. Critics claim that *Rear Window* is about film viewing, because (it is claimed) we the audience perform the identical action that Jeffries performs—in other words that *Rear Window*, through its main character, doubles or mirrors the film-goer.

Yet do we perform the *identical* action that Jeffries performs? The answer is yes, if we rely only on the obvious fact that we, the audience, see what he sees. When he sees Miss Torso dropping her halter top and stretching her legs, we do too. And so on. However, Stam and Pearson (and Wood)

confuse what is *fictionally* seen with what is *factually* seen. It is fictional —
true in the movie but not the real world — that Jeffries sees a young woman
who drops her halter top and does stretching exercises. Voyeurism is the
activity of observing people in places where they have a legitimate expectation of privacy, while doing things they would prefer not to be seen doing.
To commit voyeurism, as I'll put it, is to violate the legitimate expectations
of people to this privacy and to expose private facts of their lives, if only to
the voyeur. Fictionally — in the movie — Miss Torso has a legitimate expectation of privacy and would prefer not to be observed (though why doesn't
she draw her blinds?), and so fictionally — again, in the movie — Jeffries commits voyeurism. But do we the audience commit voyeurism? Factually —
in the real world — we, the film's audience, observe moving pictures of actors
who portray certain roles. *These* people do not have an expectation of privacy as they act their roles, rather the opposite: they expect to be viewed acting. Watching actors act is about as far from voyeurism as you can get. Hence
we do not factually commit voyeurism (though I don't doubt that many
in the audience are titillated by Miss Torso's exercises). It is for this reason that *identifying* cinematic viewing as voyeurism is nearly always incorrect.[11] (There are atypical cases in which real individuals are, without their
consent, appropriated as "characters" into a film, and so observing them
even as a member of the film's audience is, or can be, voyeuristic in fact.
Rear Window obviously does not fall into this category.)

However, there is a way in which the audience to *Rear Window* is,
factually, in the same situation as L. B. Jeffries is fictionally. Both Jeffries
and the audience members take pleasure in wondering just what Lars Thorwald is up to. Both seek and experience the thrill of seeing what happens
next. This is shown not just by the fact that the audience literally experi-
ences such a thrill, but also because of whom the audience identifies with.
Our sympathies are largely with Jeff and Lisa, though their evidence for
Anna Thorwald's murder is patchy at best, at least until the note is slipped
under Thorwald's door. Thorwald's three trips in the rain with his sample case are certainly suspicious, but Jeffries also brings in unpersuasive
evidence. "That's no ordinary look," Jeff tells Stella referring to Thorwald.
"That's the kind of a look a man gives when he's afraid somebody might
be watching him." Conversations such as the following abound:

> JEFF: I've seen it through that window. I've seen bickering and family
> quarrels and mysterious trips at night, and knives and saws and ropes,
> and now since last evening, not a sign of the wife. All right, now you tell
> me where she is...
>
> LISA: Maybe he's leaving his wife. I don't know. I don't care. Lots of peo-
> ple have knives and saws and ropes around their houses, and lots of men

don't speak to their wives all day. Lots of wives nag and men hate them and trouble starts. But very, very few of them end up in *murder* if that's what you're thinking.

JEFF: It's pretty hard for you to keep away from that word isn't it?

LISA: You could see all that he did, couldn't you?

JEFF: Of course, I —

LISA: You could see because the shades were up and, and he walked along the corridor and the street and the back yard. Oh Jeff, do you think a murderer would let you see all that? That he wouldn't pull the shades *down* and hide behind them?

JEFF: Just where he's being clever. He's being nonchalant about things—

LISA: Oh, and that's where you're not being clever. A murderer would never parade his crime in front of an open window.

When Doyle reports that a witness saw Mrs. Thorwald board the train, Jeff responds, "Well, what good's his information? It's a second-hand version of an unsupported story by the murderer himself, Thorwald" — more a whine than a knock-down argument. Then Lisa comes up with further evidence — her trade of "feminine intuition" for a bed for the night:

LISA: It doesn't make sense to me ... Women aren't that unpredictable ... A woman has a favorite handbag and it always hangs on her bedpost where she can get at it easily. And then all of a sudden, she goes away on a trip and leaves it behind. Why?

JEFF: Because she didn't know she was going on a trip. And where she's going she wouldn't need the handbag.

LISA: Yes, but only her husband would know that. And that jewelry. Women don't keep their jewelry in a purse, getting all twisted and scratched and tangled up.

JEFF: Well, do they hide it in their husband's clothes?

LISA: They do not. And they don't leave it behind either. Why, a woman going anywhere but the hospital would always take makeup, perfume, and jewelry.... It's basic equipment. And you don't leave it behind in your husband's drawer in your favorite handbag.

The left-behind jewelry finally convinces Lisa of Thorwald's guilt, but regarded objectively this is evidence that allows room for reasonable doubt.

Jeff and Lisa are not, of course, members of a jury who are supposed to disinterestedly weigh the evidence for and against Lars Thorwald's guilt. But the patchy quality of their evidence shows that the *strength* of their conviction must have some emotional drive behind it. They *want* Lars Thorwald to be a murderer; a murder is more aesthetically thrilling than a marital separation. Interestingly, it's not just that Jeff and Lisa strongly believe in Lars Thorwald's guilt despite counter-evidence; *we* do as well. Our sympathies are with the couple looking out the rear window: we like them and not only wish them well, but wish them to be correct. We too are dejected after Detective Doyle plays his final trump card (the suspicious trunk signed for in Merritsville by Mrs. Thorwald), because along with Jeff and Lisa we've found out that a man *didn't* kill his wife. Yet we have a piece of evidence in favor of Thorwald's *innocence*: only the film's audience is shown a woman leaving the apartment with Thorwald the morning after his suitcase adventures. We should be on Detective Doyle's side with respect to the evidence and Thorwald's innocence, and yet we're not. We're not because murder is aesthetically thrilling to contemplate and a woman merely leaving for the country is dull — which is exactly the attitude of Jeff and Lisa.

All of us — Lisa, Jeff, the film-goer — are aestheticizers of experience. It may be that in this sense *Rear Window* is a film-about-film. At the least it is a film about the aesthetic delights of uncovering a murder, delights for which Jeff and Lisa must pay an ethical price but which are the film-goer's just for the price of admission.

14

The Man Who Knew Too Much

Indianapolis Doctor Ben MacKenna (James Stewart), his wife Jo (Doris Day), a former star of the musical theatre, and their son Hank (Christopher Olsen) are visiting French Morocco, having attended a medical convention in Paris. On a bus they strike up an acquaintance with Louis Bernard (Daniel Gélin) when he intervenes to calm an angry husband (little Hank MacKenna had accidentally taken off the wife's veil). M. Bernard does not disclose his occupation, but invites the MacKenna's to dinner later.

Arriving at their hotel in Marrakech, Jo notices a couple observing them intently. Ben shrugs off her suspicions. Later, during cocktails with Bernard, Jo asks him about his business in Marrakech, and again he gives only the vaguest answer (he buys and sells). After making a brief phone call, Bernard informs the MacKennas that he is unable to have dinner with them tonight. At the restaurant, Jo sees the couple who had observed them earlier. "They're staring at us." "Stop imagining things," Ben responds. "I'm not." The woman asks Jo if she is "*the* Jo Conway." The couple introduce themselves as Lucy and Edward Drayton (Brenda de Banzie, Bernard Miles), in Marrakech on behalf of United Nations Relief. Edward Drayton invites the MacKennas to come to the market with them the next day.

The Draytons and MacKennas are enjoying the sights at the marketplace, when a disturbance breaks out. Police are chasing a man in Arabic dress. Out of nowhere a man, also in Arabic dress, stabs the first, who lurches towards the Draytons and MacKennas. We see that stabbed "Arab" is Louis Bernard, who pulls Ben MacKenna towards him and whispers, "A man, a statesman, he is to be killed, assassinated, in London — soon, very soon. Tell them, in London — Ambrose Chappell. Chappell." Bernard dies, and Ben, surreptitiously, makes a note of what he said.

The police ask the MacKennas to go to the police station to make a statement, and Edward Drayton says that he thinks he should go with

The dying Louis Bernard (Daniel Gélin) whispers his dangerous secret to Ben MacKenna (James Stewart): "A man, a statesman, he is to be killed, assassinated, in London — soon, very soon." *The Man Who Knew Too Much* (1956).

them. "Yes, of course," his wife responds. "But you don't want your little boy to go, do you? I think it better if I take him back to the hotel." "Would you please," Jo responds.

> JO: Why do you suppose he turned up in an Arab outfit? Wearing make-up?
>
> BEN: More important, why was he killed?
>
> JO: I bet he was a spy or something like that. What were you writing down. What was he telling you?
>
> BEN: I'll tell you later. I just feel kind of funny. Why should he pick me out to tell?

Ben tells the police that he just met Louis Bernard on a bus the day before. "Yet out of five-thousand people in a great marketplace, he comes to you when he is about to die," the police inspector points out. "Is that the action of a casual acquaintance?" The inspector reveals that Louis Bernard was a spy who had been sent to Marrakech, had discovered what he had been sent to discover, and told it to Ben MacKenna. "Why? Because he placed complete confidence in you."

An anonymous phone call to Ben MacKenna at the police station warns him, "If you tell even one word of what Louis Bernard whispered to you in the marketplace, your little boy will be in serious danger." On their way back to their hotel, Ben shows Jo what he had written. "We should go back to the hotel, pick up Hank, and get out of here as quickly as we can." She begs her husband to give the note to the American consulate.

Back at the hotel, Ben discover that the Draytons have checked out and that no one has seen Hank. In their hotel room, Ben tells Jo what he's come to know about Louis Bernard:

> BEN: He started to talk to us, and the reason he started to talk to us, and the reason he started to talk to us was 'cause he was on the lookout for a suspicious married couple.
>
> JO: There's nothing very suspicious looking about us, is there?
>
> BEN: No, because he was wrong. It was a different married couple.
>
> JO: Oh, and he was killed before he found them.
>
> BEN: No, he found them. He found them, all right....
>
> JO: You'll be telling me next it was Mr. and Mrs. Drayton.
>
> BEN: That's who it was, Jo.

Ben has to tell Jo about the threat against Hank — and that the Draytons and Hank have disappeared. Jo is prostrate with anxiety. Ben and Jo leave for London, where they believe the Draytons have gone. "This Chappell guy's our only hope," Ben tells his wife. In London, they're met by fans and photographers who remember Jo from her last stage appearance — and by Inspector Buchanan (Ralph Truman). Buchanan tells the MacKennas that unless they tell him what Louis Bernard has told them, they will become "an accessory before the fact to murder." Ben tells the Inspector that Louis Bernard had spoken in French, and he doesn't understand French.

Mrs. Drayton telephones the MacKennas at the police station, and Hank is allowed to speak to his parents: another warning that they should keep what they know to themselves. Ben seeks out Ambrose Chappell — who turns out to be a taxidermist and has no idea what Ben MacKenna is talking about. Back at the hotel Jo realizes, "It's not a man. It's a place. It's Ambrose Chapel." At Ambrose Chapel, we see Mrs. Drayton placing hymn numbers on a board, and Mr. Drayton putting on a parson's uniform and giving the assassin, Rien (Reggie Nalder), whom he went to Marrakech to hire, tickets to the Albert Hall concert that night. "Your box is *strategically* placed." Mr. Drayton rehearses to a phonograph when in the piece Rien is to shoot. "Listen for the crash of the cymbals."

Ben and Jo enter Ambrose Chapel, where they are spotted by Mrs. Drayton and while Mr. Drayton gives a sermon on life's adversities, Jo leaves to telephone Inspector Buchanan. It turns out Inspector Buchanan is attending an "important diplomatic affair at the Albert Hall" and is unreachable. The police are dispatched to Ambrose Chapel which is suddenly and mysteriously empty. Jo leaves for the Albert Hall, while Hank is taken away in a car to an (unnamed) embassy. Inside the Albert Hall, Rien recognizes Jo from Marrakech. "You have a very nice little boy, madam. His safety will depend on you tonight." A second before the storm cantata's cymbal crash, Jo screams, presumably deflecting Rien's aim (the Prime Minister receives a slight flesh wound), and Rien is killed when he jumps from the balcony.

Back at the unnamed embassy, the Draytons are excoriated by the Ambassador for their errors and, to Mrs. Drayton's horror, ordered to kill the child. Ben wrangles an invitation to the reception at the embassy from the Prime Minister who is grateful to Jo for saving his life. The "famous Jo Conway" is invited to sing for the guests, and she chooses "Que sera, sera," a song her little boy knows well. Hitchcock's camera follows the song up the stairs, until Hank hears it. Mrs. Drayton encourages him to whistle the tune, and soon Ben finds the boy. A brief scuffle ends both Mr. Drayton's life and the film.

***

Hitchcock made *The Man Who Knew Too Much* twice, in England in 1934 and in America in 1956. It was based on a story by Charles Bennett and D. B. Wyndham-Lewis, though the title actually came from a collection of mysteries by G. K. Chesterton, to which Hitchcock owned the rights and which has nothing to do with the story-line of the films he made.[1] The plot summary above is of the later version, though the principal plot points are the same in each: a dying spy whispers a secret about a political assassination to an ordinary man; his child is kidnapped so he won't reveal the information; his wife's scream at the crucial point in the concert disturbs the marksman's aim; the child is ultimately released and the villains defeated. John Michael Hayes, who wrote the screenplay for the 1955 version, said that Hitchcock would not let him see the earlier version (nor read its script) but told him the story.[2] The 1934 version opens in St. Moritz, not Morocco, and there is a subtle allusion to the first version in the second. When the servants in the (unnamed) embassy are rounded up in the corridor so that young Hank can be smuggled in, one complains, "Give me the Swiss embassy anytime."

Hitchcock himself regarded the second version as superior to the first. "Let's just say that the first version is the work of a talented amateur and the second was made by a professional."[3] Perhaps. There are, to my taste, some aspects of the English *Man* that are superior to the American *Man*. Leslie Banks's character (Bob Lawrence, the counterpart of Ben MacKenna) is sophisticated, witty, and replete with British *sang-froid*— a more enjoyable character than Stewart's irritable, rube doctor. Peter Lorre plays the ring leader in the first version, alternately repellant and fascinating to watch. His counterpart in the re-make is not exactly the plot's leader — that would be the "ambassador" who has perhaps two minutes of film time and is given hardly any characterization — but rather the marksman, played by Reggie Nalder, chillingly methodical, though not quite on par with Peter Lorre's villain. Leslie Banks in the English *Man* visits a "Geo. Barbor — Dentist" (the counterpart to James Stewart's visit to the taxidermist, Ambrose Chappell). The scene at the dentist's office is alternately comic and sinister, and Henry Oscar's (uncredited) performance as the dentist very creepy. The taxidermist scene in the second version I find neither particularly comic nor sinister. On the other hand, the re-orchestration by Bernard Herrmann of Arthur Benjamin's "Storm Clouds Cantata" in the second version allows for a longer build to the cymbal crash. (The earlier version's concert scene is short by comparison, though Hitchcock's slowly rotating camera as Edna Best looks around the Albert Hall is a small masterpiece of suspense in its own right.) The scene in which Doris Day echo-locates her son by singing "Que sera, sera" has no counterpart in the first version (which some might say is a plus for the first version). The first version is marred by an overly-long shooting match between Lorre's gang and the London police (though the second version, too, has its *longueurs*: the scene in the Marrakech restaurant, the long march down the stairs with Ben and Hank MacKenna and Edward Drayton).

***

Dangerous knowledge. Some seek it, some have it thrust it upon them. The protagonists in *Rear Window* look for information that is on its face ethically improper to come to know: the private lives of a troubled marriage. The protagonists in *The Man Who Knew Too Much* are literally forced into knowledge they do not wish to have. The dying Louis Bernard pulls Ben, an innocent bystander, down and whispers about an assassination plot. Now Ben MacKenna knows too much, and suddenly his child is in grave danger, not to mention the statesman who is the target of assassination. But it is not only Ben MacKenna who knows too much. Louis Bernard is killed because of what he knows. Rien, the assassin, jumps to his death. Young Hank MacKenna is kidnapped and *almost* killed for what

A cymbalist (uncredited) prepares for the crash during the "Storm Cantata" that will cover the assassin's shot. *The Man Who Knew Too Much* (1956).

he knows. And the prognosis for the Draytons is poor: he is killed, she (out of sight of the film's ending) is doomed as well. (The body count in the earlier version is even higher: most of Peter Lorre's gang is wiped out.)

Indeed the possible danger in knowledge is hinted at near the beginning of the film, when Jo points out to her husband how much he has revealed about himself to Louis Bernard.

JO: You don't know anything about this man, and he knows everything there is to know about you.

BEN: Oh, wait –

JO: He knows that you live in Indianapolis, Indiana. He knows that you're a doctor at the Good Samaritan Hospital. He knows that you attended a medical convention in Paris. And that you stopped off in Rome, Lisbon, and Casablanca for just a few days.

BEN: All right –

JO: And he knows that you served in North Africa in an Army field hospital.

BEN: Honey, it was just a casual conversation, that's all.

JO: You weren't just talking casually. He was asking all kinds of questions, and you were answering them. You might as well have handed him your passport.

BEN: What's the difference. We just had a conversation. I have nothing to hide.

JO: But I have a feeling that Mr. Bernard has.

BEN: I know this is mysterious Morocco, but we're not going to lose our head, are we.

The danger the MacKennas have to face, however, is not that someone knows something about them that they would wish to keep private. It is that *they* have come to know something someone else would wish to keep private. This situation comes to have a harrowing impact on their lives when their son is kidnapped to ensure that the MacKennas keep what they know to themselves. Not only is their son in grave danger. They must solve an ethical dilemma.

Do they tell what they know about the assassination attempt and thereby jeopardize their son? Or do they keep what they know to themselves and thereby jeopardize social stability? In the American *Man* the MacKennas are tempted with the offer, made by Inspector Buchanan, that "we might find your boy quite soon, indeed — if we work together." Then a threat: "I'm trying to prevent a man being murdered here, in London. If you don't tell me all you know you become an accessory before the fact to murder." The difficulty of their dilemma is acknowledged by Buchanan. "I've got a son of my own. I don't know what I'd do." Their counterparts in the English *Man* — it is their daughter who has been kidnapped — are given the stark choice, "Her life against Ropa's" (the target of the assassination). And when they refuse to divulge information they're told by an agent of the foreign office with less sympathy than in the later version, "Well, if there's any trouble, I hope you'll remember you're to blame. It isn't a very nice thing to have on your conscience."

The assassin (George Curzon) threatens the kidnapped girl, Betty Lawrence (Nova Pilbeam), in this climactic scene from *The Man Who Knew Too Much* (1934).

The anguish of being caught in an ethical dilemma is strikingly characterized by Jean-Paul Sartre in "Existentialism and Humanism":

> As an example ... I will refer to the case of a pupil of mine, who sought me out in the following circumstances. His father was quarrelling with his mother and was also inclined to be a "collaborator"; his elder brother had been killed in the German offensive of 1940 and this young man, with a sentiment somewhat primitive but generous, burned to avenge him. His mother was living alone with him, deeply afflicted by the semi-treason of his father and by the death of her eldest son, and her one consolation was in this young man. But he, at this moment, had the choice between going to England to join the Free French Forces or of staying near his mother and helping her to live. He fully realized that this woman lived only for him and that his disappearance — or perhaps his death — would plunge her into despair.... Consequently, he found himself confronted by two very different modes of action; the one concrete, immediate, but directed towards only one individual; and the other an action addressed to an end infinitely greater, a national collectivity, but for that very reason ambiguous — and it might be frustrated on the way. At the same time, he was hesitating between two kinds of morality; on the one side the morality of sympathy, of personal devotion and, on the other side, a morality of wider scope but of more debatable validity. He had to choose between those two. What could help him to choose? Could the Christian doctrine? No. Christian doctrine says: Act with charity, love your neighbor, deny your self for others, choose the way which is hardest, and so forth. But which is the harder road? To whom does one owe the more brotherly love, the patriot or the mother? Which is the more useful aim, the general one of fighting in and for the whole community, or the precise aim of helping one particular person to live? Who can give an answer to that *à priori*? No one. Nor is it given in any ethical scripture. The Kantian ethic says, Never regard another as a means, but always as an end. Very well: if I remain with my mother, I shall be regarding her as the end and not as a means: but by the same token I am in danger of treating as means those who are fighting on my behalf; and the converse is true, that if I go to the aid of the combatants I shall be treating them as the end at the risk of treating my mother as a means.[4]

The MacKennas, too, must decide between two kinds of morality: the morality of personal devotion to their son, or the morality of "national collectivity." And which is the more useful aim: helping an important political personage to live or freeing their son? Do they treat the political target as a means to their son's freedom, or their son's life as a means for social peace? For Sartre, the only choice left is — to choose, and to accept responsibility for one's choice. Ben and Jo MacKenna (as well as their English counterparts, Bob and Jill Lawrence) come to a decision almost immediately with very little discussion between them. The parents' decision in both films is made without the French existentialist histrionics of despair, forlornness, abandonment, etc. (Perhaps Hitchcock has invented an Anglo-American style of existential anguish.) The MacKennas/Lawrences decide that they and they alone will try to find their child; they will not divulge what they know. At the same time, the couples seem weighed down by their decision.

Any obvious ethical agonizing is postponed until the climactic scene in the Albert Hall. Both Edna Best and Doris Day are photographed with wordless suffering looks—and Doris Day suffers quite a bit longer given Herrmann's lengthening of the cantata. There are several interpretations of the scene: a mother is fraught with anxiety over the fate of her child; a person knows something awful might well happen and is intensely distraught; a woman is torn between familial and patriotic concerns. These are not mutually inconsistent interpretations. But given the possible meanings of her emotional turmoil, we should not think of Jo MacKenna as Antigone, staunchly defending her familial rights against the demands of the state. She is all but prostrate under the weight of the responsibility that has come with her choice. Jo's scream just before the cymbal crash is less a decision than an eruption of too much emotion.

I suspect that film audiences side with the parents—in part because their plight is foregrounded. The political consequences of their decision — apart from the possible murder of a statesman — are in the narrative left vague (but dire). One critic writes, "In all Hitchcock's apparently political spy-chase thrillers, the international issue is merely his pretext for examining quite personal and emotional issues—thus his refusal to specify a 'cause' or to identify the nation involved."[5] Still, we can read a cause of sorts out of the context of *The Man Who Knew Too Much*.

The 1956 *Man* is set in the climate of the cold war. The unnamed embassy is pretty clearly Russian or at least Soviet bloc. The Ambassador who wants the Prime Minister out of the way is aided by the Draytons, whom he describes as "English intellectuals" (surely intended to call to mind the "Cambridge spies" of the early 1950s). The staff of the embassy longs for "Swiss neutrality" and complains, "Always something funny going on at this embassy. Bringing people in in secret." Inspector Buchanan says in annoyance after the failed assassination attempt in the Albert Hall, "Trying to liquidate one of their own big shots. I wish they'd stick to their usual custom and do it in their own country."

The 1934 *Man* is, at least by dint of its date of release, probably set against the political situation brewing in Germany, which was of considerable concern to Britain. There is a *bit* of allusion to this. Peter Lorre was a German actor, but would the audience bring this to bear on the plot? Leslie Banks tries speaking German to a guard (*"Der britishe Konsul"*), but the guard is Swiss. In any case, talk of assassinations and spies in 1934 might well call Germany to the mind of the mid–1930s British film-goer.

But does it matter to our understanding of the story whether the film's villains are cold war spies or murderers sent of behalf of Hitler or entirely unspecified terrorists? I think it does. It explains, in part anyway, why the audience will be in sympathy with the parents' decision and have little truck with the authorities. Audiences will feel that cold war doings or German machinations are all "dirty business," and how awful that innocent people are caught up in it.

The notion of being caught up in something beyond one's control is given emphasis in the later *Man* (which in this respect at least is richer than the earlier). That there are dangerous currents in the world is emphasized in the various tunes that percolate throughout the film. Jo Conway's "Que sera, sera," sung to her son in his bedroom and of course the tune that locates the lost boy within the embassy, is a song about fate and our inability to do anything about it. What will be, will be. Natural disasters loom large in the film's music. In the grim hymn the parishioners grind their way through in Ambrose Chapel, we're asked to consider, "Wherefore do earthquakes cleave the ground? Why hides the sun in shame?" And the "Cantata, Storm Clouds" which opens the film and provides its climax, is about being in the grip of a storm: "And on the trembling trees came the nameless fear. And panic overtook each flying creature of the wild." Dangerous secrets like earthquakes and storms can suddenly strike. The difference is that the secret that struck the MacKennas demands an ethical choice.

Were Ben and Jo MacKenna right in their decision? Things turn out as well as can be expected under the circumstances: the Prime Minister receives a slight flesh wound, their son is unharmed, the assassin is killed by his fall, the more villainous of the two Draytons is killed (and one suspects his wife will not go unpunished). But this outcome is somewhat serendipitous. A scream tears from Jo's throat, her song actually locates her boy, Ben's lunge for Drayton's gun kills Drayton. In *Rear Window* Hitchcock sends in various characters to chastise Jeff for "peeping": Stella, Lisa, Doyle. In *The Man Who Knew Too Much* (both versions) the police warn the MacKennas/Lawrences of the consequences of their decision to remain silent. But Hitchcock's attitude towards the MacKennas/Lawrences is less judgmental than towards Jeff (and eventually Lisa)—if for no other reason than that the police warnings in *The Man Who Knew Too Much* occupy very little screen time, especially when compared with the several round-table discussions of the ethics of peeping in *Rear Window*. It may be that the decision the MacKennas/Lawrences have to make is so overwhelmingly difficult that any criticism might be too harsh. To paraphrase Sartre: Who could help them to choose?

15

The Birds

"For it is quite conceivable that, regardless of all the uniformity of natural things in terms of the universal laws, without which the form of an empirical cognition in general would not occur at all, the specific differences in the empirical laws of nature, along with their effects, might still be so great that it would be impossible for our understanding to discover in nature an order it could grasp..."
— Immanuel Kant, *Critique of Judgment*[1]

"Mitch, what's happening?" "I don't know, Melanie."
— *The Birds*

The Birds (1963) is Hitchcock's second foray into horror, *Psycho* being his first. The films belong to different sub-genres. Hitchcock's adaptation of Daphne du Maurier's novella is a "creature feature"; *Psycho* is a "slasher film." The birds in the Hitchcock's film are natural animals—crows, gulls, sparrows—that have for some reason run outrageously amok. Pre-*Birds* monsters were from outer space (*The Thing From Another World*, 1951), animals that had mutated into something huge (the giants ants of *Them!*, 1954), or other unnatural and scientifically impossible beings such as vampires, mummies, and werewolves. *The Birds* initiated the genre of natural-animals-run-amok, thereby spawning the streams of rats in *Willard* (1971), the predatory shark of *Jaws* (1975), the killer bees of *The Swarm* (1978), and the highly venomous and aggressive spiders of *Arachnophobia* (1990). There are, however, differences between *The Birds* and conventional horror stories, which I will discuss later. First I want to compare *The Birds* and its sibling, *Psycho*.

Birds of the stuffed variety decorated Norman Bates's office, and these proved almost as ominous as the live birds that attack Bodega Bay. Eyes, mouths, and wounds are prominent in both films. Eyes seem the birds' favored target. Dan Fawcett's and Annie Hayworth's eyes are pecked out. (The *images* of Dan Fawcett's pecked-out eyes—the camera going to close-

175

up in three sudden jump-cuts—are more horrible than anything we're *shown* in *Psycho*, though *Psycho* is the more horrifying film.) Lydia Brenner's reaction to Dan Fawcett's death is an open-mouthed, silent scream, not unlike the silent scream of Milton Arbogast as he is attacked by "Mother." Gulls attack Cathy Brenner as she, blindfolded, plays blindman's bluff at her birthday party. Crows at the schoolhouse go for a little girl's eyes as her glasses fall and shatter (a reprise of Miriam Haines's glasses as she is strangled by Bruno Anthony in *Strangers on a Train*). Melanie Daniels, like Norman Bates, ends the film open-mouthed, staring ahead but apparently seeing nothing. If the eyes are the windows to the soul, both Norman Bates and Melanie Daniels are shuttered up.

***

Hundreds of gulls wheel under a dark San Francisco sky, their cries continuing the bird sounds from the opening credits. A beautiful and stylish young woman, Melanie Daniels (Tippi Hedren), visits a pet shop to buy a mynah bird for her aunt, when she has a chance encounter with Mitch Brenner (Rod Taylor), a handsome attorney who is shopping for some love birds as a birthday gift for his little sister. Mitch, who recognizes Melanie from court, pretends to think she is a salesperson, and she pretends to be one. He later tells her this is retaliation for a practical joke she is supposed to have pulled that resulted in the destruction of a plate glass window. "I just thought you might like to know what it felt like to be on the other end of a gag."

But Melanie Daniels apparently has a penchant for stunts. She finds out the name of the man in the pet shop, buys a pair of love birds, and drives north of San Francisco to Bodega Bay where Mitch spends weekends. The local school teacher, Annie Hayworth (Suzanne Pleshette), tells Melanie the name of "the little Brenner girl" and hints at a past with Mitch Brenner. To add to the surprise of her visit, Melanie rents a small boat, sneaks across the bay to the Brenner house, deposits the love birds with a note to Cathy Brenner, and retreats. On the way back, a gull swoops down and wounds her.

Mitch witnesses the gull attack, and attends to Melanie's wound. Melanie lies and tells him she has come to Bodega Bay to visit her college friend, Annie Hayworth. Mitch's mother, Lydia Brenner (Jessica Tandy), is introduced to Melanie and frowns as Mitch invites her to dinner. Melanie asks Annie, who conveniently has a "Room for Rent" sign, for overnight lodging. During dinner at the Brenners', Cathy (Veronica Cartwright) squeals with delight at the love birds, Mitch exhibits some romantic interest in Melanie, while Lydia seems distant—and "naturally curious about a girl like that.... She's always mentioned in the columns, Mitch." As

Melanie leaves the Brenners, hundreds of birds sit on the utility poles and wires. Back at Annie Hayworth's, Annie reveals that she used to have a relationship with Mitch — she even moved to Bodega Bay from San Francisco because of him — but that it foundered in part because of Lydia Brenner. "You know, her attitude nearly drove me crazy." Mitch telephones and invites Melanie to Cathy's birthday party the next day. A seagull smashes into Annie's front door.

During the birthday party, Mitch and Melanie get better acquainted, and the children play games on the lawn. Suddenly they are attacked by gulls, though none of the children is seriously injured. Later, as Melanie and the Brenners eat a light supper in the living room, hundreds of sparrows swoop out of the fireplace opening, leaving the room a shambles. The next day Lydia, trying to determine why her chickens won't eat, visits Dan Fawcett, her neighbor, only to discover that he is dead, his eyes dark holes, with several gulls lying dead nearby. Shaken, Lydia asks Melanie to go to the school to check on Cathy. At the school, Melanie sits outside while the children finish singing a song. A flock of crows gathers on the jungle gym. Melanie and Annie decide they must get the children out of the school room, and instruct them to run to a nearby hotel. The crows attack and one girl is seriously injured.

At the Tides Restaurant, Melanie calls her father, who owns a newspaper in San Francisco, to tell him about the bird attacks. An amateur ornithologist, Mrs. Bundy (Ethel Griffies), declares such attacks "impossible." A drunk (Karl Swenson) declares that it's the end of the world. A fisherman, Sebastian Sholes (Charles McGraw), reports that a flock of gulls nearly capsized one of his fishing boats last week, though he eventually concedes that they were only after his fish. A salesman (Joe Mantell) advises people to get guns and "wipe birds off the face of the earth." A mother with two children (Doreen Lang) begins to panic. The proprietor, Deke Carter (Lonny Chapman), wonders why people won't believe Melanie Daniels. A debate ensues as to whether birds really are attacking people. Across the street a gull knocks down a man pumping gasoline which flows onto the street and soon explodes from a carelessly dropped match. The gulls attack in earnest, and the gas station becomes a scene of fire, chaos, and death. Women in the Tides accuse Melanie Daniels of causing the attacks.

Mitch and Melanie go to pick up Cathy at Annie Hayworth's house, but find Annie dead on the front steps, pecked to death by birds. Back at the Brenner house, Mitch boards up the doors and windows in anticipation of the next bird attack. A rising din of bird noises terrifies Melanie, Mitch, Cathy, and Lydia who scurry back and forth in the living room.

Amateur ornithologist Mrs. Bundy (Ethel Griffies, second from left) disabuses fisherman Sebastian Sholes (Charles McGraw, right) of his belief that he has been attacked: "The gulls were after your fish, Mr. Sholes. Really, let's be logical about this." Visitor Melanie Daniels (Tippi Hedren) and Deke Carter (Lonnie Chapman), owner of the Tides Restaurant, look on. *The Birds* (1964).

The gulls break windows and nearly peck apart the front door. Later, after the bird attack has apparently subsided, Melanie hears some fluttering upstairs and goes to investigate. She is viciously attacked by birds in the attic and badly injured. Mitch wants to take Melanie to a hospital in San Francisco, and gathers his mother, sister, and Melanie, leads them through thousands of birds gathered threateningly outside the house, and slowly drives off as the bird squawking intensifies.

***

For some critics, *The Birds* is a story about human relationships with a thin veneer of horror. Indeed, for some critics the veneer is *so* thin that it becomes transparent. According to Donald Spoto, "the film operates *completely on the level of symbol....* Some viewers still take it as a horror story, but it in fact has none of the characteristics of that genre."[2] In Spoto's view, "the birds operate as markers of the chaos unleashed by shallow

Sparrows behaving badly terrorize (left to right) Mitch Brenner (Rod Taylor), Cathy Brenner (Veronica Cartwright), Melanie Daniels (Tippi Hedren), and Lydia Brenner (Jessica Tandy). *The Birds* (1964).

human relationships," and he supports this claim by considering when the birds attack: a gull swoops down on her after Melanie's "coy teasing of Mitch"; a gull smashes into her front door after Annie "discusses her loneliness"; gulls attack the birthday party after "Melanie's discussion of her own childhood abandonment"; sparrows invade the Brenners' living room "as a frightened Lydia encourages Melanie (whose presence she fears) to leave Bodega Bay"; and crows attack the schoolchildren after "Lydia's talk about her fear of abandonment."[3] The bird attacks are "objective correlates for the results of those weaknesses."

It is true that the rhythm of the film alternates a vignette involving several of the characters with some sort of bird incident. The character vignettes have a closure to them: something is revealed about a character, or one character's relation with another is advanced in some respect. And then a bird incident arrives as punctuation. The narrative in this sense has a oscillating structure: ABABAB… There is also a kind of reversing tempo, as the character vignettes which are longer at the beginning grow shorter towards the end, and the bird attacks which are initially quite brief become longer and longer.

Still, Spoto's thesis is wrong for a number of reasons. In the first place, there is no "*chaos* unleashed by shallow human relationships." It is absurd to read the film as implying that Melanie and Lydia have a frosty moment which *causes* the birds to attack. This is the fallacy of *post hoc, ergo propter hoc*. There is a tension now and then (between Melanie and Mitch, Melanie and Annie, Melanie and Lydia), but, if anything, this comes about because the characters are getting *deeper* into what the other is about. Secondly, while the characters sometimes *reveal* a weakness, they often become closer during their little scenes together, which is a kind of strength. Melanie and Mitch reconcile after their tiff in the pet shop; Annie and Melanie are on their way to becoming friends; the kiss Melanie and Mitch exchange after the gruesome discovery at Dan Fawcett's farm shows a new depth in their relation; Lydia Brenner begins to confide in Melanie and calls her by her first name; Cathy and Melanie grow closer together.

Thirdly, not all the bird attacks are preceded by some revelation of human weakness. Is Melanie's visit to Bodega Bay a sign of weakness? She drives two hours by herself to a destination she knows little about — and rents a motorboat and crosses a bay in the bargain! (Melanie lies to Mitch about why she's come — she doesn't have the courage of her flirtation — but that's *after* the gull attacks her.) Annie Hayworth does have a victim's outlook. This is perhaps why her recording of *Tristan und Isolde* is prominently displayed — Isolde who died for love of Tristan — though Annie dies protecting Cathy Brenner, an act of bravery not weakness. (Unfortunately the last sounds she heard are bird squawks, not Wagner's sublime harmonies.) What weakness is shown before the crows attack the gas station across from the Tides? Disbelief in the bird attacks? Alcohol consumption? Smoking? And before the final horrific scenes in the Brenners' living room and attic? By this time the characters express little except their terror of the birds: Lydia is frantic, Cathy vomits from fear, while Mitch and Melanie hold on as best they can.

Yet another problem with Spoto's view is why the human frailties that some characters have should result in disasters of such proportion. Annie Hayworth confesses herself a bit lonely but content enough teaching in Bodega Bay (she doesn't want to give up Mitch's "friendship" — never mind that he's in San Francisco five days a week); Lydia fears abandonment; Melanie still longs for (and is angry with) her missing mother. Should these "weaknesses" portend such *doom*? The main problem these characters face is those damn birds! Lastly, the claim that the birds (or the bird attacks) are *completely* symbolic implies that they didn't happen in the fiction — that it is not a fictional truth of *The Birds* that birds attacked schoolchildren, killed Annie Hayworth and Dan Fawcett, and mauled Melanie Daniels. Are the inhabitants of Bodega Bay terrorized by a *symbol*?

In another attempt to interpret the bird attacks as caused by the film's characters, Margaret Horowitz claims that "the heroine is punished by the hero's mother because of the heroine's desirability to him." [4] In Horowitz's reading, Melanie is brought down by (Lydia's) birds, thus at the end Lydia appears "victorious" because she and the birds have "achieved dominance." [5] Camille Paglia extends Horowitz's thesis, seeing Lydia Brenner as a continuation of another jealous mother, Violet Venable of *Suddenly, Last Summer*. "The lobotomy that Violet Venable tries to inflict on her niece … is in effect performed on Hitchcock's heroine, who's out of her mind by the end." [6]

In broad outline, of course, Melanie begins as a self-confident, richly dressed and groomed beauty, and, because of the birds, ends up a bloodied, nearly catatonic invalid. She has driven her own car to Bodega Bay, and has to be driven out of it by Mitch. Read literally, though Horowitz and Paglia are on par with the hysterical mother in the Tides who accuses Melanie of causing the bird attacks, only now it is *Lydia* who stands accused. But Lydia is not presented as a sorceress with the power to command nature. Nor is Lydia the Carrie of Bodega Bay, directing the birds to lobotomize Melanie with her telekinetic powers.

What is probably intended is that the birds are symbols of or metaphors for Lydia's jealousy or insecurity. "The wild birds function as a kind of malevolent female superego," Horowitz writes, "an indirect revelation of Lydia's character." [7] But the bird attacks don't make sense even as symbol (or metaphor or indirect revelation of character). Why, for example, didn't Lydia Brenner's jealousy bring on bird attacks while Mitch was dating Annie Hayworth? Is she *especially* jealous of Melanie Daniels? Why should her jealousy pick off her friend and neighbor, Dan Fawcett, whose death so seriously disturbs Lydia that she takes to her bed, tormented by what she saw at his farm ("I keep seeing Dan's face")? For that matter, what aspect of Lydia's character is indirectly revealed by the killing of Annie Hayworth who is no longer a threat to Lydia? That she's a homicidal maniac? Why should the bird attacks *intensify* after Lydia and Melanie have bonded a bit? Why should Lydia's jealousy attack the schoolchildren — and her own daughter (three times)? Are we to take Lydia as a monstrous combination of Phaedra and Medea? In any case, a week before Melanie Daniels came to town, gulls attacked a fishing boat — "Practically tore the skipper's arm off," Sebastian Sholes reports. Who was Lydia jealous of then? The bird attacks, which nearly destroy the town of Bodega Bay and the Brenners themselves, are beginning in surrounding communities. These incidents, even if they symbolized jealousy, would exemplify the boundless rage of a psychotic, which Lydia plainly is not.

Nor does Lydia appear "victorious" at the end. She helps Mitch battle birds to rescue Melanie from the attic. "Oh, poor thing," Lydia in all sincerity cries. "Poor thing." She cleans and bandages Melanie's wounds. It's true that she resists taking Melanie to a hospital in San Francisco, but she also confesses that she's "terribly frightened" they won't make it. As she helps Mitch escort Melanie to the car, she exhibits nothing but fear of the gathered birds and concern for Melanie. Inside the car, Melanie, in the recumbent posture of a *pietà*, is held by Lydia. Her hand, nail polish chipped, gives Lydia's wrist a little squeeze. Lydia looks down tenderly and hugs Melanie a little closer. Maybe Lydia feels victorious inside, but if so, she certainly hides it well enough.

If Spoto thinks the birds punish the characters because they're shallow and weak, Robin Wood thinks that the bird attacks show how *interesting* the characters are. The very inexplicability of the attacks "focuses our attention on the development of character, situation, and relationship, on the birds' *effect* rather than on the birds themselves..."[8] It is true that the characters of *The Birds* have more interest for us than in the conventional horror film, at least from the '50s. But how much more interest? The film opens with an attempt at a screwball-comedy-style encounter between Mitch and Melanie in the pet shop (self-righteous attorney meets playgirl sophisticate). Melanie's drive up the coast with the lovebirds shows *something* about her (but what? that she's a woman of determination? that she's attracted to a stranger who has upbraided her in a pet store? that she'll go to great lengths to play flirtatious games? that she has nothing better to do?). Annie Hayworth's unrequited love for Mitch is poignantly expressed, and Melanie and Annie develop a friendship based on a mutual understanding of Mitch's attractiveness and Lydia's jealousy. Mitch's sister, Cathy, takes an immediate and sincere liking to Melanie, who responds almost in kind; Lydia Brenner makes clear her fear of abandonment; an affection develops between the initially cold Lydia and Melanie; and Melanie and Mitch begin to fall in love.

But Wood's view pushes the birds too much into the background, relegating them to mere stimuli for further character development. On the contrary, the birds are the focus of conversation and attention right from the opening credits. The film's characters spend a fair amount of time with faces upturned, staring into the sky looking out for birds. By the time

Melanie visits the school, "the development of character, situation, and relationship" has all but ceased as the inhabitants of Bodega Bay struggle to stay alive. The customers at the Tides Restaurant —*not* Mitch, Melanie, and Lydia — are the film's most interesting and lively characters: the waitress steering herself around the conversations about birds while serving fried chicken and bloody marys, the panicky mother, the drunk prophesizing Biblical retribution, the salesman who wants to kill all birds, the skeptical police deputy, and especially Mrs. Bundy, the ornithologist, who appears to have wandered into northern California from one of Hitchcock's English locales— Isolbel Sedbusk of *Suspicion* redux.

Despite some nicely limned emotional interactions, the main characters' relationships don't get very far. Annie Hayworth is killed. Melanie Daniels, called on to exhibit courage in the face of the unnatural and terrifying, somewhat rises to the occasion, but she is nearly done in before she has a chance to prove herself, and in any event does not attain significantly greater wisdom and maturity. Her character is already presented as having risen above her previous wild, playgirl self. She works for Travelers' Aid at the airport, studies General Semantics at Berkeley, and raises funds to send a "little Korean boy" through school. We don't know whether her ordeal at Bodega Bay advances Melanie's personality development, though, really, how could it? The short bit during Cathy's birthday party in which Melanie reveals her anger and hurt at being abandoned by her own mother *might* play a role in her emerging closeness with Lydia, but even this much is cut short by the abrupt end of the film. Lydia moves us with her fears of weakness and abandonment, but her most interesting cinematic moments come with her near-wordless visit to Dan Fawcett's farm. The customers in the Tides— Mrs. Bundy, the drunk, the panicky mother, etc.— are never revisited.

The film tells us nothing about what happens to Mitch, Melanie, Cathy, and Lydia as they drive off at the end. For all we know the birds kill them; or Melanie succumbs to her wounds and dies; or having recovered, she and Mitch never really hit it off; or Annie Hayworth turns out to be right: "Maybe there's never been anything between Mitch and any girl" (hmmm); or Melanie and Mitch marry and live happily? unhappily? ever after. (As crows gather on the jungle gym behind Melanie Daniels, coolly smoking a cigarette, the schoolchildren sing about a wife who swept the floor but once a year, who churns butter in an old boot, who lets the horse her husband brought her get away, and who, when asked to wash the floor, gives her husband his hat and shows him the door. Is this the prophecy of a Greek chorus about what a marriage between socialite Melanie Daniels and country boy Mitch Brenner would be like?)

For a film supposedly about character and relationships, *The Birds* ultimately fizzles. Hitchcock himself agreed that *The Birds* without the birds is not much of a story. "I think it still suffers, like all 'event' stories, from the conflict between the personal story and the event — the coming of the birds," he told Peter Bogdanovich. "That was the big problem with *The Birds*. The personal story was not too consequential. The central figure of the girl was nothing.... In other words, you were saying: 'Look. All these inconsequential people — their lives going on in a very humdrum way — but all of a sudden, *come the birds*. Now their comparative equanimity is disturbed.'"[9]

***

Despite critical opinion to the contrary, *The Birds* is fundamentally a horror movie with monsters, although an unconventional one. The film famously eschewed music in favor of bird noises (using a new electronic technique of mixing sound). Hitchcock was especially proud of surmounting the technical difficulties in using real birds,[10] and certainly the "special effects" in *The Birds* are head-and-shoulders above their monster-movie predecessors. Spoto thinks *The Birds* exhibits none of the characteristics of the horror genre. But this simply isn't true. The film exhibits *most* characteristics.

It will be instructive to map *The Birds* against the horror movie as dissected in a famous essay by Susan Sontag.[11] (1) The "emergence of the monsters." *The Birds* opens with hundreds of gulls wheeling in the sky above San Francisco. A solitary gull attacks Melanie Daniels. Sparrows flood the Brenners' living room. Children at the birthday party and later at the schoolhouse are attacked by gulls and crows. (2) "Confirmation of the hero's report by a host of witnesses to a great act of destruction." Melanie Daniels tries to get the customers at the Tides Restaurant to believe that birds have attacked the schoolchildren, and Mitch Brenner tries to convince the police that birds killed Dan Fawcett. Some believe them, some do not. As customers debate whether the birds really are attacking people — or are just after fish or have gotten lost in a fog or whatever — all are witness to a bird attack that causes a fiery explosion. (3) "Conferences between scientists and the military ... A national emergency is declared." But in *The Birds* scientific conferences and military intervention are at best in the future. A radio news broadcast near the end of the film mentions the bird attacks on Bodega Bay with minor attacks on Sebastopol and Santa Rosa. "No decision has been arrived at yet," it concludes, "as to what the next step will be, but there's been some discussion as to whether the military should go in." (4) "Further atrocities. At some point the hero's girlfriend is in grave danger." The hero's former girlfriend is pecked to death by birds, and his current girlfriend is left severely wounded and nearly catatonic after a horrendous attack in the Brenners' attic. (5) "Final repulse of the monster" as their vulnerability is discovered and they are vanquished. In contrast, *The Birds* ends with the birds seemingly victorious and poised for further attack.

The Birds' most striking departure from Sontag's formula is its lack of authoritative explanation of why the birds are behaving so strangely — hence the missing scientific conferences and the typical victory over the creatures. Another writer, Noël Carroll, thinks such "scientific" explanations are near-definitional of horror movies which, he says, are "dramas of discovery and confirmation." Our curiosity about the monsters is "whetted by the prospect of knowing the putatively unknowable, and then satisfied through a continuous process of revelation, enhanced by imitations of (admittedly simplistic) proofs, hypotheses, counterfeits of causal reasoning, and explanations whose details and movement intrigue the mind in ways analogous to genuine ones."[12]

The problem is that many explanations of conflicting types are offered in *The Birds*. Indeed, from the first spoken words, nearly every character speculates on what's going on:

> MELANIE (looking at the sky): Have you ever seen so many gulls? What do you suppose it is?
>
> MRS. MACGRUDER (proprietor of the pet shop): Well, there must be a storm at sea. That can drive them inland, you know.

After the gull attacks Melanie crossing the bay, Mitch hints at something unnatural going on:

> MELANIE (after a gull attacks her in the rowboat): What do you suppose made it do that?
>
> MITCH: That's the damnedest thing I ever saw. It seemed to swoop down on you, deliberately.

Annie Hayward looks towards the sky and sees a flock of gulls:

> ANNIE: Don't they *ever* stop migrating?

A gull smashes into Annie Hayworth's front door:

> ANNIE: Poor thing. Probably lost his way in the dark.
>
> MELANIE: But, it isn't dark, Annie. There's a full moon.

After sparrows invade the Brenners' living room, Deputy Al Malone (Malcom Atterbury) is called to investigate. The Brenners and Deputy Malone dispute whether the birds attacked or panicked:

> MITCH: Well, the birds invaded the house.
>
> AL: What's more likely, they got in the room and just panicked.
>
> MITCH: All right, I'll admit a bird will panic in an enclosed room. But they didn't just *get* in. They *came* in, right down the chimney!

Lydia mentions the attack at Cathy's birthday party:

> AL: Were the kids bothering the birds or something? 'Cause if you make any kind of disturbance near them, they'll come after you.
>
> LYDIA: Al, the children were playing a game. Those gulls *attacked*.
>
> AL: Now, Lydia, "attack" is a pretty strong word, don't you think? I mean, birds just don't go around attacking people without no reason. Kids probably scared 'em, that's all.

The debate goes full steam ahead at the Tides Restaurant where Melanie Daniels is on the phone, telling her newspaperman father about the attack on the school by crows or blackbirds, she's not sure which.

> MRS. BUNDY: I hardly think either species would have sufficient intelligence to launch a massed attack. Their brain pans are not big enough to—
>
> MELANIE: I just came from the school, madam. I don't know anything about their brain pans, but—
>
> MRS. BUNDY: Well, I do. I *do* know. Ornithology happens to be my avocation. Birds are not aggressive creatures, miss. They bring beauty into the world.... It is mankind, rather, who insists upon making it difficult for life to exist upon this planet. Now, if it were not for birds—
>
> DEKE CARTER: Mrs. Bundy, you don't seem to understand. This young lady said there was an attack on the school.
>
> MRS. BUNDY: Impossible

Sebastian Sholes thinks that birds behaved very strangely — possibly unnaturally — when they attacked one of his fishing boats.

> SEBASTIAN SHOLES: A whole flock of gulls nearly capsized one of my boats. Practically tore the skipper's arm off....
>
> MRS. BUNDY: The gulls were after your fish, Mr. Sholes. Really, let's be logical about this.

Melanie Daniels is sure the birds are behaving unnaturally:

> MELANIE: What were the crows after at the school?... I think they were after the children.
>
> MRS. BUNDY: For what purpose?
>
> MELANIE: To kill them.
>
> MRS. BUNDY: Why?
>
> MELANIE: I don't know why.
>
> MRS. BUNDY: I thought not. Birds have been on this planet, Miss Daniels, since archaeopteryx, 140 million years ago. Doesn't it seem odd that they'd wait all that time to start a — a war against humanity?

Mrs. Bundy eventually convinces Sholes that there is a natural explanation for the bird attack on his boat, and there is a confrontation between the naturalism of Mrs. Bundy and the anti-naturalism of Melanie Daniels:

> SHOLES: Those gulls must have been after the fish.
>
> MRS. BUNDY: Of course....
>
> SHOLES: You know, maybe we're all getting a little carried away by this. Admittedly, a few birds did act strange, but that's no reason to believe that —
>
> MELANIE: I keep telling you, this isn't a few birds. These are gulls, crows, swifts —
>
> MRS. BUNDY: I have never known birds of different species to flock together. The very concept is unimaginable. Why, if that happened, we wouldn't have a chance! How could we possibly hope to fight them?

A salesman in the restaurant brings up a recent bird "invasion," which gives Mrs. Bundy a chance to advance another naturalistic explanation.

> SALESMAN: Say, something like this happened in Santa Cruz last year. The town was covered with seagulls....
>
> MRS. BUNDY: That's right, sir, I recall it. A large flock of seagulls got lost in a fog and headed in to the town, where all the lights were.... The point is that no one seemed to be upset about it. They were all gone next morning, just as though nothing at all had happened. Poor things.

Deputy Malone joins Sholes and Mrs. Bundy in skepticism about the bird attacks:

> MITCH: [Dan Fawcett] was killed last night. By birds.
>
> AL MALONE: Now hold it, Mitch. You don't know that for a fact.

MRS. BUNDY: What are the facts, Mr. Malone?

AL: Santa Rosa police think it was a felony murder. They think a burglar broke in and killed him.

MITCH: How do they explain the dead birds all over the floor?

AL: Well, Santa Rosa police figure they got in after the old man was killed.

Explanations of the birds' behavior based on evil are advanced by two minor yet memorable characters in The Tides.

DRUNK: It's the end of the world! "Thus saith the Lord God unto the mountains and the hills and the rivers and the valleys. Behold I, even I, shall bring a sword upon you, and I will devastate your high places." Ezekiel, chapter six....

MRS. BUNDY: I hardly think a few birds are going to bring about the end of the world.

After the birds attack the gas station outside The Tides, a panicked mother says this to Melanie:

MOTHER (to Melanie Daniels, after the gulls attack the gas station): They said when you got here, the whole thing started! Who are you? What are you? Where did you come from? I think you're the cause of all this. I think you're evil. *Evil!*

These explanations fit into one of three types. (1) Natural explanations. These attempt to explain the birds' behavior by appeal to what experience has told us about birds. According to the scientific explanations, the birds aren't attacking or trying to kill anyone. A storm might have driven them inland, or they're migrating, or they've lost their way in the dark, or the children scared them, or they got in the living room and panicked, or they were simply after fish, or they got lost in a fog. Mrs. Bundy and Deputy Al Malone are the principal advocates of natural explanations. (2) Preternatural explanations. These believe that the birds are behaving contrary to past experience. The preternaturalists explain the birds as behaving with malevolent intent (and not out of fear or disorientation). The birds *came* down the chimney; they didn't just *get* in. The birds *attacked* the children; they *tried* to kill them. The birds *tried* to capsize the fishing boat. Melanie and Mitch are the principal preternaturalists. (3) Theological explanations. These take the birds to be instruments of divine justice or emanations of evil. The drunk in the Tides and the hysterical mother are the only theologians in the film (though Hitchcock himself later claimed to side with the drunk[13]).

The naturalists attempt to refute the preternaturalists (no one takes the theologians seriously). Birds don't have big enough brain pans to act in concert, they're not aggressive, different species never flock together, and besides, birds have not attacked humans in 140 million years. But the audience is forced to side with the preternaturalists. We see Dan Fawcett's eyes; we see the birds attack the children at the school; we see the body of Annie Hayward; then both we and the scientists at The Tides see the birds attack the filling station (a shot of a cowed Mrs. Bundy after the attack indicates the naturalists' capitulation to the preternaturalists); and finally we see the birds' horrific attack on the Brenners' house.

However, the preternaturalists don't have much of an explanation. They're convinced that the naturalists aren't right — and so is the audience. The birds, contrary to what we know of nature, attack and try to kill, but why the preternaturalists can't say. Neither can we. This flouts Carroll's discovery-and-confirmation formula for horror films for no one — no team of scientists, say—comes forward to clear everything up. *The Birds*, then, is ultimately about incomprehension. The birds' inexplicability — not the film's thin characters and their inconsequential relations— is the film's subject. Once the uniformity of nature is demonstrably upset, as it is in *The Birds*, there is no explanation forthcoming. Mrs. Bundy expounds the uniformity of nature as our experience has it. But the birds of Hitchcock's film confound our experience. We have then no basis for explaining the birds' behavior. *The Birds* is not about fear of the unknown, but fear of the unknowable.

***

Postscript on the film's sources. The Birds was advertised, "Based on Daphne du Maurier's classic suspense story!" Screenwriter Evan Hunter said he kept only the story's title and its premise that birds are attacking people.[14] But there is a quite a bit more of du Maurier's story in his screenplay than Hunter credits. The major characters of Hitchcock's film — Melanie, Mitch, Annie, Lydia — are, of course, Hunter's inventions. The wonderful scene in the Tides Restaurant, though written by Hunter, was suggested by Hitchcock. Du Maurier's story is more sparsely populated than Hitchcock's film. Nat Hocken, on pension from a war-time disability, works part-time at a farm on the Cornish coast. He has a wife and two small children.

But there are many parallels between the film and its literary source. Both du Maurier's story and Hitchcock's film are set in seacoast locales, hers in Cornwall, his in Bodega Bay. Nat Hocken is the first attacked, and he is attacked by gulls (he suffers more serious injuries than Melanie Daniels did in her boat); and the authorities are incredulous when he reports the bird attack. Birds of different species flock together apparently for purposes of attacking humans. The bird attacks come in waves followed by periods of quiescence (du Maurier, but not Hitchcock, tied the onset of the attacks with the coming of high tide). Explanations are offered for the birds' behavior by various people including the BBC (in du Maurier's tale, the Arctic cold and the Russians are blamed). Eyes are the birds' favored targets in both story and film. Schoolchildren are attacked by birds in story and movie (but du Maurier's birds kill their little victims). The Hocken family huddles inside their boarded-up kitchen, listening to the sounds of birds as they attack it (du Maurier, like Hitchcock, emphasizes bird sounds throughout her story). Birds manage to get down the Hockens' chimney and later into an upstairs bedroom. When Nat goes to the farm where he works, he discovers the farmer and his wife killed by birds (shades of Dan Fawcett). The Cornish postman is discovered by the road, pecked to death (like Annie Hayworth). Birds in du Maurier and Hitchcock spend time perched on trees and wires, watching. The phone eventually goes dead. The Hockens like the Brenners are still alive as du Maurier ends her tale.

Du Maurier's story is more apocalyptic than Hitchcock's film. Radio reports describe birds massing on roof-tops in London. Soon a national emergency is declared because of bird attacks. Government planes apparently trying to kill birds are brought down as birds hurl themselves into propellers. Nat is reduced to stuffing broken windows with the bodies of dead birds. Hawks and other birds of prey, absent in Hitchcock's flocks, tear at the wooden doors of the Hockens' house with their talons. Radio broadcasts, even from foreign stations, cease entirely, and for all the Hockens know they are the last people alive.

Hitchcock gave Evan Hunter newspaper articles on unexplained bird attacks, "so we weren't dealing entirely in fantasy," Hunter explained.[15] One of these described migrating gulls apparently lost in a fog who wandered into Santa Cruz, crashing into cars and antennas, and getting into houses.[16] The Santa Cruz episode is alluded to in the film at the Tides Restaurant.

Chapter Notes

Preface

1. Robert J. Yanal, *Paradoxes of Emotion and Fiction* (University Park, PA: Penn State University Press, 1999).

Chapter 1

1. Aristotle, *The Poetics*, IX 1451b, trans. G.M.A. Grube (Indianapolis: Hackett Publishing Co., 1987).

2. Aristotle, *On Rhetoric* 1393a (2.22), trans. George A. Kennedy (New York: Oxford University Press, 1991).

3. Aristotle, *On Rhetoric* 1395b (2.22).

4. Aristotle, *On Rhetoric*, 1394a (2.20).

5. Aristotle, *On Rhetoric*, 1393b (2.20).

6. Aristotle, *On Rhetoric*, 1394a (2.20).

7. Aristotle, *On Rhetoric*, 1393a (2.20).

8. This and the following quotes in this paragraph are from Aristotle, *Topics* 1.12, trans. W. A. Pickard-Cambridge (HyperText Presentation: Procyon Publishing, 1995).

9. Jean-Paul Sartre, *Being and Nothingness*, trans. Hazel E. Barnes (New York: Washington Square Press, 1966), Part One, Chapter Two "Bad Faith".

10. Judith Jarvis Thompson, "A Defense of Abortion," *Journal of Philosophy and Public Affairs*, 1 (1971).

11. Hilary Putnam, "The Meaning of 'Meaning,'" *Philosophical Papers, Vol. 2: Mind, Language and Reality* (New York: Cambridge University Press, 1975).

12. Robert Nozick, *Anarchy, State, and Utopia* (New York: Basic Books, 1974), Part Two, Chapter 7, "How Liberty Upsets Patterns."

13. Ludwig Wittgenstein, *Philosophical Investigations*, trans. G.E.M. Anscombe (Oxford: Basil Blackwell, 1953). The "builder" example opens the *Investigations*. The "diary" is a central example in the *Investigation*'s discussions of private language, beginning at §243. The "boiling pot" example occurs at *Investigations*, §297, and questions the real existence of sensations.

14. Descartes, *Meditations*, First Meditation, Anscombe and Geach, pp. 61–65.

15. Sidney Gottlieb, ed., *Hitchcock on Hitchcock: Selected Writings and Interviews* (Berkeley: University of California Press, 1995). François Truffaut, *Hitchcock* (New York: Simon and Schuster, 1966). Peter Bogdanovich, *Who the Devil Made It: Conversations with Legendary Film Directors* (New York: Ballantine Books, 1997).

16. Dan Auiler, *Hitchcock's Notebooks* (New York: Avon Books, 1999), pp. 206–209, 496–505.

17. Alfred Hitchcock, "The Enjoyment of Fear," in *Hitchcock on Hitchcock*, p. 117.

18. Hitchcock, "The Enjoyment of Fear," p. 120.

19. See for example Marcia Eaton, "A Strange Sort of Sadness," *Journal of Aesthetics and Art Criticism* 41 (1982): 51–63.
20. Truffaut, *Hitchcock*, p. 109.
21. Truffaut, *Hitchcock*, p. 113.
22. Bogdanovich, *Who The Devil Made It?*, pp. 528–530.

Chapter 2

1. Descartes, *Meditations on First Philosophy* (1642), in *Descartes: Philosophical Writings*, trans. Elizabeth Anscombe and Peter Geach (London: Thomas Nelson and Sons Ltd., 1969), First Meditation, p. 65.
2. Descartes, *Meditations*, Fifth Meditation, p. 107.
3. Descartes, *Meditations*, Sixth Meditation, p. 124.
4. Descartes, *Meditations*, Fourth Meditation, pp. 96–97.

Chapter 3

1. Descartes, *Meditations on First Philosophy* (1642), in *Descartes: Philosophical Writings*, trans. Elizabeth Anscombe and Peter Geach (London: Thomas Nelson and Sons Ltd., 1969), First Meditation, p. 61.
2. Ludwig Wittgenstein, *On Certainty*, ed. G. E. M. Anscombe and G. H. von Wright; trans. Denis Paul and G. E. M. Anscombe (New York: Harper Torchbooks, 1972), §378.
3. François Truffaut with Helen Scott, *Hitchcock* (New York: Simon and Schuster, 1967), p. 95.
4. Hilary Putnam, "Brains in a vat," *Reason, Truth, and History* (New York: Cambridge University Press, 1981).
5. For example, by Vito Russo in *The Celluloid Closet* (New York: Harper and Row, 1981), p. 256.
6. Tania Modleski, *The Women Who Knew Too Much: Hitchcock and Feminist Theory* (New York: Methuen, Inc., 1988), p. 53.
7. I owe this suggestion to Herb Granger who thinks Fontaine only *pretends* to faint to stop Maxim from revealing too much. The scene as played in the film does not mark the faint as pretended; though of course a successful pretended faint must look for all the world like a real faint. It was also Herb who persuaded me that Fontaine achieves a sort of self-actualization as Maxim's companion and who pointed out how she comes to understand Maxim's weaknesses.
8. Robin Wood, *Hitchcock's Films Revisited* (New York: Columbia University Press, 1989), p. 266.
9. Donald Spoto, *The Dark Side of Genius: The Life of Alfred Hitchcock* (New York: Ballantine Books, 1983), p. 220. This much is garnered from Selznick's memo to Hitchcock denouncing the script as "cheap beyond words" etc.
10. Spoto, *The Dark Side of Genius*, p. 221.

Chapter 4

1. Ludwig Wittgenstein, *Philosophical Investigations*, trans. G. E. M. Anscombe (New York: The Methuen Company, 1953), IIxi, p. 224e.
2. Ludwig Wittgenstein, *On Certainty*, ed. G. E. M. Anscombe and G. H. von Wright, trans. Dennis Paul and G. E. M. Anscombe (New York: Harper & Row, 1972), §223.
3. Quoted by Donald Spoto, *The Dark Side of Genius: The Life of Alfred Hitchcock* (New York: Ballantine Books, 1983), p. 257.
4. Leonard Maltin et al, *Leonard Maltin's 2001 Movie and Video Guide* (New York: Signet Books, 2000).
5. Tania Modleski, *The Women Who Knew Too Much: Hitchcock and Feminist Theory* (New York: Methuen, Inc., 1988), p. 57.

6. Donald Spoto, *The Dark Side of Genius: The Life of Alfred Hitchcock* (New York: Ballantine Books, 1983), p. 254.

7. Dan Auiler, *Hitchcock's Notebooks* (New York: Avon Books, 1999), p. 62.

8. Spoto, *The Dark Side of Genius*, p. 256.

9. Joan Fontaine interviewed by Gregory Speck, "Hollywood: Joan Fontaine & Olivia de Havilland," *Interview* XVII (1987), p. 64. Fontaine goes on to say that Cary Grant had always assumed his character would kill hers, and offers her opinion that in the released version "the film just stops—without the proper ending."

10. Auiler, *Hitchcock's Notebooks*, pp. 63–92.

11. François Truffaut, with the collaboration of Helen G. Scott, *Hitchcock* (New York: Simon and Schuster, 1967), p. 102. Hitchcock also described the same preferred ending to Peter Bogdanovich, *Who the Devil Made It* (New York: Alfred A. Knopf, 1997), p. 509.

12. Truffaut, *Hitchcock*, p. 31.

13. Truffaut, *Hitchcock*, p. 102.

14. Leslie Brill, *The Hitchcock Romance* (Princeton: Princeton University Press, 1988), p. 149.

15. Brill, *The Hitchcock Romance*, p. 177.

16. Spoto, *The Dark Side of Genius*, p. 256.

17. Robin Wood, *Hitchcock's Films Revisited* (New York: Columbia University Press, 1989), p. 71.

18. David Sterritt, *The Films of Alfred Hitchcock* (Cambridge: Cambridge University Press, 1993), p. 19.

19. George M. Wilson, *Narration in Light: Studies in Cinematic Points of View* (Baltimore: Johns Hopkins Press, 1986), p. 88.

20. Truffaut, *Hitchcock*, p. 103.

21. Descartes, *Meditations on First Philosophy* (1642), in *Descartes: Philosophical Writings*, trans. Elizabeth Anscombe and Peter Geach (London: Thomas Nelson and Sons Ltd., 1969), Fourth Meditation, p. 98.

22. Peter Bogdanovich, *Who the Devil Made It: Conversations with Legendary Film Directors* (New York: Ballantine Books, 1998), pp. 509–10.

23. Richard Allen, "Hitchcock, or the Pleasures of Metaskepticism," in Richard Allen and S. Ishii-Gonzalès, ed., *Alfred Hitchcock: Centenary Essays* (London: British Film Institute, 1999), acknowledges the ambiguity of Johnnie Aysgarth's motives, pp. 225–226.

Chapter 5

1. Plato, *Republic* 476c, trans. Robin Winterfield (New York: Oxford University Press, 1993).

2. René Descartes, *Meditations on First Philosophy*, trans. Elizabeth Anscombe and Peter Geach (London: Thomas Nelson and Sons Ltd, 1954), First Meditation, p. 63.

3. Jean-Paul Sartre, *Being and Nothingness*, trans. Hazel E. Barnes (New York: Washington Square Press, 1966), pp. 59–60.

4. *Obsessed with Vertigo: New Life for Hitchcock's Masterpiece*, a documentary on the Universal Studios DVD of the film.

5. Tania Modleski, *The Women Who Knew Too Much: Hitchcock and Feminist Theory* (New York: Routledge, 1988), p. 91.

6. Richard Wagner, *Tristan und Isolde*, II.2. This translation, uncredited, is from the libretto accompanying the Deutsche Grammophon recording conducted by Karl Böhm.

7. Dan Auiler, *Vertigo: The Making of a Hitchcock Classic* (New York: St. Martin's Griffin, 2000), p. 141.

8. Denis de Rougemont, *Love in the Western World*, trans. Montgomery Belgion (1940; New York: Fawcett world Library, 1966), p. 30. For his version of the twelfth century myth, de Rougemont relies on five sources which he lists on page 27, fn. 1.

9. Matthew Arnold, "Tristram and Iseult" (1852), in *The Poems of Matthew Arnold*, ed. Kenneth & Miriam Allott (2nd ed.; New York: Longman, 1979).

10. François Truffaut with Helen G. Scott, *Hitchcock* (New York: Simon and Schuster, 1967), p. 185.

11. An insight I owe to Herb Granger.

12. Auiler, *Vertigo*, pp. 85–88.

13. Peter Bogdanovich, *Who the Devil Made It? Conversations with Legendary Film Directors* (New York: Ballantine Books, 1997), p. 530.

14. Dan Flory sees Scottie's failure to understand what's going on as Hitchcock's "critique of the rigidly scientific understanding of human nature." ("Hitchcock and Deductive Reasoning: Moving Step by Step in *Vertigo*," *Film and Philosophy* III (1996), p. 48.) On the contrary, Scottie is not scientifically rigid enough.

15. Modleski, *The Women Who Knew Too Much*, p. 81.

16. Descartes, *Meditations*, First Meditation, Anscombe and Peter Geach, p. 62.

17. Samuel Taylor Coleridge, Letter to Daniel Stuart of May 13, 1816, *The Collected Works of Samuel Taylor Coleridge*, ed. James Engell and W. Jackson Blaine (Princeton: Princeton University Press for the Bollingen Foundation, 1983), Vol. 7.ii, p. 6, fn. 2.

18. Descartes, *Meditations on First Philosophy*, First Meditation, p. 65.

19. Celia Green and Charles McCreery, *Lucid Dreaming: The Paradox of Consciousness During Sleep* (London: Routledge, 1994), p. 1.

20. Green and McCreery, *Lucid Dreaming*, pp. 95–97.

21. John R. Cole, *The Olympian Dreams and Youthful Rebellion of René Descartes* (Urbana: University of Illinois Press, 1992), pp. 36–37.

22. Robin Wood, *Hitchcock's Films Revisited* (New York: Columbia University Press, 1989), pp. 128–129.

23. Auiler, *Vertigo*, p. 130.

Chapter 6

1. Plato, *Republic*, 598b, trans. Robin Waterfield (New York: Oxford University Press, 1993).

2. George M. Wilson, *Narration in Light: Studies in Cinematic Point of View* (Baltimore: The Johns Hopkins Press, 1986), p. 77.

3. Peter Bogdanovich, *Who the Devil Made It? Conversations with Legendary Film Directors* (New York: Alfred A. Knopf, 1997), p. 531.

4. Wilson, *Narration in Light*, p. 77.

5. Stanley Cavell, "*North by Northwest*," in Marshall Deutelbaum and Leland Poague, ed., *A Hitchcock Reader* (Ames, IA: Iowa State University Press, 1986), p. 253.

6. Peter Alexander, Introduction to *Hamlet*, in *The Complete Works of William Shakespeare* (London: William Collins Sons & Co., Ltd., 1958), Vol. III, p. 441.

7. Dan Auiler, *Hitchcock's Notebooks* (New York: Avon Books, 1999), pp. 202–205.

8. Donald Spoto, *The Dark Side of Genius* (New York: Ballantine Books, 1983), p. 435–436.

9. Auiler, *Hitchcock's Notebooks*, p. 24. See also Hitchcock's interview with Herb Lightman, "Hitchcock Talks About Lights, Camera, Action," in *Hitchcock on Hitchcock*, ed. Sidney Gottlieb (Berkeley: University of California Press, 1995), p. 313.

10. Spoto, *The Dark Side of Genius*, p. 440.

11. Bogdanovich, *Who the Devil Made It?*, p. 531.

12. Wilson, *Narration in Light*, p. 64.

Chapter 7

1. Descartes, *Meditations on First Philosophy* (1642), in *Descartes: Philosophical Writings*, trans. Elizabeth Anscombe and Peter Geach (London: Thomas Nelson and Sons Ltd., 1969), Second Meditation, pp. 70–71.

2. Descartes, *Meditations*, Second Meditation, p. 73.

3. Ludwig Wittgenstein, *Philosophical Investigations* II, trans. G. E. M. Anscombe (Oxford: Basil Blackwell, 1953), pp. 222–4.

Chapter 8

1. Ludwig Wittgenstein, *Philosophical Investigations*, trans. G. E. M. Anscombe (New York: Macmillan, 1981), II, p. 223.

2. Tania Modleski, *The Women Who Knew Too Much: Hitchcock and Feminist Theory* (New York: Routledge, 1988), p. 13

3. Meg Wolitzer, "*Shadow of a Doubt*: Fat Man and Little Girl," in David Rosenberg, ed., *The Movie That Changed My Life* (New York: Penguin Books, 1993), p. 32. I'm grateful to Mark Huston for this reference.

4. Thorton Wilder's script emphasizes Young Charlie's push more than Hitchcock's film. From Wilder's script: "Cut to UNCLE CHARLIE and YOUNG CHARLIE in a furious struggle. ... As JACK appears on the platform he is in time to see YOUNG CHARLIE give her uncle a tremendous push. YOUNG CHARLIE: 'You won't!' UNCLE CHARLIE weakens. She gives him a second push, just as the oncoming train is about to pass the open door. UNCLE CHARLIE's hold is broken and he falls. DISSOLVE in a crash of noise and lights." Dan Auiler, *Hitchcock's Notebooks* (New York: Avon Books, 1999), p. 125. Auiler reprints about twenty-six pages of the script in Wilder's hand.

5. François Truffaut with Helen Scott, *Hitchcock* (New York: Touchstone Books, 1967), p. 111.

6. Robin Wood, *Hitchcock's Films Revisited* (New York: Columbia University Press, 1989), p. 301, my emphasis.

7. Wood, *Hitchcock's Films Revisited*, p. 299.

8. Truffaut, *Hitchcock*, p. 111.

9. Truffaut, *Hitchcock*, p. 109.

10. Truffaut, *Hitchcock*, pp. 109–110.

11. Descartes, *Meditations on First Philosophy* (1642), translated and edited by Elizabeth Anscombe and Peter Geach (London: Thomas Nelson and Sons, 1954), Second Meditation, p. 75.

12. This is the epistemological version of the problem of other minds. There is an ontological version: Is another being which is in many respects like me — a human body that moves, uses language, smiles, and so on — a mere machine or a person possessed of consciousness? As Descartes put it, "I chanced ... to look out of the window, and see men walking in the street; now I say in ordinary language that I 'see' them ... but what can I 'see' besides hats and coats, which may cover automata?" *Meditations on First Philosophy*, Second Meditation, p. 73.

13. David Hume, *Dialogues Concerning Natural Religion* (1779; Indianapolis: The Bobbs-Merrill Company, 1947), Part II, p. 144.

14. Wood, *Hitchcock's Films Revisited*, p. 300.

15. Wood, *Hitchcock's Films Revisited*, p. 300.

Chapter 9

1. Ludwig Wittgenstein, *Philosophical Investigations*, trans. G. E. M. Anscombe (New York: Macmillan, 1981), II, p. 223.

2. François Truffaut with Helen Scott, *Hitchcock* (New York: Simon and Schuster), p. 142.

3. Raymond Chandler, "Notebooks on *Strangers on a Train*," in Albert La Valley, ed., *Focus on Hitchcock* (Englewood Cliffs, NJ: Prentice-Hall, 1972), p. 101. Chandler was speaking specifically of why Guy doesn't go to the police after Bruno tells him he's murdered Miriam.

4. Vito Russo, *The Celluloid Closet: Homosexuality in the Movies* (New York: Harper & Row, 1981), p. 94. Donald Spoto, *The Art of Alfred Hitchcock: Fifty Years of His Motion Pictures* (New York: Anchor Books, 2nd edition, 1992), p. 192.

5. Russo, *The Celluloid Closet*, p. 95.

6. Robin Wood, *Hitchcock's Films Revisited* (New York: Columbia University Press, 1989), p. 347.

7. Truffaut, *Hitchcock*, p. 146. Hitchcock also told much the same thing to Peter Bogdanovich, "Granger was miscast.... It should have been a much stronger man." *Who the Devil Made It: Conversations with Famous Directors* (New York: Ballantine Books, 1997), p. 519.

8. I owe this thought to Herb Granger.

9. Truffaut, *Hitchcock*, p. 147.

10. Peter Bogdanovich, *Who the Devil Made It?*, p. 519.

11. Hediod, *Theogony*, trans. Hugh G. Evelyn-White (Cambridge: Harvard University Press, 1914), lines 767–773, p. 135. It was Herb Granger who brought this passage to my attention.

12. Lesley Brill recognizes Guy's (partial) culpability for Miriam's murder, and also the "blurred line between hero and villain" in this film. *The Hitchcock Romance* (Princeton: Princeton University Press, 1988), p. 82.

13. Wood, *Hitchcock's Films Revisited*, pp. 43–49.

14. Wood, *Hitchcock's Films Revisited*, p. 301.

15. Hitchcock, it would appear, imports a feature of Wimbledon – Kipling's lines about "Triumph and Disaster" are inscribed above its center court.

16. Donald Spoto, *The Dark Side of Genius* (New York: Ballantine Books, 1983), pp. 349, 350.

17. Patricia Highsmith, *Strangers on a Train* (1950; London: Vintage, 1999), pp. 163, 228.

18. Truffaut, *Hitchcock*, p. 144.

Chapter 10

1. Ludwig Wittgenstein, *The Blue and Brown Books* (New York: Harper Torchbooks, 1965), p. 62.

2. As told by Joseph Stefano in the documentary, "The Making of *Psycho*," on the Universal Studios DVD of the film

3. François Truffaut with Helen Scott, *Hitchcock* (New York: Simon and Schuster, 1967), p. 206.

4. Norman Bates in Robert Bloch's novel, *Psycho* (1959), decapitates Marion (in the novel "Mary") Crane. Ed Gein, the Wisconsin serial killer, was the model for Norman Bates. Stephen Rebello gives an account of Ed Gein's crimes, and what Robert Bloch knew and did not know about them – the Wisconsin newspapers of the time suppressed the really ghastly details. Suffice it to say that Gein's atrocities were far more horrible than Norman Bates's. *Alfred Hitchcock and the Making of Psycho* (New York: St. Martin's Griffin, 1990), Ch. 1. The psychotic criminals Jame Gumb ("Buffalo Bill") and Hannibal Lecter of *The Silence of the Lambs* (1991) are, jointly, closer to the real Ed Gein.

5. John Locke, *An Essay Concerning Human Understanding* (1690), II.xxvii.15, "Of Ideas of Identity and Diversity." From the Everyman edition abridged and edited by John Yolton (London: J. M. Dent and Sons, 1977).

Chapter 11

1. David Hume, *A Treatise of Human Nature* (1740), ed. L. A. Selby-Bigge & p. H. Nidditch (Oxford: Clarendon Press, 1978), I.III.ix, pp. 107–108.

2. This is how Ingrid Bergman remembered it. Donald Spoto, *The Dark Side of Genius: The Life of Alfred Hitchcock* (New York: Ballantine Books, 1983), p. 262, fn.

3. Spoto, *The Dark Side of Genius*, p. 511.

4. Peter Bogdanovich, *Who the Devil Made It: Conversations with Legendary Film Directors* (New York: Ballantine Books, 1997), p. 539.

5. See for example Robin Wood, *Hitchcock's Films Revisited* (New York: Columbia University Press, 1989), pp. 179 ff.

6. Sigmund Freud, "The Unconscious," in *The Freud Reader*, ed. Peter Gay (New York: W.W. Norton & Company, 1989), p. 580.

7. Freud, "The Unconscious," p. 576.

8. Descartes, *Meditations on First Philosophy* (1642), in *Descartes: Philosophical Writ-*

ings, trans. Elizabeth Anscombe and Peter Geach (London: Thomas Nelson and Sons Ltd., 1969), Second Meditation, p. 75.

9. Dan Auiler, *Hitchcock's Notebooks* (New York: Avon Books, 1999), p. 523.

10. Spoto, *The Dark Side of Genius*, p. 289.

11. François Truffaut with Helen Scott, *Hitchcock* (New York: Simon and Schuster, 1967), p. 228.

12. Evan Hunter's letter to "Hitch" in Auiler, *Hitchcock's Notebooks*, p. 242.

13. See Hitchcock's treatment and Evan Hunter's story notes, Auiler, *Hitchcock's Notebooks*, pp. 219–241.

Chapter 12

1. Plato, *Republic* 475e, trans. Robin Waterfield (New York: Oxford University Press, 1993).

2. René Descartes, *Rules for the Direction of the Mind* (c. 1630), in *Descartes: Philosophical Writings*, trans. Elizabeth Anscombe and Peter Geach, (London: Thomas Nelso and Sons, Ltd., 1954), Rule XII, p. 165.

3. Jonathan Sawday, *The Body Emblazoned: Dissection and the Human Body in Renaissance Culture* (London and New York: Routledge, 1995), p. 148.

4. David Hume, *An Enquiry Concerning Human Understanding*, Section IV, Part I, ed. Tom L. Beauchamp (New York: Oxford University Press, 1999).

5. Hume, *Enquiry*, Section IV, Part II.

6. Hume, *Enquiry*, Section V, Part I.

7. Reported by Donald Spoto, *The Dark Side of Genius: The Life of Alfred Hitchcock* (New York: Ballantine Books, 1984), p. 487n.

Chapter 13

1. Trans. W. D. Ross, Bk. I, Ch. 1.

2. Woolrich's story was originally titled, "It Had to Be Murder," published in *Dime Detective*, 1942. It was reprinted in the Woolrich anthology, *After-Dinner Story* (1944), as "Rear Window," and generally kept this title as it made its way through later anthologies. I'm grateful to Howard Spindel for this information.

3. A thought from Gina Granger.

4. Søren Kierkegaard, *Either/Or*, trans. David F. Swenson and Lillian Marvin Swenson (vol. I), and Walter Lowrie (vol. II), (Princeton: Princeton University Press, 1959), vol. I, pp. 337, 405, 410, 376.

5. A thought I owe to Herb Granger.

6. François Truffaut with Helen Scott, *Hitchcock* (New York: Simon and Schuster, 1967), p. 162.

7. Kierkegaard, *Either/Or*, vol. II, pp. 110–111.

8. Robin Wood, *Hitchcock's Films Revisited* (New York: Columbia University Press, 1989), p. 103.

9. Robert Stam and Roberta Pearson, "Hitchcock's *Rear Window*: Reflexivity and the Critique of Voyeurism," in *A Hitchcock Reader*, ed. Marshall Deutelbaum and Leland Pogue (Ames, IA: Iowa State University Press, 1986), pp. 198, 197, 193.

10. John Fawell, *Hitchcock's* Rear Window: *The Well-Made Film* (Carbondale: Southern Illinois University Press, 2001), pp. 123–124.

11. Berys Gaut has criticized the view that film-goers are voyeurs along similar lines. "On Cinema and Perversion," *Film and Philosophy* I (1994), pp. 3–17.

Chapter 14

1. Patricia Hitchcock O'Connell, interviewed in "The Making of The Man Who Knew Too Much," on the Universal studios DVD.

2. John Michael Hayes, interviewed in "The Making of The Man Who Knew Too Much," on the Universal studios DVD.

3. François Truffaut with Helen G. Scott, *Hitchcock* (New York: Simon and Schuster, 1967), p. 65.

4. Jean-Paul Sartre, "Existentialism and Humanism," trans. Philip Mairet, in *Existentialism from Dostoevsky to Sartre*, ed. Walter Kaufmann (New York: Meridian Books, 1956), pp. 295–296.

5. Donald Spoto, *The Art of Alfred Hitchcock: Fifty Years of His Motion Pictures* (New York: Anchor Books, 1992), p. 38.

Chapter 15

1. Immanuel Kant, *Critique of Judgment* (1790), trans. Werner S. Pluhar (Indianapolis: Hackett Publishing, 1987), Introduction V, p. 186.

2. Donald Spoto, *The Art of Alfred Hitchcock: Fifty Years of His Motion Pictures* (2nd edition; New York: Anchor Books, 1992), p. 330. Emphasis in original.

3. Spoto, *The Art of Alfred Hitchcock*, pp. 334–335.

4. Margaret Horowitz, "*The Birds*: A Mother's Love," in Marshall Deitelbaum and Leland Poague, eds., *The Hitchcock Reader* (Ames: Iowa State University Press, 1986), p. 279.

5. Horowitz, "*The Birds*: A Mother's Love," p. 286.

6. Camille Paglia, *The Birds* (London: British Film Institute, 1998), p. 87.

7. Horowitz, "*The Birds*: A Mother's Love," p. 281.

8. Robin Wood, *Hitchcock's Films Revisited* (New York: Columbia University Press, 1989), p. 167.

9. Peter Bogdanovich, *Who the Devil Made It: Conversations with Legendary Film Directors* (New York: Ballantine Books, 1997), p. 537.

10. Bogdanovich, *Who the Devil Made It*, pp. 536–537. For an enlightening and entertaining look at the technical problems and their solutions, see "All About *The Birds*" on the Universal Studios DVD.

11. Susan Sontag, "The Imagination of Disaster," in *Against Interpretation* (New York: Dell Publishing, 1969).

12. Noël Carroll, *The Philosophy of Horror, or Paradoxes of the Heart* (New York: Routledge, 1990), p. 184.

13. "Isn't the film also a kind of vision of Judgment Day?" Bogdanovich asked Hitchcock. "Yes, it is," he responded. "And we don't know how they are going to come out." *Who the Devil Made It*, p. 535.

14. Interview with Evan Hunter in "All About *The Birds*," a documentary on the making of the film on the Universal Studios DVD.

15. Interview with Evan Hunter in "All About *The Birds*."

16. Camille Paglia reproduces the front page of the *Santa Cruz Sentinel* of August 18, 1961, bearing the headline, "Seabird Invasion Hits Coastal Homes." She reports that Hitchcock requested a copy of the *Sentinel* be sent to him. *The Birds*, p. 11.

Bibliography

Alexander, Peter. Introduction to *Hamlet*. *The Complete Works of William Shakespeare*. London: William Collins Sons & Co., Ltd., 1958.

All About "The Birds." Dir. Laurent Bouzereau. The Alfred Hitchcock Collection. Universal Studios Home Video, 2000.

Allen, Richard. "Hitchcock, or the Pleasures of Metaskepticism." *Alfred Hitchcock: Centenary Essays*. Ed. Richard Allen and S. Ishii-Gonzalès. London: British Film Institute, 1999.

Aristotle. *Metaphysics*. Trans. W. D. Ross. Internet Classics Archive.

_____. *On Rhetoric*. Trans. George A. Kennedy. New York: Oxford University Press, 1991.

_____. *The Poetics*. Trans. G.M.A. Grube. Indianapolis: Hackett, 1987.

_____. *Topics*. Trans. W. A. Pickard-Cambridge. HyperText Presentation: Procyon, 1995.

Arnold, Matthew. "Tristram and Iseult" (1852). *The Poems of Matthew Arnold*. Ed. Kenneth and Miriam Allott. New York: Longman, 1979.

Auiler, Dan. *Hitchcock's Notebooks*. New York: Avon, 1999.

_____. *Vertigo: The Making of a Hitchcock Classic*. New York: St. Martin's Griffin, 2000.

Bloch, Robert. *Psycho*. New York: Tom Doherty Associates, 1989.

Bogdanovich, Peter. *Who the Devil Made It: Conversations with Legendary Film Directors*. New York: Ballantine, 1997.

Boileau, Pierre, and Thomas Narcejac. *The Living and the Dead (Vertigo)*. New York: Dell, 1958.

Brill, Leslie. *The Hitchcock Romance*. Princeton: Princeton University Press, 1988.

Carroll, Noël. *The Philosophy of Horror, or Paradoxes of the Heart*. New York: Routledge, 1990.

Cavell, Stanley. "*North by Northwest*." *A Hitchcock Reader*. Eds. Marshall Deutelbaum and Leland Poague. Ames: Iowa State University Press, 1986.

Chandler, Raymond. "Notebooks on *Strangers on a Train*." *Focus on Hitchcock*. Ed. Albert La Valley. Englewood Cliffs, NJ: Prentice Hall, 1972.

Cole, John R. *The Olympian Dreams and Youthful Rebellion of René Descartes*. Urbana: University of Illinois Press, 1992.

Coleridge, Samuel Taylor. Letter to Daniel Stuart of May 13, 1816. *The Collected Works of Samuel Taylor Coleridge*. Ed. James Engell and W. Jackson Blaine. Princeton: Princeton University Press for the Bollingen Foundation, 1983.

Descartes, René. *Descartes: Philosophical Writings*. Trans. Elizabeth Anscombe and Peter Geach. London: Thomas Nelson, 1969.

du Maurier, Daphne. "The Birds." *The Birds and Other Stories*. New York: Penguin, 1963.
_____. *Rebecca*. New York: Avon, 1971.
Eaton, Marcia. "A Strange Sort of Sadness." *Journal of Aesthetics and Art Criticism* 41 (1982): 51–63.
Fawell, John. *Hitchcock's* Rear Window: *The Well-Made Film*. Carbondale: Southern Illinois University Press, 2001.
Flory, Dan. "Hitchcock and Deductive Reasoning: Moving Step by Step in *Vertigo*." *Film and Philosophy* III (1996).
Freud, Sigmund. "The Unconscious." *The Freud Reader*. Ed. Peter Gay. New York: W.W. Norton, 1989.
Gaut, Berys. "On Cinema and Perversion." *Film and Philosophy* 1 (1994): 3–17.
Gottlieb, Sidney, ed. *Hitchcock on Hitchcock: Selected Writings and Interviews*. Berkeley: University of California Press, 1995.
Green, Celia, and Charles McCreery, *Lucid Dreaming: The Paradox of Consciousness During Sleep*. London: Routledge, 1994.
Hesiod. *Theogony*. Trans. Hugh G. Evelyn-White. Cambridge: Harvard University Press, 1914.
Highsmith, Patricia. *Strangers on a Train* (1950). London: Vintage, 1999.
Hitchcock, Alfred. "The Enjoyment of Fear." *Hitchcock on Hitchcock: Selected Writings and Interviews*. Ed. Sidney Gottlieb. Berkeley: University of California Press, 1995.
Horowitz, Margaret. "*The Birds*: A Mother's Love." *The Hitchcock Reader*. Eds. Marshall Deitelbaum and Leland Poague. Ames: Iowa State University Press, 1986.
Hume, David. *Dialogues Concerning Natural Religion*. Indianapolis: Bobbs-Merrill, 1947.
_____. *An Enquiry Concerning Human Understanding*. Ed. Tom L. Beauchamp. New York: Oxford University Press, 1999.
_____. *A Treatise of Human Nature* (1740). Ed. L. A. Selby-Bigge and P. H. Nidditch. Oxford: Clarendon, 1978.
Iles, Francis. *Before the Fact*. New York: Perennial Library, 1980.
Kant, Immanuel. *Critique of Judgment* (1790). Trans. Werner S. Pluhar. Indianapolis: Hackett, 1987.
Kierkegaard, Søren. *Either/Or*. Trans. David F. Swenson and Lillian Marvin Swenson (vol. I) and Walter Lowrie (vol. II). Princeton: Princeton University Press, 1959.
Locke, John. *An Essay Concerning Human Understanding* (1690). Ed. John Yolton. London: J. M. Dent, 1977.
The Making of "Psycho." Dir. Laurent Bouzereau. The Alfred Hitchcock Collection. Universal Studios Home Video, 1999.
The Making of "The Man Who Knew Too Much." Dir. Laurent Bouzereau. The Alfred Hitchcock Collection. Universal Studios Home Video, 2000.
Maltin, Leonard, et al. *Leonard Maltin's 2001 Movie and Video Guide*. New York: Signet, 2000.
Modleski, Tania. *The Women Who Knew Too Much: Hitchcock and Feminist Theory*. New York: Methuen, 1988.
Nozick, Robert. *Anarchy, State, and Utopia*. New York: Basic, 1974.
Obsessed with "Vertigo." Dir. Harrison Engle. The Alfred Hitchcock Collection. Universal Studios Home Video, 1999.
Paglia, Camille. *The Birds*. London: British Film Institute, 1998.
Plato. *Republic*. Trans. Robin Winterfield. New York: Oxford University Press, 1993.
Putnam, Hilary. "Brains in a Vat." *Reason, Truth, and History*. New York: Cambridge University Press, 1981.
_____. "The Meaning of 'Meaning.'" *Philosophical Papers, Vol. 2: Mind, Language and Reality*. New York: Cambridge University Press, 1975.

Rebello, Stephen. *Alfred Hitchcock and the Making of Psycho.* New York: St. Martin's Griffin, 1990.

Rougemont, Denis de. *Love in the Western World* (1940). Trans. Montgomery Belgion. New York: Fawcett World Library, 1966.

Russo, Vito. *The Celluloid Closet: Homosexuality in the Movies.* New York: Harper and Row, 1981.

Sartre, Jean-Paul. *Being and Nothingness.* Trans. Hazel E. Barnes. New York: Washington Square, 1966.

_____. "Existentialism and Humanism." Trans. Philip Mairet. *Existentialism from Dostoevsky to Sartre.* Ed. Walter Kaufmann. New York: Meridian, 1956.

Sawday, Jonathan. *The Body Emblazoned: Dissection and the Human Body in Renaissance Culture.* London and New York: Routledge, 1995.

Sontag, Susan. "The Imagination of Disaster." *Against Interpretation.* New York: Dell, 1969.

Speck, Gregory. "Hollywood: Joan Fontaine & Olivia de Havilland." *Interview* 17 (1987).

Spoto, Donald. *The Art of Alfred Hitchcock: Fifty Years of His Motion Pictures.* 2nd ed. New York: Anchor, 1992.

_____. *The Dark Side of Genius: The Life of Alfred Hitchcock.* New York: Ballantine, 1983.

Stam, Robert, and Roberta Pearson. "Hitchcock's *Rear Window*: Reflexivity and the Critique of Voyeurism." *A Hitchcock Reader.* Eds. Marshall Deutelbaum and Leland Pogue. Ames: Iowa State University Press, 1986.

Sterritt, David. *The Films of Alfred Hitchcock.* Cambridge: Cambridge University Press, 1993.

Thompson, Judith Jarvis. "A Defense of Abortion. " *Journal of Philosophy and Public Affairs* 1 (1971).

Truffaut, François, with Helen Scott. *Hitchcock.* New York: Simon and Schuster, 1966.

Wilson, George M. *Narration in Light: Studies in Cinematic Points of View.* Baltimore: Johns Hopkins Press, 1986.

Wittgenstein, Ludwig. *The Blue and Brown Books.* New York: Harper Torchbooks, 1965.

_____. *On Certainty.* Ed. G. E. M. Anscombe and G. H. von Wright. Trans. Denis Paul and G. E. M. Anscombe. New York: Harper Torchbooks, 1972.

_____. *Philosophical Investigations.* Trans. G.E.M. Anscombe. Oxford: Basil Blackwell, 1953.

Wolitzer, Meg. "*Shadow of a Doubt:* Fat Man and Little Girl." *The Movie That Changed My Life.* Ed. David Rosenberg. New York: Penguin, 1993.

Wood, Robin. *Hitchcock's Films Revisited.* New York: Columbia University Press, 1989.

Woolrich, Cornell. "Rear Window." *The Cornell Woolrich Omnibus.* New York: Penguin, 1998.

Yanal, Robert J. "The End of *Suspicion*: Hitchcock, Descartes, and Joan Fontaine." *Film and Knowledge: Essays on the Integration of Images and Ideas.* Ed. Kevin Stoehr. Jefferson, NC: McFarland, 2000.

_____. *Paradoxes of Emotion and Fiction.* University Park PA: Pennsylvania State University Press, 1999.

_____. "*Rebecca*'s Deceivers." *Philosophy and Literature* 34 (2000): 67–82.

Index

Aesop 5, 7
Aesthetic life 155–6, 158–9, 161–2
Against Interpretation 198
Alexander, Peter 194
Alfred Hitchcock and the Making of Psycho 196
Alfred Hitchcock: Centenary Essays 193
All About "The Birds" 198
Allen, Jay Presson 139–40
Allen, Richard 193
Ambrogio, Anthony vii
Analogical reasoning 94–5
Anderson, Judith 21, 23
Aristotle 3–7, 148, 191
Arnold, Matthew 53, 193
The Art of Alfred Hitchcock: Fifty Years of His Motion Pictures 195, 198
Auiler, Dan 8, 53, 66, 75, 191, 193, 194, 197

Baker, Diane 133
Balsam, Martin 117
Banks, Leslie 167, 173
Bates, Florence 18, 20
Bedazzled 91
Before the Fact 38
Being and Nothingness 47, 191
Bel Geddes, Barbara 48
Benjamin, Arthur 167
Bennett, Charles 166
Bergman, Ingrid 73, 82, 126, 127, 128
Berner, Sara 148
Best, Edna 167
The Birds 2, 3, 8, 54, 85, 129, 146, 175–90; du Maurier's story 189–90
The Birds (Paglia) 198
Bloch, Robert 122, 196
The Blue and Brown Books 115, 196
Body Emblazoned: Dissection and the Human Body in Renaissance Culture 197

Bogdanovich, Peter 8, 9, 45, 75, 191–4, 196, 198
Bogdasarian, Ross 148
Boileau, Pierre 47
Boyer, Charles 46
Brill, Lesley vii, 40, 193, 196
Bruce, Nigel 34
Burr, Raymond 148, 149

Cady, Frank 148
Cambridge spies 172
Carey, Macdonald 86
Carroll, Leo G. 34, 68, 101, 127
Carroll, Noël vii, 183, 189, 198
Cartwright, Veronica 176, 179
Cassidy, Jack 115–6
Cavell, Stanley 74–5, 194
The Celluloid Closet 195
Chandler, Raymond 100, 127, 195
Chapman, Lonny 177, 178
Chekhov, Michael 127
Chesterton, G. K. 166
Citizen Kane 36, 47
Coleridge, Samuel Taylor 60–1, 194
Collected Works of Samuel Taylor Coleridge 194
Collinge, Patricia 86
Connery, Sean 82, 126, 130
Cooper, Gladys 22
Corey, Wendell 149
Cotten, Joseph 82, 84, 86, 88
Critique of Judgment 173, 198
Cronyn, Hume 85
Crowther, Bosley 36
Cummings, Robert 73
Curzon, George 170

Dalí, Salvador 128
Darcy, Georgine 148

The Dark Side of Genius 192, 193, 194, 196
Davenport, Havis 148
Day, Doris 163, 167
de Banzie, Brenda 163
Deception 13–5, 19–20, 24–5, 26–7, 31–2,
  43–5, 48, 50–1, 59, 67, 77–8
Denny, Reginald 22
D'Entre les Morts 47, 55
De Rougemont, Denis 53
Descartes, René 1, 3, 8, 13–4, 16, 20, 24,
  28, 44–5, 47, 81, 82–3, 93, 109–10, 145,
  155, 191–6
Dewey, Ken vii
Dial M for Murder 2
Dialogues Concerning Natural Religion 94,
  195
Doubles 56–7, 89–91, 102–4, 114, 119
Dracula 93
Dreams 17, 29–30, 47, 56–7, 59–61, 62–5,
  127–8
du Maurier, Daphne 16, 30, 189–90

Eaton, Marcia 192
Either/Or 155–7, 197
Elliott, Laura 100
*Enquiry Concerning Human Understand-
  ing* 146, 197
Enthymeme 4–5
*An Essay Concerning Human Understand-
  ing* 196
L'Éternel retour 54
Ethics 145–6, 152–7, 158–9, 171–4; *see also*
  Good and evil
Evelyn, Judith 148
Examples in philosophy 6–7
Existentialism and humanism 171
Existentialism from Dostoevsky to Sartre 198
Explanations 188–9

Fables 5–6, 7
Fawell, John 159, 197
Fellini, Federico 147
*Film and Knowledge: Essays on the Integra-
  tion of Images and Ideas* vii
Films of Alfred Hitchcock 193
Flory, Dan 194
Focus on Hitchcock 195
Fontaine, Joan 1, 18, 23, 31, 33, 38–9, 43,
  193
Foreign Correspondent 73, 75, 156
Frenzy 84
Freud, Sigmund 135, 196
The Freud Reader 196

Gabel, Martin 130
Gaslight 46

Gaut, Berys 197
Gavin, John 115
Gélin, Daniel 163, 164
The Godfather 4
Good and evil 112–3, 125, 140–1; *see also*
  Ethics
Gottlieb, Sidney 8, 191, 194
Granger, Farley 1, 82, 100, 102, 110
Granger, Gina vii, 197
Granger, Herb v, vii, 192, 194, 196
Grant, Cary 1, 31, 33, 38, 41, 44, 46, 67,
  68, 71, 73, 75, 139
Green, Celia 194
Griffies, Ethel 177, 178
Guernsey, Otis 75

Halloween 115
Hamlet 74–5, 194
Harper, Rand 148
Hayes, John Michael 166, 198
Hays Code 38, 66
Hecht, Ben 100, 127
Hedren, Tippi 82, 127, 129–31, 176, 178,
  179
Helmore, Tom 48
Herrmann, Bernard 53, 69, 115, 130, 167
Hesiod 8, 109, 110, 196
Highsmith, Patricia 100, 113–4, 196
Hitchcock 191–6, 198
Hitchcock, Alfred: *The Birds* 184, 189,
  190, 198; enjoyment of fear 8–9, 191;
  Lifeboat 9; *The Man Who Knew Too
  Much* 166, 167; *Marnie* 139; *North by
  Northwest* 75; *Psycho* 115, 122; *Rebecca*
  30; *Shadow of a Doubt* 91; *Strangers on
  a Train* 100, 108–9, 114, 196; *Suspicion*
  31, 38–9, 45; *Vertigo* 9, 51, 54, 59
Hitchcock, Patricia 101, 197
Hitchcock on Hitchcock 8, 191
A Hitchcock Reader 194, 197, 198
The Hitchcock Romance 193
Hitchcock's Films Revisited 192, 194, 195,
  196, 197
Hitchcock's Notebooks 191, 193, 194, 197
*Hitchcock's Rear Window: The Well-Made
  Film* 197
Holden, William 106
Homosexuality 27, 104–7, 183
Horowitz, Margaret 181–2
How Green Was My Valley 36
Hume, David 3, 94, 126, 146–7, 195, 196,
  197
Hunter, Evan 8, 139, 189, 190, 197, 198
Huston, Mark vii

Iles, Francis 38

Illusion 67, 76–7
Incest 96–7
Incorrigibility 81–2
Ishii-Gonzalès, S. 193

Jaws 175

Kant, Immanuel 3, 145, 175, 198
Kaplan, George 67–70, 77–8
Kelly, Grace 139, 145, 148, 154
Kierkegaard, Søren 145–6, 155, 156–7, 197
King Lear 21
Kipling, Rudyard 113, 196
Knight, Deborah vii

The Lady Vanishes 73
Landau, Martin 69
Landis, Jesse 70
Lang, Doreen 177
Latham, Louise 82, 130
Launer, S. John 130
Lee, Auriol 35
Lehman, Ernest 67, 75
Leigh, Janet 83, 115, 116, 120, 122
Leonard Maltin's 2001 Movie and Video Guide 192
The Living and the Dead see *D'Entre les Morts*
Locke, John 124, 196
Lorne, Marion 104
Lorre, Peter 167, 172–3
Love in the Western World 193
Lucid dreaming 63–64
Lucid Dreaming: The Paradox of Consciousness During Sleep 194

The Maltese Falcon 36
Maltin, Leonard 36, 192
The Man Who Knew Too Much 2, 8, 146, 163–74; two versions 166–7
Mantell, Joe 177
Marnie 82, 126–7, 129–41
Mason, James 67
The Matrix 4
McCarthyism 152
McCrea, Joel 73, 75
McCrery, Charles 194
McGraw, Charles 177, 178
McIntire, John 117
Meditations on First Philosophy 8, 13–4, 16, 44–5, 47, 81, 191–6
Memory 126, 128, 133, 135–7
Metaphilosophy 4–7
Metaphysics 148
Metz, Christian 159
Miles, Bernard 163

Miles, Vera 117
Mind *see* Self
Modleski, Tania 27–8, 50, 84, 192, 193, 195
Money 107, 119–21, 123
The Movie That Changed My Life 195
Murder 30, 35–6, 37, 39, 40, 41–2, 44–5, 49–50, 65, 101, 108, 109, 110–2, 117, 122

Nalder, Reggie 165, 167
Narcejac, Thomas 47
Narcissism 95–96
Narration in Light: Studies in Cinematic Points of View 193, 194
North by Northwest 1, 2, 14, 15, 17, 67–78, 115, 156; alternative titles 75
Notorious 2, 73, 85, 129, 133, 136
Novak, Kim 48, 51
Nozick, Robert 7, 191

Oakland, Simon 118
Obsessed with Vertigo: New Life for Hitchcock's Masterpiece 193
Olivier, Laurence 18, 38
Olsen, Christopher 163
On Certainty 16, 31, 46, 192
Ormonde, Czenzi 100
Oscar, Henry 167

Paglia, Camille 181–2, 198
Paradoxes of Emotion and Fiction 191
Pearson, Roberta 159–60, 197
Peck, Gregory 82, 126, 128
Perkins, Anthony 1, 82, 116, 120, 122
Philosophical Investigations 31, 81–2, 84, 100, 191, 192, 194, 195
Philosophy of Horror 198
Pilbeam, Nova 170
Plato 47, 67, 76–7, 98, 145, 193, 197
Play Misty for Me 115
Pleshette, Suzanne 176
The Poems of Matthew Arnold 193
Poetics 191
The Possession of Joel Delaney 124
Privileged access 81–2, 93–4
Psycho 1, 82, 84, 115–25, 129, 130, 175–6; Bloch's novel 122, 196
Psychoanalysis 128, 134–5, 138
Putnam, Hilary 6, 191

Rains, Claude 73
Raphaelson, Samson 38
Rashômon 4
Rear Window 2, 3, 4, 145, 148–62, 173; Woolrich's short story 151–2, 197
Rebecca vii, 1, 3, 14, 16–30, 50, 77, 84, 85; du Maurier's novel 30

Republic 47, 67, 193, 194, 197
Rhetoric 4–6
Ritter, Thelma 148, 154
Roman, Ruth 101
Rope 2
Rozsa, Miklos 127
Rules of the Direction of the Mind 197
Russo, Vito 105, 192, 195

Saboteur 73
Saint, Eva Marie 67, 71, 73
Sanders, George 16
Sartre, Jean-Paul 6, 47, 171–2, 191, 198
Sawday, Jonathan 197
Seeing 118–9, 148
Self 81, 83, 119, 120, 121–2, 123–4, 137–8
Self-deception 47, 52, 61–2, 64
Selznick, David 17, 30
Shadow of a Doubt 2, 3, 4, 56, 82, 84–99,
   123
Shakespeare, William 74–5
Shayne, Konstantin 48
Sontag, Susan 184–5, 198
Spellbound 82, 126–9, 133–8
Spencer, Larry vii
Spindel, Howard 197
Spoto, Donald 30, 38, 114, 178–181, 192,
   193, 196–8
Stam, Robert 159–60, 107
Star Trek 93
Stefano, Joseph 115, 122
Sterrit, David 40, 193
Stewart, James 48, 145, 148, 156, 163, 164
Stoehr, Kevin vii
Strangers on a Train 1, 3, 8, 56, 82, 100–4,
   123, 127, 176; Highsmith's novel 113–4
Suspicion vii, 2, 3, 14, 15, 31–46, 50, 51,
   77, 84, 85; *see also Before the Fact*
The Swarm 175
Swenson, Karl 177

Tandy, Jessica 176, 179
Taylor, Rod 176, 179
Telepathy 92–3
Texas Chainsaw Massacre 115
Them! 175

Theogony 196
The Thing from Another World 175
The 39 Steps 2, 72–3, 76, 136, 138, 156
Thompson, Judith 6, 191
To Catch a Thief 2, 139
Tragedy 51, 65
Travers, Henry 86
A Treatise of Human Nature 126, 196
Tristan and Iseult 52–6, 180
Truffaut, François 8–9, 39, 40, 114, 191,
   192, 195, 196, 198
Truman, Ralph 165
Twins 86, 95, 112

Vertigo 2, 3, 8, 14, 47–66, 67, 76, 77, 130
Vertigo: The Making of a Hitchcock Classic
   193, 194
Voyeurism 159–60

Wagner, Richard 52, 55–6, 65, 180, 193
Waking Life 4
Walker, Robert 1, 82, 102, 110, 114
Waxman, Franz 17
Welles, Orson 10
*Who the Devil Made It: Conversations with
   Legendary Film Directors* 192, 193, 194,
   198
Wilder, Thorton 9, 87, 93, 195
Willard 175
Wilson, George 41, 72, 73, 76, 193, 194
Winston, Irene 148
Wittgenstein, Ludwig 3, 7, 16, 31, 46,
   81–2, 191, 192, 194, 195, 196
Wolitzer, Meg 85, 195
The Women Who Knew Too Much 192,
   193, 194, 195
Wonacott, Edna May 91
Wood, Robin 29, 40, 92, 96–7, 98, 105,
   112–3, 159–60, 182–4, 192, 194–6
Woolrich, Cornell 151–2, 197
Wounds 119
Wright, Teresa 82, 84, 86, 88
Wyndham-Lewis, D. B. 166

Yanal, Elizabeth v
Yanal, Robert J. 191